BEAT OF A DIFFERENT DRUM

BEAT OF A DIFFERENT DRUM

THE UNTOLD STORIES OF AFRICAN AMERICANS
FORGING THEIR OWN PATHS IN WORK AND LIFE

DAX-DEVLON ROSS

NEW YORK

Library of Congress Cataloging-in-Publication Data

ISBN: 1-4013-0784-1

Hyperion books are available at special quantity discounts to use as
premiums or for special programs, including corporate training.
For details contact Michael Rentas, Assistant Director, Inventory
Operations, Hyperion, 77 West 66th Street, 11th floor, New York,
New York 10023, or call 212-456-0133.

FIRST EDITION

10 9 8 7 6 5 4 3 2 1

*To my father, Claude Linwood Ross, Jr.,
for teaching me how to fly.*

We miss you, Dad.

*To my mother, Evelyn Chambers Ross,
for always keeping me grounded.*

Love ya, Ma.

CONTENTS

Introduction

> "Brothers and sisters my text this morning is the 'Blackness of Blackness.'"
>
> And a congregation of voices answered, "That blackness is most black, brother, most black . . ."
>
> —RALPH ELLISON

My life had followed a fairly tight script. I'd gone through high school, through college, and through law school with relative ease. I'd moved to New York, I'd gotten a job that I liked, I was writing my first novel—things were moving according to plan. Then, I got laid off. Getting axed wasn't the problem, though. The problem was, I couldn't find a job that paid more than the unemployment stipend I received every week. The problem was, none of the jobs listed on any of the Web sites I canvassed daily over the next six months sounded even remotely appealing to me. The problem was, everyone around me had an opinion about what I should do. In retrospect, I don't know what would've become of me had I not noticed Po Bronson's *What Should I Do with My Life* at the bookstore, and had the presence of mind to buy it on the spot.

The book told all of these wonderful stories about people searching for their calling, people struggling to make the right choices in life, people making radical life changes in order to pursue their idea of happiness. I can't begin to explain how comforting it was to read about others who, like me, didn't want to just settle for a life that left them wondering what else they could have done. As I read, I felt my six-month malaise slowly peel away. What remained was the realization that the reason I didn't like my occupational options was because they weren't *my* options. They were what I had been taught that as an educated young black man from an integrated, middle-class background I was supposed to pursue, but they didn't belong to me, Dax-Devlon Ross. Frankly, I wasn't interested in being the next Johnny Cochran or Vernon Jordan. My dream of being the next Michael Jordan had ended with high school, and any ideas I'd had about a career on the stage or screen (be it small or big) had been dashed with an elementary school performance of *The Wizard of Oz*, where I floundered about the stage as the Cowardly Lion. So what did that leave me with? What could I do with *my* life outside of the boundaries that seemed so stringently set for blacks living in America?

It's often the case that African-Americans themselves don't acknowledge the range of experiences within the so-called black experience. Looking back, I see now that what I was looking for was guidance from other black folks who had taken the road less traveled. If only to know it had been done before, I needed to hear these stories. I came from a traditional southern family where everyone pretty much followed the rules. My father was part of the generation of African-Americans who were the first in their families to graduate from college. After graduation he worked as an electrical engineer for the rest of his life. My mother has worked as a small-business consultant for the District of Columbia for almost twenty years. They never openly discouraged my interests or voiced doubt about my choices, and I thank them enormously for that, but because I was entering territory they had never explored, there came a point when even they couldn't help me find my way.

As I see it, the problem is this: We often encounter anecdotes of black upward mobility in America, tales of success in the "land of plenty," but those tales tend to confine the definition of success to three things: money, fame, and status. African-Americans are only considered successful by both themselves and others if they earn a significant amount of cash, are seen on the screen, perform heroic acts on the playing field, or have a certain set of letters following their names. While this is arguably true of any ethnic group in America, what inevitably tends to happen when these stories are regurgitated is that they wind up sounding, at best, superficial. They aren't inspiring or uplifting; what they are is formulaic and shallow. Invariably, the standard African-American success story grazes over the rough spots in order to serve up the literary equivalent of a microwave dinner: something comforting, bland, and artificial. What's more, the customary "African-American" success story is so limited in scope that it never reflects any ideals apart from the ones sanctioned by the same institutions that have historically oppressed African-Americans. Even as the black upper and middle class expands, we rarely see a critique of the entrenched political, legal, and economic hegemony that has systematically depressed the lives of millions of black folks for hundreds of years.

None of this is meant to diminish the inroads African-Americans have made, particularly those in the last half of the twentieth century. With each new face of color in the White House, on Wall Street, in the inner circles of the Fortune 500, or in the halls of justice, African-Americans chip a little more at the legacy of Jim Crow and debunk that nagging inferiority myth. But I find it difficult to believe that when Dr. King prayed for a day when African-Americans would be judged by the "content of their character" and not the color of their skin, his idea of "character" had to do with only cash and class. I am certain that his definition included words like strength, courage, integrity, ingenuity, independence, generosity, creativity, and fortitude—all qualities I found in the people whose stories fill the pages of *Beat of a Different Drum*; all qualities that have come to define the highest virtues of humanity.

What distinguishes this book from others that have preceded it is that by sharing the stories of people who have chosen unique paths, it challenges the ingrained ways that we tend to think about African-Americans and success. These stories probe the nature of one's search for purpose and clarity by looking beyond race, beyond even the so-called souls of black folks, and into the corridors of one's particular struggles, triumphs, complexities, and perplexities. And in doing so, *Beat of a Different Drum* reveals what it means to be part of a group, but also an individual.

When I set out to write this book I wanted to discover inspiring stories that forced me to think beyond my comfort zone and into the realm of limitless possibility. I let that standard guide me. The next step involved research. I made a list of fields, like the marine sciences, in which African-Americans were under-represented. Then, I sent introductory e-mails to the people I came across. If I couldn't find an e-mail address, I cold-called. From the very outset, people responded favorably. Each afternoon I sent out dozens of e-mails to people I'd never met, and each morning I'd open my in-box to find as many, if not more, replies. People forwarded the e-mail to others. Some contacted me directly with names of people they thought that I should interview. Everyone who wrote back to me was astonishingly encouraging. They'd tell me how glad they were that someone—particularly a black someone—had taken an interest in their stories; many thought it was simply a thought-provoking concept; several just really wanted to tell their stories; most saw it as a way to reach out to young people. A handful of the people who contacted me doubted that their stories would qualify for the book, but they wanted to encourage me nonetheless. Everyone related in some way, shape, or form to the book's basic theme.

In the life summaries I asked many people to write for me, they'd invariably tell of unusual interests they'd had as children, formative experiences they'd had in their teens or early twenties, and choices they'd made at some or another point to pursue their passion—often against the wishes of their parents or in opposition to the pressure to conform they felt coming from other black folks. Given the dark period I was emerging from, this was an especially exciting time for me. As the bitter northeastern winter thawed outside, the people I began meeting—in their homes, at their workplaces, or in the many cafés and diners I came to know well—warmed me inwardly with the inspiration and motivation to continue on even when I didn't know where I was being led.

In the beginning, I was merely looking to document the stories of African-Americans with careers in unusual professions. My original plan was to take each interview and weave it into a monologue, à la Studs Terkel. However, I found over time that the initial career-focused conversation I had sought to have unintentionally launched us into deeper discourses about identity and society. At the same time, I was finding that race, while still an issue, was not the defining issue in these people's lives. Put another way, the stories I was hearing struck me as human ones grounded in the reality that skin color has played (and continues to play) a significant role in our society. In fact, I was surprised and refreshed by how rarely and even reluctantly we talked directly about race. Of course, it came up. No discussion among black folks would be a truly honest one if race weren't broached. The people I met were weary of shallow images of blackness. They wanted parity in their portrayals: for the world, and other black Americans, to gain a more authentic perspective on who they are, where they come from, and who they can be. But they also hungered for a truer, deeper sense of themselves and their reason for being. To that end, they demanded that the same freedom to define one's self—a freedom that every other American enjoys—be granted to them as well.

Slowly, and perhaps reluctantly, I allowed the original concept to layer itself with questions that I hadn't entertained at the outset. The more people opened up to me, the more I felt it was crucial that each story reflect the individual as much as the career path they'd chosen. Actually, as I began listening to the interview tapes, career started sounding less significant; it was the speaker's spontaneous insight and life wisdom that I found myself responding to. The people themselves ranged from the modestly successful, to the mildly famous, to those who struggled to make ends meet. They were a virtual hodgepodge, bearing little surface similarity. But I never doubted that within each story lay a piece to a puzzle that, once arranged, would tell an alternative tale about the experience of being both black and American.

The changes in the book were reflective of the changes I was going through while I was writing it. When I started *Beat of a Different Drum* I was single, I didn't have a job, and my father was in perfect health. By the time I finished, I'd been married close to a year, I'd been teaching middle school in Brooklyn for almost two, and my father had passed, from a brain tumor doctors had discovered less than a year earlier. As I entered each new stage of maturity, so, too, did the book. In the midst of my struggles with my father's mortality, my seventh graders' hormones, and the prospect of starting a family of my own, writing about people like Ray Hill (an entrepreneur from St. Louis who resigned from a $70,000-a-year job with the federal government at age twenty-eight to pursue his passion for beer brewing, while raising his twelve-year-old son by himself) kept me afloat.

During the periods, and there were several, when I doubted this book would have much of an impact, there was always a tape I needed to listen to or a transcript that I needed to read, and without fail it put me back on track. I hadn't foreseen coming to depend on these voices for inspiration and support, but I don't know how I would have finished without that push they provided. When I was depressed about my father, I wrote. When I was questioning whether I was cut out for teaching, I wrote. When I was anxious about my impending wedding when all I'd known of marriage had been divorce, I wrote. On weekends, late at night, early in the morning, on planes, trains, and buses, in cafés from New York to Paris, before school, during school, and after school, both for the reader whose eye would one day catch this title and be inspired, and for the part of me that would have been lost otherwise, I wrote.

I share all of this at the outset not to brag about my dedication, but to underscore the urgency I felt. Each time I met someone who was boldly pursuing his or her bliss, I was reminded that I still wasn't marching to the beat of my own drum. Yes, I was writing, and in many ways the ritual itself is the point. But no, I hadn't delivered myself entirely. Writing this book ultimately allowed me to confront my inner conflicts about what I wanted versus what, deep down, I thought I was worthy of. I suspect I'm not alone on this score. Many of us talk about the life we want to live; at the very least we complain about wanting to find "that thing" that best suits us. The number of conversations I've had on this subject alone in the last two years boggles my mind. What's really staggering, though, are the fictions we create in order to justify remaining dissatisfied:

"School loans."

"Lack of experience."

"I wouldn't know where to begin."

"It isn't practical."

"It's too late to start over now."

"Next year."

I've heard them all and my response to them is the same as the one Bill Collins, teacher turned sailor turned chef, offered to me: "In the final analysis we're on this earth for a blip. We ain't here that long." Watching my father wither away over a ten-month period gave me firsthand knowledge about the frailty of life. After working and raising children for almost forty years, he was finally positioning himself to open a new chapter in his life, the one he'd put on hold for four decades; then he started having headaches. Less than a month later, his life was upside down. Less than a year later, he was gone.

So much of *Beat of a Different Drum* stems directly from my father's influence on my life. Because he never judged my siblings and me or pressured us to conform; because he always supported our interests whatever they were and said, from as early as I can recall, "You never know, the thing you wind up doing for a living may not even exist yet"; because he was the first person I talked to about this book, the person whose approving nod I looked to before anyone else's—because of all of that, and much, much more of course, his untimely death was not in vain. Before he passed on, he conveyed to me the wisdom of his later years: "Do what you want and let everything else fall in line."

A few months back I found myself in a conversation with a young woman who, like me, had been teaching middle school English for the past two years. Although we'd entered New York City's Teaching Fellows program at the same time and had had a number of the same classes at Brooklyn College, we'd never previously spoken to each other. We didn't even know each other's names. But that didn't stop her from opening up to me about her experience in the classroom. She said she was miserable. Teaching wasn't for her. She couldn't handle the kids, nor could she stomach the bureaucracy. At the same time, she didn't know what else to do. The primary reason she'd gone into teaching in the first place was because she'd majored in literature in college and her family and friends had told her teaching would be a good way to share her love of books. I asked her what she really wanted to be doing.

"I've been thinking about publishing," the woman replied. "I can see myself as an editor."

Immediately, a change came over her. Her face brightened; her tone lightened. For whatever reason, perhaps simply because I listened, she felt comfortable telling me what she secretly longed to do. But while she was excited about publishing, she didn't know who to talk to or where to begin. As much as the idea of being an editor appealed to her, I sensed that she didn't believe she could make the career change, nor did she have a meaningful support system, and so she would likely languish in the classroom for another year or two before she did anything to change her situation.

In many ways this woman reminded me of Stacey Barney, a teacher turned book editor I had interviewed. They had both majored in literature. They had both been told they'd make good teachers. They had both been unhappy teachers.

I told the woman about Stacey, about what she had gone through and where she was now, and while she seemed interested, I don't know if she really got it. Like the saying goes, "seeing is believing." Had I had a copy of *Beat of a Different Drum* with me at that moment, the woman could've seen and heard Stacey. Maybe then she would have grasped what my words alone couldn't convey.

What my encounter with this young disgruntled teacher showed me is that as the doors to access and opportunity open for African-Americans, the search for fulfillment in life and work is undoubtedly deepening and becoming richer as well.

And as the discovery is made that there is no script to follow, no perfect job that awaits, and no amount of money that can replace the pursuit of a passion, I foresee more black Americans breaking from the herd and moving to the beat of their own drum. Ultimately, the stories herein are but the beginning of a dialogue about the nature and purpose of existence, one that has been a long time coming. We must remember how new we are to this whole experience called the American Dream. For so long it was just another dream deferred.

THE LAST TRAILBLAZERS

These six stories are the backbone of this book. From zoo curator to guitar maker, from world-class gymnast to the world's greatest show, from artificial intelligence to environmental conscience, the spectrum of their experiences and occupations informs us, if we didn't know already, that we have the capacity to define our own destiny. Of course, this isn't a new mantra by any stretch. Starting with the end of legal segregation in the 1950s, each generation of African-Americans has had its ax to grind, its point to prove, and its burden to bear. So much of the war that's been waged for the last fifty years has been about black folks proving their competence in classrooms, courtrooms, and boardrooms while disproving one pseudoscientific stereotype after another. Our most memorable shared moments as a race have been moments of triumph and defeat in black and white. Consider the following as but a starting point:

Brown v. Board of Education
The Little Rock Nine
James Meredith's admission to the University of Mississippi
Passage of the Civil Rights and Voting Rights Acts
Assassinations of Malcolm X and Martin Luther King
Jesse Jackson in 1984
Clarence Thomas in 1991

Rodney King
Reginald Denny
Denny's
O.J.
Magic vs. Bird (Celtics vs. Lakers)
The Cosby Show
Can a black quarterback win a Super Bowl?
The Bell Curve
DWB (Driving While Black)
Venus and Serena Williams
Tiger Woods
The Confederate flag
affirmative action

At one moment or another each of these contentious issues (and dozens more) emerged as the litmus test that let blacks and whites alike know how far we'd come and how far we had to go.

But what happens when race doesn't raise eyebrows any longer, when encountering an African-American in an atypical setting doesn't cause alarm, incite undue curiosity, or warrant special attention? In short, what happens when the stories in this chapter are irrelevant? What happens when race is relieved of the weight it carries in society and all we're left with are stories about human beings? What, then, will we find instructive about these people and their lives? What will endure even after their significance as "pioneers" fades? These were the questions with which I approached the subjects in this chapter. Rather than portray Jonathon, Lisa, Jair, James, Woody, and Darryl as lone black voices in largely white fields, mere mouthpieces in other words, I tried to focus on the depth of their passion and their wide range of experiences to reveal a fuller, more captivating plotline.

For Lisa and Darryl it was their early encounters with nature that set them on their path. Meanwhile, Woody and James had a native curiosity about the way certain things worked that guided them to their callings. Jonathon spent his entire teenage years traveling the world with the Harlem Boys Choir, while Jair spent his adolescence on parallel bars, balance beams, and pummel horses from Paris to Puerto Rico. Whatever the precise details were, they'd all gone their own way. At a young age, Jair grew to savor the separate worlds he inhabited, the different parts of himself each allowed him to experience and explore. In a similar vein, Woody relished the time he spent inventing gadgets on his own. Even as Lisa and James and Darryl recall the ridicule they endured because they didn't always fit in with other blacks in the neighborhood or at school, they do so with the understanding that, in the long run, being odd relieved them of the pressure to comform to the standards by which others attempted to measure them; moreover, it freed them to be who they wanted to be at an early age.

The Panda Lady

Lisa Stevens: Zoo Curator

"Everybody wants to find their little niche in their community. Why? The world's so rich. There's all kinds of people. You don't have to have this little community that you fit in. You should have this community that you're proud of, that's part of you, but there's a whole world out there."

Once in your life visit a zoo just as it opens, before the crowds arrive. Just walk and listen, take your time and reflect. Then imagine if instead of heavy traffic and crowded trains, your daily routine included a walk through the zoo. For Lisa Stevens, a forty-seven-year-old curator at the National Zoo in Washington, D.C., this is her reality.

"The zoo is wonderful early in the morning. I love the animal sounds. I love the peacefulness of it before the visitors come," she says. "I really enjoy watching the animals. I really like coming here every morning."

The enthusiasm Lisa feels for her occupation shows on her youthful face, in her gentle voice. The silver strands streaking her long brown hair are the only notable signs of her age. Her coworkers joke that she's a living example of how doing what you love keeps you young. Today, like most days, she's casually dressed in a pair of sneakers, jeans, and a sweater. In the summer the jeans are replaced by a pair of shorts, the sweater by a short-sleeved shirt. The dozens of keys jingling like loose change when she walks down the hall or swivels in a chair, however, are worn year-round.

Lisa Stevens was one of the first people who came to mind

when I started writing this book. At the time I didn't know her name, didn't know exactly what she did at the zoo or even if she was still working there. I'd seen her on television years earlier talking about a pair of pandas, Ling-Ling and Hsing-Hsing. I remembered wondering, then, where she came from and how she'd found her way into her profession. The truth of the matter is we don't often we see nonwhites in positions like Lisa's.

"This field is not diverse at all," Lisa says. "There certainly are more women in management than there were when I started, but certainly in terms of blacks or other minorities there are very few of us. To my knowledge, I'm one of only a few black curators in the country. There was one other gentleman at the Akron Zoo, but I haven't seen him in years. There is also another woman who just recently left Zoo Atlanta to take a curatorial position at the Lincoln Park Zoo. I don't know of anyone else. There may be a few more out there, but I don't know them. I think part of it is that it's an unusual profession. Just like I didn't think this was a career path when I went off to college, I think most [black] people don't think of this as a career path either. It's just a totally foreign area.

"Most people get into this profession by chance. Not a lot of people plan to be a zookeeper or a zoo manager, although certainly more people do now than in my day. There are very few programs in the country that teach zoo biology. Most people are people like me who were interested in medicine, either veterinary or traditional medicine, studied biology or zoology, got that degree, and then thought, 'I don't think I want to go to medical school or vet school, so what do I want to do with my life.' The zoo profession also ends up being a potential outlet for people who want to work and bond with animals. I think the people drawn to this profession not only like animals or have an interest in biology, but they also tend to be educators. They're people who care about conservation and want to educate people about animals and conservation. I have keepers who come into the zoo from a variety of backgrounds. Some of them have never gone to college, so it's a real broad range."

Lisa's own background is a unique one. She was born in Ohio in 1956, the year the Montgomery bus boycott began after Rosa Parks refused to relinquish her seat on a public bus. It was the middle of the century and the civil rights movement was gripping the nation. Two years earlier, the Supreme Court had outlawed segregation in public classrooms. One year earlier, Emmett Till's body had been fished from a river in Money, Mississippi. A year later, nine black students would integrate Central High School in Little Rock, Arkansas. While her generation would be indelibly marked by these events, Lisa would leave the country with her family before she was old enough to attend school. Her father, who was U.S. Army Special Forces, was sent to Okinawa. Later, he would be transferred to Thailand. In total she spent nine years abroad, isolated from America's racial troubles. Though her skin color made her an outsider, it was never a source of discrimination. Southeast Asia's people, culture, and pace shaped her.

"As I was growing up in the tropics I had a lot of time alone. Nature and pets were my companionship; I also learned to be very comfortable being alone, not having my buddies around to socialize with all the time. Living in the tropics, first of all, living in an environment where you have a lot of contact with wildlife and nature, is really unique. If you live in the tropics you have to look out for snakes, and there are insects everywhere and all types of fascinating birds. There was an opportunity to explore wildlife that doesn't necessarily exist in an urban setting unless you go to the zoo. I also started riding horses when I was living in Thailand. I first started riding on the beach. We'd rent a horse and ride bareback."

Moving frequently at a young age meant Lisa's family was her stabilizing force. She couldn't rely on a consistent community or a consistent set of friends, but she could always rely on her parents. Military life, while not lucrative, ensures security and stability for enlisted officers and their families. Army bases provide housing, recreation, safe communities, low-cost food, even free health care, so the pecuniary dilemmas that have traditionally afflicted black families for centuries were not an overriding preoccupation for Lisa's family. She was raised humbly, but with a sense of assuredness that enabled her to inquire about the world confidently.

In particular, Lisa's mother validated her interests at a young age, despite the prevailing attitudes about gender roles at the time. Lisa's fondness for getting dirty in the woods would have tormented some mothers to no end, but Lisa's mother always accepted her daughter and encouraged her curiosity. But just as Lisa was being exposed to a different lifestyle than her urban counterparts, she was also maturing without an awareness of the issues affecting black Americans at home. She didn't know that the schools black kids attended were inadequately equipped. She'd never seen a ghetto, had never heard of communities being swallowed by riots and drugs. She didn't know of the injustice, the economic inequity, the sadness, the waste. All she knew was her secluded, safe life in a foreign land she called home. In 1969—the year of Woodstock, Neil Armstrong's landing on the moon, and the Supreme Court's ruling to end racial segregation nationwide—that would all change.

When she was thirteen, Lisa's family moved back to Washington, D.C., where she attended a public high school in the city. Suddenly, she was inserted into a community rife with racial tension. She lived on the east side of Rock Creek Park, which normally meant she would have attended Coolidge High School. However, since school systems across the country were instituting busing practices to assist in school integration, she was sent to Wilson High School (on the west side of the park) to help boost its minority population.

If you knew D.C. prior to its recent gentrification process, then you know that 16th Street was the line typically dividing the races. A predominant number of city blacks from every economic stratum lived east of the line, while a predominant number of affluent whites lived west of the line. As one might imagine, a heavy concentration of the city's wealth also resided west of the line. Lisa was overwhelmed by the racial tension with which she was faced, and perplexed by the general apathy of many of the students. She'd never been in an environment where so many students didn't want to learn. "They weren't motivated," she recalls, "and most of those students were black." What she didn't consider at the time was that many of the African-American students she encountered at Wilson came from overcrowded, underfunded junior high schools.* Within the span of a year she'd been removed from a tranquil tropical environment and thrown into a hostile urban setting where white and black students didn't get along. The whites resented having their school overrun with blacks and the blacks were bitter about being bused across town. On more than one occasion this tension resulted in school violence. Yet because of her experience living abroad, Lisa was able to make friends across the color line. This opened her up to criticism from the black students. In their eyes she was trying to be white, betraying the race.

Along with the typical angst that accompanies adolescence, Lisa was suddenly faced with several confusing questions regarding race. In her absence the civil rights movement had given way

---

*To this day, Washington, D.C., public schools are among the worst performing in the country. In 2002 the city's average SAT score was roughly 800 while the national average stood at 1,020.

to the Black Power movement. The new black radical leadership was more style-conscious than its predecessors, more concerned with an aesthetic that celebrated the very Afrocentric attributes blacks had been shamed by for so many centuries. They wore dark shades, black sweaters, Afros. They spoke of armed confrontation, seized university buildings, and made direct demands rather than patient appeals. They also claimed to represent and reflect the values of a poor and working-class black America whose socioeconomic status hadn't changed with integration. Being black now meant being "down for the cause," and Lisa's dialect, disposition, and dress all seemed to clash with the tenor of the times.

Once again, Lisa found herself on the outside looking in. During that rough transition she really began appreciating the self-confidence her mother had instilled in her at an early age. "I learned from my mother that it was okay to be sensitive, but that you had your own life to live," she says. In her new environment Lisa eventually began valuing her differences. She was the child who liked animals, the one who was quite content to sit in the woods and just listen to the birds, or look at the different leaves. She was very comfortable in nature. "I wasn't into the makeup and the hair. I just really liked to do different things than most of my friends. Of course, you end up finding the friends who like those things and I had a very diverse group of friends."

Still, being categorized and labeled by people who didn't know her bothered Lisa. Even today she sees that urge to group people in our society. "That's the way we think in the United States," she says, visibly troubled. "I'm thinking about black people because I'm black, but I see the same thing with white people or Hispanic people. Everybody wants to find their little niche in their community. Why? The world's so rich. There's all kinds of people. You don't have to have this little community that you fit in. You should have this community that you're proud of, that's part of you, but there's a whole world out there."

During high school Lisa decided she wanted to become a veterinarian. She wanted to work with animals and, as she remembers, "there were no other careers with animals *other* than being a veterinarian." Ultimately, Lisa chose Michigan State because it was the closest school to D.C. that her parents could afford that had a veterinary school. "I also went there because I really hadn't lived anywhere where there was really a winter. I thought it would be really cold up there. Crazy me."

By the time Lisa graduated in 1978, zoos across the country were in the midst of a major overhaul. With the passage of the Endangered Species Act of 1973, zoos were suddenly required to provide better care for their animals. Rather than collecting more wild animals once the ones in their care died, zoos had to start thinking about how they could sustain and manage their animal populations. In order to do that, the profession had to evolve from one in which people with janitorial skills were taking care of animals to one in which people with zoology and biology degrees were being hired in entry-level positions as zookeepers. Zoos needed to think about the psychology of the animal. They needed to think about behavior. They needed to think about creating more enriched environments where animals could thrive and breed. Meanwhile, Lisa's time at Michigan State had shown her that she didn't want to be a veterinarian. Although she had a passion for animals, she wasn't thrilled about the prospect of veterinary school. Nevertheless, Lisa was armed with a background in science, which made her a perfect candidate for a job opening as a zookeeper at the National Zoo.

Lisa was managing about half the zoo by 1987. Included under her care were the giant pandas, perhaps the zoo's biggest draws.

"That was a big year," she recalls, her voice mellowing as she recalls that memorable period in her life. Ling-Ling, the zoo's female panda, had a set of twins in 1987, which was a big deal for the National Zoo as well as for the international zoo community. Three years had passed since the female panda had carried a cub to term. Media from around the world came to get pictures and stories. Quite unexpectedly, Lisa found herself standing in front of the cameras, giving interviews, taking live shots. "It was incredible," she says. "I'm one of these people who can talk about animals till the cows come home. You ask me about something else or about myself and I'm like, 'Well, you know, whatever.' But I could very easily talk to the media about pandas; it was no problem."

That first experience in front of the camera made her into a hero. Thousands of people saw her and were affected by her presence on the screen. Overnight her life began to change. Suddenly, when she was out and about in D.C., people would come up to her and say things like "You're the lady at the zoo. I'm really proud of you." Or they'd turn to their kids and say something like "That's the lady who works with the animals at the zoo. She has a really interesting job."

"People would come over and chat with me and I started getting letters from students saying they'd always been interested in animals, but never knew they could do something like this. Then they'd ask if I could tell them how I got to do what I do."

Up until that point in her life, Lisa had always considered herself a lone wolf. She had found her passion and was perfectly comfortable pursuing it in anonymity. Her life was changing, however, and Lisa had to reevaluate her position. Without intending to become one, she was now a role model. She responded to the letters with encouraging words. She began appearing at Career Day in local schools. She also began making it a point for African-American kids who came to the zoo to see her going about her job. Even now, if she knows there's a group from an inner-city school visiting the zoo, she takes time from her day to talk to them. Lisa's visibility is crucial. It informs the child who might have similar aspirations that there is someone who has already traveled the road.

There isn't much space to sit in Lisa's office. The couch planted near the rear of the room is covered with folders and documents and books. Her desk, stacked high and wide with papers and Post-its, is just as unruly. There's obviously an order to her chaos, however. Just by watching her maneuver around the office I can tell that she knows exactly where everything is, that if someone were to clean up her clutter they'd only make her job more difficult. Here in her office, watching and listening, patiently waiting for her to finish with a coworker or answer an important phone call, I learn a curator's job isn't all direct contact with the animals. There's plenty of paperwork, and there are meetings and conference calls. Curating also entails a number of managerial responsibilities. Lisa handles five exhibits: the Giant Pandas, the Great Ape House, Gibbon Ridge, Lemur Island, and Think Tank. She brings animals into the zoo and ships others out; she handles media inquiries; she oversees specialized interpretation and enrichment programs for the large mammals; and she even designs enclosures for the animals.

This morning she met with her staff about putting their newly acquired orangutans together for an exhibit. After that she had a meeting with the public affairs office concerning the pandas. Mei Xiang, the zoo's new female panda, is in the early stages of estrus, a female panda's breeding period. In early April she and the male panda, Tian-Tian, briefly mated. Since female pandas come into heat for only two to three weeks a year, zoo staff, as well as the media, are eager to learn if she is pregnant.

This afternoon Lisa says she has another conference about the pandas. Before that, though, she has a meeting with a researcher who's working on a language project with the orangutans in the Think Tank exhibit. Later on she'll have to slog through paperwork. A colony of leaf-cutter ants is being brought in for an exhibit at Think Tank, and a gibbon that is headed to Australia by way of California has to be shipped out. The office, Lisa says, looking around, looks the way it does because it is the dumping ground as she runs back and forth.

"There's no routine in the business. You're always juggling. I've worked at the zoo for twenty-five years. This job can drive you crazy, but it can also be fun. You're constantly stimulated, there's always something new, and the end of the day comes very fast. The days just zip by all the time. I'm doing something I love. I feel very lucky about that, because a lot of people go to a job and it's just a job to pay the bills. I really like coming here every morning. I really enjoy the connection I have with the animals. Certainly, working with primates, they know you. It's very rewarding to be recognized by the animals you care for.

"I think what's really rewarding for me is the kind of things that just happen. Subtle things like knowing that the animal's comfortable with you on a day-to-day basis. You see how they act toward strangers versus how they act toward you. Just the little things like an orangutan soliciting you to play with them, or you're out in the visitor area and you see this kind of recognition, that's just very rewarding. I think also being able to go and sit and watch them and have them kind of look at you and realize you're there and then totally go about their business, ignoring you as though you're part of the group—that's also very rewarding. So it's paying attention to me, but it's also ignoring me. The fact that I can sit there and watch them and I might as well be a speck of dirt on the floor. It's kind of neat to make contact with them and have that relationship. Again, the parameters are different. It's not about holding them and all that kind of stuff, it's really about that connection we have based on respecting their biology as a wild animal, respecting the rules that are based on that animal's biology.

"Zookeepers and zoo curators are always a hit at a party. People always want to talk to you about your job and about animals. On the negative side, I suppose, the things that are tough are when you get people who are disrespectful. They're yelling, they want to throw things at the animals, they're just being obnoxious and they're loud. Their minds are closed and all they can focus on is how an animal smells or the fact that it just defecated or something like that. That's a very teenage thing. Probably of all the groups in the zoo that I interact with, the teenagers are the toughest to capture. But, usually, if I talk about sex that gets their attention. If you bring in sexuality, man, you get 'em just like that. That's usually the hook. And then I might be able to throw in some conservation stuff."

On my way out of the zoo I stop by the panda house. Somehow my visit to the zoo wouldn't have been complete otherwise. Dozens of other patrons are already lined up against the wall, looking into the grassy habitat just beyond a slim stream of water. Mei Xiang and Tian-Tian are both in the shade, indifferent to the fascinated onlookers. In person they're not as pristine as I'd pictured them. Their fur isn't a pure white, they both seem a little heavy and sluggish. And although the zoo's Web site faithfully documents the daily lives of these two burly creatures, as if they were a pair of pop icons, I find it difficult figuring out exactly what the excitement and interest surrounding them is all about. That is, until I'm reminded how few pandas still exist in the wild (roughly eleven hundred, according to the latest statistics), making them one of the most endangered species known to humankind. Then I'm struck with the irony of two endangered pandas in the care of a lone African-American curator.

On July 9, 2005 Mei-Xiang at last gave birth. At the time *Beat* went to publication the baby panda was six weeks old. None of the previous cubs had lived longer than a few days. Once again a media frenzy descended on the National Zoo, and once again Lisa Stevens stood proudly at the forefront.

Shaking the Stigma

Darryl Keith: Oceanographer

"I didn't want to just be *in* the water, but *of* the water."

Following a series of short e-mails and one clipped phone conversation, I drove up to Rhode Island one dreary May morning to spend the day with Darryl Keith. Initially, I didn't know what to expect or whether the trip would be worth it in the end. All I really knew was what most of us know: that African-Americans are underrepresented in the sciences and almost nonexistent in the marine sciences; also, that those who choose that route do it fully aware that it's a lonely path, and that it certainly isn't paved with gold. I wanted everything else, from Darryl's physical appearance to his day-to-day duties, to come as a surprise.

What I recall most clearly about my initial appraisal of Darryl, besides the jolly, open laugh with which he greeted me, was that he looked every bit the part of a scientist. Plainly dressed in slacks, a short-sleeved shirt, and tie, Darryl was the picture of the modest man of science who would rather devote his time to complex mathematical formulas than the way the colors in his shirt set off the patterns in his tie.

From as far back as he can remember, Darryl Keith has been a lover of water. Some of his earliest memories are of watching the popular television series *Sea Hunt*, starring Lloyd Bridges as sea diver Mike Nelson. Back then scuba diving was still new enough to have the air of adventure and danger about it, which made Mike Nelson into the subaquatic equivalent of Bruce Wayne. Week after week, like millions of kids across America, Darryl tuned in to watch Nelson solve mysteries, battle the elements, embark on rescue missions, and thwart crimes—all underwater. That the show's hero was a middle-aged white man didn't much matter to him. It didn't limit Darryl's sense of his own possibility or cause him to think he couldn't also carve out a similar life. His parents were college graduates, as were his grandparents, so early on he knew he could achieve, even against the odds.

"I was born in coastal North Carolina," Darryl says, once we'd settled into his office, where his walls are populated by family photos and shots of himself at sea. "The water, the beaches, weren't that far away. My neighborhood was a middle-class African-American neighborhood. Some of those folks were able to have summer homes on the shore. There was an enclave of African-American families in Topsail Beach, North Carolina, that had homes. We didn't, but we knew people who did, so we had access to the shore."

That access gave him a front-seat view of North Carolina's surfing culture. At the time, a buddy of his was already into surfing, and one day Darryl decided to try it himself. He didn't feel inhibited because he was black and the rest of the surfers were white. Surfing was something he wanted to do, so he did it. "As far as we knew," Darryl says, "we were the only black kids who had surfboards from the North Carolina border to the Virginia border."

Soon after, his father bought him his own board, and with the beach just ten miles from home, he and his friend were surfing as often as they could get a car. Unsurprisingly, they caught flack for breaking an unspoken taboo from both sides of the racial divide. Neither the white kids on the beach nor the black kids in the neighborhood were ever able to grasp the idea of two otherwise normal African-American teenagers spending their summers on the beach surfing. As far as everyone around them was concerned, black people didn't surf; as far as Darryl was concerned, surfing was fun. "We did it because we liked it," he says. "We didn't really care what people thought."

When Darryl eventually did put down his board, he didn't do so because of pressure to conform. His parents thought he was getting too old to be idling his summers away on the beach. It was time to get a job. But the summer between his junior and senior years of high school, Darryl was offered an opportunity that Mr. and Mrs. Keith couldn't pass up.

"In my junior year the English teacher at our high school wanted to put together a group to go to Europe. At that time you could go to Europe pretty cheaply. The trip was like one thousand dollars, which in the 1970s was still a lot of money, but my parents saw it as an opportunity. It was one of those things that said, 'We've made it. We can send our children to Europe like the white parents.' So we went to Europe for six weeks. For three of those weeks we were on land and for three of those weeks we toured the Mediterranean. There were dolphins and good weather and I was on a ship. That trip to Europe was a kind of culmination of all the experiences I had had before that. That opened the door and set the course because I started navigating into studying the science of the ocean. I always liked science and my father always encouraged me to do science. He bought me chemistry sets. He and my mother would buy me engineering and building toys. I just knew that my course was going to be in science and oceanography, once I found it. It was a science I could understand. I didn't want to just be *in* the water, but *of* the water. I hadn't really even thought about any cultural implications."

Something had changed in Darryl when he returned to North Carolina for his senior year: "It did something to my spirit. It gave me a spirit of independence. There was also the feeling and sense that the veil had been lifted. That yes, I'm part of a group, but I'm also an individual."

While Darryl had always been his own person and gone his own way, there was now something of the nonconformist in him. When the school instituted a random locker-search policy to curb the flow of drugs, Darryl boycotted the locker system altogether and carried his books from class to class in protest. He refused to allow school administrators to rummage through his belongings at their discretion. Then he decided to enroll in all of the advanced science and math courses. Darryl was one of the few African-American students at his predominantly white high school to choose that route. Yet again, people from both sides of the color line wondered about him. Black students, he was repeatedly told, didn't study science and math. What made people really wonder about him, though, was when he started riding his bike back and forth to school. He made the ten-mile trip nearly every day with a full load of books on his back, but he enjoyed the exercise. Even more, he enjoyed the challenge. The fact that others thought it peculiar simply made it all the more appealing to him.

At North Carolina A&T, Darryl continued walking his own walk. When he learned that MIT's marine sciences department was interested in recruiting minority students for a summer program, he quickly wrote back to Professor John Southern expressing his interest. In turn, Southern invited Darryl to Boston to work as a laboratory technician.

Darryl calls that summer experience his first "lucky break." Not only did he do hands-on work, he spent time at the highly regarded Woods Hole Oceanographic Institution, where he met world-renowned oceanographers. At the end of that summer Darryl caught his second break. Professor Southern asked him if he'd like to come back to Boston again the following summer.

Then, after a second summer in Boston, Southern asked Darryl if he'd be interested in attending MIT for a semester. "I said sure, I'd give it a try, thinking there was no way I'd ever survive at MIT. I went up and I started out in five courses and settled into three. I'm sitting in a math class with people who can multiply four-digit numbers in their heads, going, 'This is nice.' "

After the semester at MIT, Darryl decided he was ready to take on another challenge. When he was still in high school his parents had cautioned him against going to an integrated university. They'd had wonderful experiences at all-black colleges, but their friends' children who'd headed off to integrated schools had come home complaining of isolation and campus tension. At eighteen, he had accepted their advice at face value, but at twenty, and with his own experiences under his belt, he needed to see for himself. Darryl transferred to the University of North Carolina–Chapel Hill, where, again, he developed a friendship with a professor who ultimately helped him along his path. Coming out of college, he had three job offers: two in North Carolina and one at Woods Hole. With the encouragement of his professor, Darryl took the job at Woods Hole.

The next four and a half years of Darryl's life were a young oceanographer's dream. He met interesting people; he was paid well; and he traveled throughout South America. But Darryl also realized the limitations of his job. If he was willing to accept his position as a technician, he could remain at Woods Hole his entire life. But if he wanted to do his own research, he needed to get his Ph.D. He chose to go back to school.

Part of the impetus behind the move was, again, his independent nature. Darryl didn't want to spend the rest of his career processing other people's data, cleaning out their beakers, exploring their ideas. Sure, he'd get credit when a discovery was made. He might've even gotten to present certain aspects of the work. But only as a lead researcher would he get to come up with his own ideas and actually explore them, because in the scientific world, as opposed to the business world, a different set of values shape the culture.

"In an environment like this," explains Darryl, "you write a proposal that outlines what you want to do so you can get the money to do the research. After you've done the research, you write to publications and do presentations and establish a reputation for having done research in a particular aspect of the ocean sciences. For scientists, that's kind of the golden nugget."

In the sciences, money is seen as a means to an end, not necessarily the end in itself. The objective for the individual scientist is to create breakthroughs, to add her or his brick to the wall of humanity. And yet there's still a competitive, hierarchical structure in place, which, alas, is where race fit into our discussion.

Early on in his Woods Hole days, a supervisor asked Darryl to help recruit students at historically black colleges. Darryl was glad to help. The institute wanted to set up a program that would bring minority students to Woods Hole for the summer. They'd get a sense of what was going on, and hopefully get encouraged to apply to the MIT–Woods Hole doctoral program. Darryl and his supervisor visited historically black colleges to present their case: Oceanography is a great career path to pursue for a number of reasons, they insisted. One, you get to travel; two, you can help preserve the environment; and three, you can ultimately make discoveries that benefit humanity.

But the more Darryl spoke to people about the profession, the more he found himself in the awkward position of having to reconcile his public image as an African-American role model with his professional duties as a glorified lab tech. Though he'd always been race conscious, he'd also always been an adamantly independent soul. He believed that a person should shape his own life according to his personal philosophy, not a group mentality. Then, all of a sudden, he was in this position where he could affect change in a field that desperately needed it. Historically, there hadn't been a place for African-Americans in the marine sciences. Only when he was coming out of college had Woods Hole begun to do serious outreach, and only then because their big funding agencies were demanding it. It was critical, then, both to his sense of personal integrity and racial pride, that he not be seen as the ineffectual poster boy for integration. He wanted, had always wanted, to be the real deal.

"If you were to talk to the few African-American oceanographers that are out there, one of the common threads I think you will find is the desire to be the leader of the group, not to be a follower within the group," says Darryl. "You don't want to be part of the crowd. You want to get out there—that way you're being the role model for the next generation that comes through to look at you and say, 'Well, here we have an African-American scientist who is the leader, he's really doing the research, he's out there, he's getting the notoriety.'"

What has always troubled Darryl is the stigma that is often attached to the African-American scientist's work. "Some look at your science from the perspective of a black man doing science rather than science being done by a black man," he says, adding, "There's a distinction in that some people think science being done by a black scientist might not be as up to par as a white colleague's. That's a perception I continue to see now. It's not overt; it's a very subtle kind of thing."

The "subtlety" of racism came up repeatedly in my conversations with people, and what I ultimately found, as Darryl and I mined this issue together, was that this insidious variety of doubt and disbelief is even more antagonizing than outright racism because it makes you question your abilities—even after you have jumped through all the hoops and followed all the directions you were told would lead to full inclusion in the American meritocracy.

That is, unless you're able to resist those negative impulses.

Darryl acknowledged the unspoken bigotry, devised a plan, and quietly plodded along beneath the race radar. He went back to school, got married, had three children—all boys—earned two master's degrees, and taught some before landing his present job as a research oceanographer with the Environmental Protection Agency's Atlantic Ecology Division in Narragansett, Rhode Island. In other words, he got on with his life.

Darryl's work here centers around supporting the EPA's regulatory measures. Compared to his days cruising the coasts of Cuba and Haiti in his twenties, working for the government doesn't sound nearly as interesting or exciting. Back then, he was part of a team that explored purely for the sake of human knowledge; now he's part of a team that researches in the interest of environmental preservation. Among other things, Darryl studies water pollution levels stemming from chemical waste in order to draw links between toxicity levels and illnesses in local populations. For the last two years he's been working on a method of measuring chlorophyll concentration in the phytoplankton population, the basis of the food chain.

"Planktons take in light and photosynthesize the energy to produce nutrients that we live on," he says, providing me with a cursory refresher course in biology. "The higher the color, the greater the concentration. What I'm doing is coming up with ways to measure the chlorophyll concentration, and the way I do it is by aircraft. We fly along the Rhode Island shoreline and the Massachusetts shoreline. I use reflected light, light that comes out of the basin, to determine what the concentration is."

Darryl's idea isn't exactly new. NASA has been using satellites to measure the same concentration levels for years. But

NASA can't use the same satellites to measure inland bodies of water such as bays and estuaries, because these areas are generally too small and surrounded by too much land to ever get a clear reading. What Darryl figured out was a way to use light aircraft to carry a smaller satellite throughout these inland areas. In the past, researchers have had to manually gather samples all along a shoreline in order to measure these same levels. In his basement laboratory he shows me the particle analyzer scientists presently use to measure these levels. Water samples, he explains, are first placed into a beaker, then filtered and situated into a test tube where two laser beams shoot through the tube so a detector can measure the emanating light. A shoreline study can generate upwards of four hundred samples at a cost of $500 each. Annually, the cost of testing these samples runs into the millions. With the method Darryl has developed, both time and cost can be dramatically diminished.

"The first year was the concept year," he says, a tinge of nervousness rising in his otherwise mild voice. "This is the year that will decide if it's any good."

"But why does it matter if the chlorophyll concentrations rise?"

"If the fish start to die and the water turns green, there are the economic implications right there. The 'who cares' is if you have green water, tourists won't come; if you have fish dying, the fishing industry will suffer. You've got two industries that are major players in the state."

Darryl's is but a piece in a much larger environmental puzzle, the objective of which is to measure and regulate the amount of excess nutrients flowing into water systems from agricultural and industrial waste. Nevertheless, in a world where efficiency (both of cost and time) is the top priority, a breakthrough of this order has the potential to be more than just a minor scientific innovation. As for Darryl, there'll be no bonus, no promotion. All he'll get is the satisfaction of knowing that his work is making a difference, of disproving his doubters, and of setting a positive example for the next generation of scientists. Before any of that can happen, though, he'll have to spend several months studying, writing, then publishing his findings. After that, he'll have to defend them and then quietly recede back into his laboratory.

"Someone once told me, when I first started working here years ago, to be prepared to give away whatever it is you come up with," Darryl says, smiling insouciantly. "Once we've refined it to the point that it's been accepted by the scientific and environmental community, we'll transport the technology to whoever's interested."

Meanwhile, Darryl is also pursuing his Ph.D. in oceanography in the evenings. He won't get paid any more by the EPA once he's earned it, nor will he be promoted to the office in the corner, the one with the view of the Narragansett River. But, again, that's not what he's after.

"There will be a sense of personal satisfaction. At the same time, I can move ahead on educational initiatives to get more minority kids interested in the hard sciences. Also, [it shows] any African-American or Hispanic students or Chinese students if I can do it, you can do this. You just need the drive and some lucky breaks here and there."

Respecting the Gift

Jonathon Lee Iverson: Ringmaster

"You couldn't dream this thing up. A guy calls me and asks if I want to do the Greatest Show on Earth."

Picture Madison Square Garden, March 26, 1999. It's the official world premiere of The Greatest Show on Earth. It's also your homecoming, and Mayor Rudy Giuliani has just given you an award for being the first New Yorker to serve as a Ringling Brothers ringmaster. Your family and friends are in the stands watching you work the crowd. Everything's running smoothly, the people are having a great time. Then, right in the middle of the show, something eerie happens. You can't explain it, you just know something's different. You feel calmer, perhaps like someone's coaching you.

At the end of the show you go out to greet your family, exhilarated from the rush of performing in your hometown. But then you see your best friend moping and you start asking yourself if you're going to have to deal with petty jealousy issues. Then you look at your mother and she's straight-faced, too. Something's up, but no one says a word. You look around for Dad, but you don't see him. You don't want to ask, but in your spirit you know. Finally, your mother tells you your father passed away while you were performing.

Though Jonathon Lee Iverson's father had been ill for some time, his passing was still a blow. In the last five years they'd grown closer, and as early as the night before they'd had a lengthy conversation about their relationship. "It was still a beautiful night," Jonathon says. "It was beautiful and tragic. That was when I began to understand the circus. That's what keeps people coming back. It's the only place where you can actually see someone tread the fine line between triumph and tragedy, life and death. It's like a boxing match. You just know things can go either way. Death and life are looking each other in the face. One misstep can turn that show into reality. That's the thing, we're actually working against nature. We've been doing that for 133 years. It's the place where fantasy and reality meet. And that's what people are really there to see.

Within the first five minutes of our conversation Jonathon's phone rings. After looking at the number, he tells me it's his mother. I turn off the tape recorder and sip on the ice water our waitress just delivered. We're just outside the city of Brotherly Love, Philadelphia, in a diner that looks like thousands of others dotting the American landscape, and this is the first moment all morning I've had to relax; I savor it.

Jonathon Lee Iverson is a broad-shouldered twenty-something. In person he looks ten years younger than in the posters I saw plastered all over New York just a month or so earlier. He's somewhere in the range of six-four, has mocha-colored skin, is clean-shaven, and, today at least, he keeps his neatly cropped hair beneath a baseball cap. His dark shades coupled with his size lend him the mystique of a ballplayer, though once I hear him sing and watch him perform I'll more accurately describe him as a modern-day Paul Robeson.

The phone call concerned his uncle's funeral arrangements. Jonathon and his wife, Priscilla (who is the show's dance captain), are expected to fly to the funeral from Providence, Rhode Island, the show's next stop. "His health was bad," he says when I offer my condolences, "so it was kind of expected."

Jonathon and his uncle had grown close when he moved to

Wisconsin to perform in a dinner theater, which was about five years ago now. Wisconsin was cold, lonely, and exceptionally slow for a kid from New York City. Pretty soon Jonathon was making trips to nearby Chicago on his days off to see his uncle. He became a father substitute when Jonathon needed guidance and support.

"That's when he gave me 'the talk.' The last time he'd seen me was when I was about eight, so I was too young for it then. He was the one who gave the talk to all of the male children. It was always very raw, no-holds-barred. He told me about all of his life experiences, mistakes he'd made, things he'd done. There was a period in his life when he considered himself the devil incarnate."

Jonathon's uncle also told him he had never expected to live past twenty. "That's why it's not such a mournful period, at least not for me. I don't even think really for anybody in my family, because that's how [my uncle] lived. He wasn't afraid of dying and he wasn't afraid of life. He was a really cool guy, really wise. He taught me how to live life without fears."

The year he was living in Wisconsin and traveling to Chicago to see his uncle on his days off was also the year Ringling Brothers Circus was looking for a new ringmaster. They wanted someone fresh, someone who could draw in new crowds, and for the first time in the show's history, someone who could sing. As it happened, the director of the dinner theater where Jonathon was working also directed for Ringling. He thought Jonathon would be perfect for the job, so he set up an audition with Kenneth Feld, the show's proprietor. Despite Jonathon's age (he was twenty-two at the time), Feld saw his potential right away and hired him on the spot. Jonathon remembers his first performance before an audience well:

"December 25, 1998, in Tampa Bay. It was in front of all these circus performers from across the country. Ringling is the top dog, so no matter what anybody says, you're always trying to see what the top dog's got. It's kind of pathetic. You see how abused a lot of these people are, how they have to create these fictions, so a lot of them come to the shows with a certain attitude. It was still so exciting. And when I got through I was like, 'I can do this.' "

Once the initial exhilaration of simply being in The Greatest Show on Earth wore off, though, Jonathon found himself caught in the usual trappings of stardom. In less than a year he'd gone from being an obscure Wisconsin dinner-theater performer to a main attraction in an American institution. The change overwhelmed him to the point that he nearly lost control of himself. He became preoccupied with how he looked in pictures, the kind of reviews he was receiving, and the types of interviews he was getting.

"I was such a selfish person. I think there are two forms of selfishness. There's the good selfish and the really bad selfish. The good selfish is knowing that you have to make sacrifices. Anybody who's going to accomplish anything worth an eagle's nest is going to have to be alone. There are certain people, certain elements, certain things that you're going to have to cut off in order to get where you're trying to go. That can be perceived as selfish, but it's not. Then there's the bad selfish, where you actually do accomplish certain things.

"The first year I had this job I was selfish with my own spirit. I was selfish in not taking care of my health. I was selfish in not taking care of my gifts. I was selfish in not really regarding the people who really loved me. I've never been too good at keeping in contact with people, and it's sad, but then it was so much about getting things and getting money. Healthwise, during that first year, I was eating everything. I was spending my money on all types of crap."

"What woke you up?" I ask.

"I was in Chicago or New Orleans and the audience was very small. I'm just going through the motions. At the end of the show one of the teamster guys told me a lady wanted to meet me. I ran out to meet her. She was bawling. She said, 'I've been coming to the circus for seventeen years and seeing you has been so wonderful.' She could barely talk. When I heard her words, finally, I said, 'Wow!' That was something else. It really humbled me. That's what really made me realize what entertaining people is all about.

"Once I started realizing the power of what I do, I started seeing the way people responded to me. I'd say stuff over the mike, man, and people would react! It's funny. It's a very honest job, too. People can see if you're not enjoying yourself. People can see you, that's why a lot of people can't do this for a living. It's like being naked in Macy's window. People can see right through you. For you to be an excellent, excellent performer no matter how good you are, you've got to expose yourself. That takes a helluva lot of humility. You can actually be humble in that single regard and be a jerk in every other way. That's why some of the most tremendous artists suck as people.

"Now I see what I do as a form of service. Getting a bunch of interviews isn't important unless I'm going to share something that's going to shed some light on the life I live. Before I would talk in interviews just to hear myself speak, just to see the reaction in the interviewer. It was about my self-worship. My own self-righteousness. I had to break that mold because it was just destroying me in a lot of ways. It chips away at you. When I got my health under control, somewhat, I kind of came back to earth. I just started seeing what it is I do. When a singer sings or a speaker speaks it's a religious act. Life and death are in the tongue. We use the voice for so much. The voice is used for mourning. It's [used] for celebrating. There's something about singing that really— The words that come out of your mouth can really affect people.

"When I started realizing that every interview I had, every autograph I signed, every line I sang I'm immortalized in some person's mind as an image, I started respecting myself more. I have to make sure I'm feeding the spirit of the people I touch. At the end of the day that's all blessing means. In heavenly language blessing means investment. People say, 'Oh, God, just bless me.' Are you sure? When He blesses you that means He's investing in you. In our language we see blessing as the 'bling-bling,' the this and the that. Having a big house and all that. That's not blessings. All that prosperous stuff is fine, but really that's all symbolic. I see what I do as a service and that's what motivates me."

Jonathon was born in New York City in the mid-seventies and grew up on the Upper West Side of Manhattan near Central Park. From as far back as he can remember, his mother encouraged him to enjoy his own company, to never run with the crowd, and to think for himself. In time he learned to use his imagination in order to fill the empty space a gang of friends would have occupied. Living in New York meant never having to search for inspiration—the muse of creation was always nearby. But what he couldn't help seeing was how hard people in his community worked and how little most of them had to show for it. "I knew at an early age that I didn't want to work paycheck to paycheck at something I hated. All most people do their whole lives is work. They never have a career. They just work." Even then Jonathon knew he wanted to do something that would allow him to live life as he saw fit.

When Jonathon was eleven his mother asked him if he'd be interested in joining the Harlem Boys Choir. This was his first chance to pursue his passion for entertaining; he jumped at it. Joining the choir would mean traveling around the world, singing in large concert halls, meeting legislators, dignitaries, celebrities: the continuation of his imaginative inner life. After he was accepted he discovered that joining one of the world's elite choirs also meant paying his dues.

"That was a lesson in itself, because for two years I did nothing other than train. At that time the singing group had a training, a preparatory, and a concert choir. The concert choir was composed of about thirty or thirty-five members who actually performed publicly in countries as far away as South Africa. It was such a *thrill* to be called up to the concert choir. You'd be in the middle of your training class and all of a sudden you'd get pulled aside and told you just made the concert choir. It was like being drafted. You never knew when that day was going to come, either."

Jonathon didn't get his shot at performing with the concert choir until he was thirteen, two years after he'd joined and at the very moment he was ready to quit. He'd grown weary and jaded waiting for his time to come.

"I remember walking in the hallway after rehearsal, moping. The performing choir was going to Pittsburgh the next day and all I had to look forward to was another day of practice. Then out of nowhere my teacher came up to me and said, 'I need you to go home and pack your stuff. I need you to come to Pittsburgh.' One of the other boys had gotten sick. Man, I ran straight home and told my mother I was going to Pittsburgh. I don't even know what I packed that night. I just know I was happy."

That Jonathon fell in love with the road over the next five years likely explains why he's comfortable living in a little apartment on Ringling's traveling train. Instead of a fixed apartment in the city or a house in the suburbs, the train is what gives his life a sense of continuity. "It's like a city with no zip code. Wherever we are, we're at home. It's cool."

As the centerpiece of an American tradition, Jonathon Iverson has had to understand his role in the larger context of race. He's proud to be the first African-American to lead the show, but he also realizes his success is a "double-edged sword," and most of his opposition has come from other African-Americans. Shortly after Jonathon was hired, Richard Pryor wrote him a letter in regards to the animals used in the show. The letter read in part, "[w]hile I'm hardly one to complain about a young African-American making an honest living, I urge you to ask yourself just how honorable it is to preside over the abuse and suffering of animals." What exactly Pryor expected from Jonathon as a result of the letter is unclear. Perhaps he hoped Jonathon would make an appeal to Ringling's management based on the letter. The question that troubled me most, when I discovered the letter while searching the Internet one afternoon, was whether Pryor would have written the same letter to Jonathon if he was white.

When I ask Jonathon about the incident with Richard Pryor, he laughs. "Who is Richard Pryor to pass judgment on anyone?" he says, amused. "What's sad is that he's being used and I don't know why." What's even sadder, he later adds, is that most animal rights activists have never even seen the facilities the animals are housed in, even though the show invites them to see the animals' living conditions for themselves.

Pryor hasn't been the only detractor Jonathon has encountered in his time with Ringling. A few years back, while performing in Cincinnati, Jonathon almost got into a fight with an African-American radio host following a promotional interview. In the host's opinion, Jonathon was an Uncle Tom, a sellout. He told Jonathon that if it wasn't for UniverSoul (a renowned African-American circus) he wouldn't have a job, and that the only reason Ringling even hired him in the first place was because it wanted to take UniverSoul's audience. The host's insinuations instigated an embarrassing and regrettable on-air argument.

Although Jonathon lightheartedly dismisses the episode, race does play a role in the circus's sordid history. In 1835, P. T. Barnum achieved his first success as a showman by passing off an elderly slave named Joice Heth as a century-and-a-half-old ex–wet nurse of George Washington. The pair toured the country for two years, drawing crowds wherever they went. Despite the extravagance of Barnum's claim, people were too fascinated by the oddity of a 150-year-old ex-slave to resist the show's allure. His success at the time merely illustrated the racist ideology that used pseudoscience and religious dogma to distinguish the humanity of blacks from that of whites. (Remarkably, the fascination surrounding the 1994 book *The Bell Curve* wasn't very different.) During Barnum's time, many Americans already believed in the inhumanity of blacks. He merely offered them the physical evidence to corroborate those beliefs. When Heth finally passed away, Barnum even profited from her death by selling tickets to an autopsy that ultimately revealed her true age of eighty. By then, though, he'd made his name as a showman.

The point is that circuses in general exploit people's fascination with the unusual and peculiar. Looking at it from that perspective, a six-foot-four-inch black man who looks and sounds like a young Paul Robeson would be quite a draw for whichever "big top" he worked under. Nonetheless, assuming that Jonathon is merely a naive pawn—as the radio host and Pryor did—deprives him of his independence and intellect. Jonathon knows Ringling Brothers Barnum and Bailey Circus is still the shrewd enterprise it was in P. T. Barnum's day. Otherwise, it wouldn't have the celebrated reputation it has, nor would it have survived this long.

"They know that black people set the trend, at least I hope they know, in everything, so they were going to have to do something to keep up," Jonathon points out. "They were going to have to put somebody out there that can relate to the public. The thing is, if I sucked, what good would it be? That's what it comes down to, and my talent transcends all of it. I have more little white kids writing me than anybody. One little girl's mother wrote me about how all her daughter talked about at Show and Tell was the show. I try to understand how much the show mattered to this little girl. For her I'm just a guy in a top hat she enjoys running around pretending to be. It's the same thing with Tiger Woods. He's got all of these kids pretending they're him. They're not going, 'Oh wow, look at his skin color.' That's us adults, which is why my favorite audiences are kids and the elderly. They don't have those inhibitions."

The show starts in less than an hour, but I seem to be more anxious about the time than Jonathon is. He'll be fine, he assures me as we wait for the bill. He does this show every day, sometimes, like today, twice a day. Eventually, we do head back to the arena and descend into a tunnel area. I follow him backstage, watch him joke with a few performers. Everyone's relaxed, some are grabbing a bite to eat. Jonathon introduces me to everyone we pass. For him it's natural to see all of these peculiar people from around the globe collected under the "big tent." They're all his family. The Chinese, he says, pointing to a man stretching, have an amazing work ethic. The Russians, he says, passing a woman on the telephone, are famously meticulous. The South Americans, he says, after a brief banter with a triumvirate of gymnasts, are the spirit of the show. Watching them risk their lives every day makes him think his job is easy. But they respect him for what he does, what he brings, and they often tell him so. To know that they respect his contribution to the show humbles

Jonathon. After a few minutes backstage Jonathon hands me a ticket and a backstage pass. In turn I tell him I've only got one more question.

"What do you think of everything that's happened so far in your life?"

"You couldn't dream this thing up. A guy calls me and asks if I want to do The Greatest Show on Earth. I was fresh out of college. That goes to show [that] when you really do seek your true self, it's the same thing as pursuing God; it's going to come to you. You can't outdo God. It's going to come to you in ways you can't even imagine. It's not something of my own doing. People always say we have destiny, but I think we have options. I don't think things are just going to happen, that what's going to be will be. I don't believe that. It really is what you choose. I have various options every day, various roads that I can take. It's about you choosing certain paths to lead you to certain places. It scared me a little bit because I knew how big [Ringling] was, but I left myself open for this kind of thing to happen in my life.

"I look at it in this perspective: I'm in America and I'm privileged to do really great work. Even though there are a lot of politics, it's really not bad at all. I am happy. Sometimes you have to make yourself happy. And you make yourself happy by looking at life as a whole. Do I have everything I want? No. Do I need everything I want? No. I'm not all the way fulfilled and that's my fault. I need to be fulfilled in every area of my life so I can move on to a higher level. I think that's how God works. I *know* that's how God works."

The Lone Luthier

Sherwood "Woody" Phifer: Inventor/Guitar Maker

> "If people want to stop me, I'll go around the wall. If you want to block me there, I'm going to blow the wall down. I'm going to make something so bad it's just going to blow you away and there's just going to be no denying it."

The Great American Guitar Show is a necessary evil for a guitar maker. Trade shows are an important way to showcase a product and to network with others in the industry all in one place. Cards get exchanged; promises are made; competition is evaluated. These kinds of annual events are the lifeblood of a fledgling enterprise, someone operating in a smaller market, or a company from overseas. A vendor who drove up from Florida with a car full of imported sitars tells me that despite the tepid turnout—and the fact that he's headed back home with a full car—it's been worth the trip. The Japanese collectors in the booth just behind him seem pleased as well. Their vintage guitars are priced so high they don't even bother putting price tags on them. The theory, I suppose, is if you have to ask you can't afford. At $120,000, a 1959 Gibson Les Paul is the highest list-priced guitar here. At every booth—and there are hundreds of them here—I encounter a different brand of guitar, each with its own flair. The buyers and sellers are just as interesting.

For a first timer this is quite an entertaining scene, but for Woody Phifer it's just another day at the office, worse in fact. At the office, or in his case his workshop, he could be working on one of his custom built "Woodys," two of which are due to rapper/

actor Mos Def later in the summer. At an expo like this one he has to stand around for hours, waiting for a sale he's all but positive won't happen here. Other luthiers—guitar makers—and sellers stop by to chat. Mostly they talk about how sluggish this year's show has been. Everyone appears to be struggling in this stumbling economy. One vendor tells me he's selling a pair of guitars for a previously well-to-do collector who needs some quick cash. When the occasional customer does stop by his booth, the other vendors hastily step aside while Woody graciously answers questions. Because his instruments are so meticulously crafted, people tend to shy away from touching them. This is exactly what Woody doesn't want.

"You can pick it up," he says to the customer. "It's okay."

Woody encourages the customer to plug it into the amp and strum it. Unlike their vintage counterparts, Woody's guitars are meant to be played, not gawked at. For many, guitar collecting is more than an expensive hobby, it's a kind of cultural nostalgia where older automatically means better, more valuable. Most vintage guitars, Woody tells me after the customer has moved on to another booth, won't even get played after they're bought. They'll get locked in a safe, hung on a wall, or sold again. That just doesn't make much sense to Woody. An instrument is meant to be played, he says. An instrument is a tool for musical expression first, an object of aesthetic appreciation a distant second.

The last time I had seen Woody was more than a year earlier in his Garnerville, New York, workshop, where his wife, Kristen, had led me on a tour. Kristen, a film editor, figures heavily into Woody's story. Without her I would have never pinned Woody down for an interview. He means well, but like most ingenious souls he tends to get caught up either in his inner world of ideas or in the daily struggle to keep the lights on. Kristen prepped me for the interview by showing me the machines Woody uses to build his custom bridges and tailpieces. He cuts his own wood (maple, sitka spruce, and mahogany), then carves it and builds the internal structures to support the instrument's unique tonal qualities. Legendary jazz guitarist George Benson, Kristen proudly said that day, had called just a few days prior to tell Woody the world "needed" his instrument. The call had put him on cloud nine for the rest of the week.

Woody and Kristen met in Manhattan more than twenty years ago. He was coming up Forty-ninth Street on his motorcycle and she was crossing Sixth Avenue. Their eyes locked while she was crossing and again when she reached the other side. After the second look, Woody motioned for her to come back across. She replied with a sign to meet her halfway. "If he hadn't understood what the sign meant," said Woody's extroverted wife, "I was going to keep on walking."

With such an auspicious beginning, you'd think romance would've been on the immediate horizon, but for the next couple of years they remained good friends only. Even after they got together, they were never a traditional couple. Kristen was working in film and Woody in music, so their relationship, in order to work, had to be flexible and friendly: a matter of give and take. "We're trying to forever grow. I don't want to put him in a box and he doesn't want to put me in a box," Kristen said, as the sound of Woody tuning a guitar flooded the workroom. "We don't live our life through the stereotype of what a man's supposed to be or a woman's supposed to be. We figure out each other in our relationship."

Passionate and opinionated, Kristen plays the role of office manager, public relations director, and lead cheerleader for her inventive husband. She answers phones, arranges trips, and sends out press packets, all so Woody can focus on his work.

"I think what he's doing is pioneering," she said. "I really do believe that, and I'm not just saying that because I'm his wife. If

I knew about this guy that was doing what he's doing I would feel the same."

What Kristen means when she says Woody's work is pioneering is that her husband's creations are a radical departure from the standard guitar. Just as a scientist might spend his or her career working on a cure for a disease, Woody has spent his entire adult life studying, playing, and thinking about the guitar. He's taken apart thousands, built hundreds, and along the way he's made discoveries that have altered the way he believes the instrument should look, feel, and sound.

"Every time I look at something I break it down to its components," Woody explains. "I'm trying to figure out how I can make this work better. With the guitar, I look at it from a natural standpoint. It's an acoustic instrument, so I break it down to an organic state and try to make it mimic nature. There's a certain theme that runs through all living things. There're laws in terms of structure, and I'm trying to follow those same laws and step away from some of the things that seem to be obviously man-made laws. Things that to me, just in terms of looking at them, are obvious contradictions to the way things should work. I look at a guitar and how the bracing is inside and how they expect sound to travel through this instrument and it doesn't make sense to me. This is something I know, something I feel when I pick up the instrument. I'm not drawing a blueprint; I'm looking at this piece of wood and *it* basically dictates, as I'm looking at it, what will work best, what's going to vibrate best, what shape's going to work, and with that shape, what structure's going to work in this instrument to make it sing. Within that I keep tweaking the formula, but the basic idea that I come up with is very organic. It has nothing to do with studies or book knowledge. I'm just taking a block of wood and freehand I start drawing what's supposed to happen."

What Woody is best known for are his solid-body or electric guitars and basses, but what he wants to talk about these days is an acoustic guitar he's been working on for twenty years and has nearly perfected.

"Acoustic instruments are centuries old and the part the acoustic guitar played in music was as an accompaniment instrument to play chords. Nowadays everybody's a solo artist. They're the front man. Where a horn was the front man before, the guitar player is the front man now. He's playing all of the melody lines and he has to be heard, so you need to rethink the construction of the instrument so that the bass register, which is the heart of the chord, is not that prominent. What's prominent is the upper register, so you have to change the way the instrument is constructed in order to do that."

Woody started testing his theories by making his guitar with a smaller bass side and a larger treble side. He figured out where, internally, the sound of the instrument was being created, then how to reconfigure that internal makeup to manipulate the sounds of the strings to match the correct tone of the instrument. In simpler terms, he rerouted the internal system to fit with the natural flow of sound and managed to create a crystal clear–sounding instrument that's been called a "Rolls-Royce with strings."*

"No one has been doing that," Woody says. "Everyone has been taking the same old instrument and adding in a little more electronics. Being in the repair business so long, you see the things people bring to your attention." Once he explains his thinking to me, it makes perfect sense. What I wonder is why he saw things so differently from anyone else in the industry. Beyond that, what gave him the confidence to believe he could take a centuries-old instrument and make it better? Then again,

*Jude Gold, *Guitar Player Magazine*, February 2002.

why the guitar in the first place? Why had he chosen to devote so much of his life to this particular thing and not some other thing?

The last question is the easiest to answer: Jimi Hendrix. Woody was taken by the sounds Jimi was making with his guitar in the late sixties and early seventies. He was coming of age just as Hendrix was stepping into his prime, and, like a lot of young people in his generation, he was viscerally affected by what he was hearing. Woody wanted to be the next Jimi. He had always been good with his hands. As a boy he built go-carts and bicycles and kites. As a track star at Taft High School in the Bronx he wore a pair of lightweight track shoes that he'd designed himself. As it turned out, Woody had a gift for the guitar as well, and when he came home from college one summer it radically altered the course of his life.

"I decided to go into the city to Forty-eighth Street to buy a new set of pickups. I got on the wrong train and ended up on Forty-seventh Street by mistake. I started walking down Forty-seventh Street and saw a small sign that said 'Guitar Lab' so I went in. I started talking to the proprietor, Charles Lobue, and not only ended up with the pickups but ended up with a summer job. He became my mentor and initially taught me guitar construction. I never did make it to Forty-eighth Street."

Or back to college. He spent the next five years apprenticing at the Guitar Lab while spending four to six hours a day practicing guitar. Within a couple of years he was playing every night of the week with bands throughout the city. His reputation as both a player and an expert repairman soared through the 1970s. However, after he lost the tip of a finger on his playing hand in a machine accident, he began focusing all of his energies on the design side.

Woody's belief in his ideas comes from his capacity to see what isn't there. It's a skill he has spent years developing, one that's required many long hours in what he likes to call "the room." According to Woody, "the room" is where you face yourself, where you deal with your inner thoughts, where you get to the core of the problem you're faced with. If you keep going into "the room" often enough, he says, you're bound to make a breakthrough. But as long as you're not willing to go into "the room," you're never going to find out what you're capable of.

At a certain point in our conversation, Woody picks up one of his guitars and starts playing. The partially severed finger doctors said was gone for good has since healed and he can play again, though he modestly denies any claims to glory. We've been talking for over an hour, and with Kristen's help Woody and I have found our common ground. My dad was an engineer like his dad, like him. His oldest son is a writer.

Initially, Woody had promised me only an hour, but as the hour passes we both seem to get lost in the ease of the afternoon. Woody's workshop is in the back of a small industrial park in a quiet town less than an hour outside of the Bronx. He chose this place because it became too difficult to work in the city. There were too many outside distractions. People felt they could stop by anytime. If you don't have a car—and most New Yorkers don't—you can't get out to his new place.

Woody's inaccessibility shouldn't be taken as an indication of his character, though. He is a kind, gentlemanly man who isolates himself so he can be productive. Despite the acclaim he's received for his creations, repair work still accounts for a sizable share of his steady income, and it takes up a significant amount of his day. His evenings and weekends are set aside exclusively for design work. That it typically takes Woody well over one hundred labor hours to produce a single guitar explains why each one carries a $5,000 price tag. With such a high price, it's little wonder that only a handful of musicians can afford one. If he were willing to sacrifice some of the craftsmanship, he could save money and time, which would then allow him to lower his selling price, increase his production, and hire a staff of builders. After that, if he felt so inclined, he could pursue his high-end aspirations at his leisure.

But that's not Woody's way. He wants to elevate the playing experience. That's why he does what he does. "Details," he says after I propose this very scenario to him, "are what my instruments are all about." Woody's *other* inventions are where he hopes to make the big money. One is a motorcycle and bicycle lock he patented ten years ago; another is an aquatic propulsion system that requires no mechanical parts. When it comes to ideas, Woody's are never in short supply. What he lacks is the money to support them, or the time to pursue them.

Kristen steers Woody's and my conversation back on course by asking me if I've heard of Wyclef Jean. "He's another of Woody's clients," she says. "He showed him his instruments down at Wyclef's studio. Woody brought a variety of instruments. When he took out that red one his whole body reacted. He was like, 'You made this?' When they came out of the studio together I could tell that they'd made the deal. Both of them were smiling from ear to ear. You live for those reactions. All the work that you put in and sometimes it's just the positive in somebody's reaction. It's just them saying, 'I'm on board.'"

I turn back to Woody: "How *do* artists respond to you?" I ask him. Though I leave the question intentionally vague, Woody intuitively grasps that what I'm really curious about is his experience as the only African-American luthier in the business.

"It's a new experience for most people. I showed [one of my guitars] to this brother and he looked at me and said, 'You made that? Wow. Who made the bridge?'

" 'I made it.'

" 'Who did the paint?'

" 'I *made* it.'

" 'Who did the electronics?'

" 'I *made* it.'

" 'You didn't do all of this.'

" 'No, I did *everything.*'

"People are always amazed," Woody adds.

Others flat out can't believe Woody does what he does. Take the year he went to a National Association of Musical Merchants (NAMM) Conference in California. Out of the 670 merchants, he was the only African-American. He'd been given a booth in the basement, but because he wanted to demonstrate his guitar for another merchant on the floor above, he gathered his belongings and headed up the steps. En route, a security guard stopped him and asked for identification. Woody pointed to the name "Woody" on the guitar, then to his badge that read "Owner, Woody Phifer." Still, the security guard didn't believe the guitars belonged to Woody. He even radioed for backup.

Even more absurd than his California experience was the one in Atlanta. "I was taken into custody by security because I had two cases and I didn't have a booth that time. I was just going to see someone who was there." Again, he had on a badge and again he pointed to the names on the guitars. Plus, Woody was walking into the convention, not out. The guards took his guitars and placed him in a holding room until the vendor he was going to see came to vouch for him.

There's also an infamous bank-loan story. When Woody first opened his Garnerville shop two decades ago, he called a local bank to see about a loan. He had $60,000 worth of equipment and he wanted a small loan for operating capital. "I talked to the branch manager, who was actually the person in charge of the loans. I told him I could collateralize my equipment." The manager said he'd be right over so they could get the ball rolling. "I opened the door and the man asked, 'Is Mr. Phifer here?' I stuck my hand out and his face dropped. He came in here and stayed five minutes. He called me ten minutes later and said, 'Sorry, we can't help you.'"

Far from being embittered by these and other experiences, Woody laughs as he recalls them. When he isn't inside of his head, he has a clever sense of humor. His observations of the absurd and ridiculous coupled with a slight lift in his eyebrow, widening of his eyes, or tilting of his head reveal a natural comedian beneath his serious surface. But while he is able to find humor in each slight now, when the wounds were still fresh he had to wonder if he was being victimized by racism or his own sensitivity to racism.

What becomes clear to me as Woody reveals the inner workings of his mind is that his is the new dilemma facing African-Americans. Each time an African-American rises to unprecedented heights of social and economic prominence, it becomes that much more difficult to charge the system or its agents with out-and-out racism. Meanwhile, even the most prejudiced whites are let off the hook while someone like Woody remains burdened with the psychological baggage of an entire society. They alone, or in small group settings, are left to replay each incident in their heads over and over again: Maybe the security guards who hassled him were just protecting the vendors by stopping him. And perhaps the bank manager didn't think his equipment would be worth the hassle if he defaulted on a loan. The trouble is he wasn't inside their heads.

"How do you look past all of that?" I ask.

"I look at my work. I look at what I'm doing, because all of the nonsense and rhetoric takes place in the hall. It doesn't affect what I do. It doesn't enter my room. I go in there and I do what I do. If people want to stop me, I'll go around the wall. If you want to block me there, I'm going to blow the wall down. I'm going to make something so bad it's just going to blow you away, and there's just going to be no denying it."

In the three hours I spend at the Great American Guitar Show I talk to Woody for a total of ten minutes. We take a photo together and he fixes a pair of my sunglasses that I mistakenly sat on, but mainly I try to stay out of the way and watch, not just him, but everything happening around him. I decided to come because I was intrigued by the idea of guitar culture, but more than that I was curious about Woody's horror stories. I didn't arrive expecting to see Woody harassed or taken into custody, but I did wonder how his peers perceive him and his work, and whether his race would play negatively or positively into that perception. The vendors and buyers I speak to have nothing but good things to say about Woody and his work. They all see his vision and admire his commitment, though one buyer in particular expresses his doubts about the practicality of producing such an expensive instrument amid a deluge of lower-priced competition. He likes Woody, he says, he just worries that he can't survive in this market, even as a boutique luthier.

What I think about but don't say to the critic is that perhaps the purpose Woody is serving is far greater than any bottom line. After all, he's part of a community that twenty, thirty years ago didn't have any African-Americans to speak of. Just by being exceptional at what he does, maybe he's changing people's attitudes. In our conversation a year earlier I asked Woody if he thought he was a trailblazer, and without even flinching he replied, "Oh yeah." He and Kristen are very aware of race and the implications of black ingenuity. They know people don't pursue what they don't believe they can succeed in, and that typically people need models in order to believe in their own possibilities for success. In his own way, and while doing his own thing, Woody Phifer shows us all just what might happen if you get on the wrong train.

Focused

Jair Lynch: Olympian/Real Estate Developer

"I knew I had a small window of time. Like a head of lettuce, I knew it would go bad. If you don't know who you are before you get there, then someone else will define you."

My earliest memory of Jair Lynch is watching him perform backflips in his backyard. By then, I'd heard all about Jair, the gymnastics prodigy. He was four years ahead of me, but we knew each other in the way of neighborhood kids. You play in the same parks; you walk the same streets; you ride bikes through the same alleys; you go to the same elementary school. My sister and her friends sometimes talked about Jair. Plus, our parents ran in the same social set. Shepard Park was a predominantly African-American middle-class neighborhood straddling the D.C.-Maryland line. Many of our parents were first-generation college graduates. They were professors, engineers, doctors, lawyers: people who had worked hard and cracked through the system that had held previous generations in check. Now they were living the dream. Beautiful homes. Late-model automobiles. Vacations in the islands. Private school educations for the kids. By no means was it easy street, but it was the neighborhood norm.

I'd never seen Jair show his stuff in public prior to that day. He wasn't a show-off. What struck me even then was his focus; I doubted he even noticed me. In fact, when I tell him the story he says, simply, "I don't remember any of that stuff."

But I do. The question is why that specific image has endured for two decades. I couldn't have been more than nine or ten at the time, which would've made Jair thirteen or fourteen. I remember thinking that I couldn't do what he was doing. I could play soccer, basketball, run track, throw a football. But I could never hurl my body in the air in rapid succession and land on my feet, gracefully.

As the years progressed, so did the legend of Jair, which means "one who sees the light" in Senegalese. By sixteen, he was a Junior Olympics national champion and competing internationally. Few people in the neighborhood had actually seen him perform, and yet it was commonly acknowledged that he was something of a wunderkind. For those of us coming up, having someone you knew making a name for himself in a sport other than football or basketball or baseball was fascinating, and that he was never around anymore only added to his legend.

"That was the start of the compartmentalizing of my life," Jair says sixteen years later. "I was starting to compete internationally so I would be gone. I was in Paris, Japan, Puerto Rico. In high school it felt like I was going to college because I went to class and I left. I wasn't around. I just wasn't there."

So Jair's life became three separate worlds that never intersected. In the morning he had practice. During the day he was in school. After school he was back at practice. When he did have free time, he spent it with his friends from the neighborhood. His parents felt it was important that despite his athletic gifts he experience a normal kind of childhood. Gymnastics was his dream and they were certainly going to do everything in their power to support him, but they also felt he should be allowed to develop and explore and make choices for himself.

"I'll never forget my dad saying, 'I'm gonna let you run with the boys. But please don't make me have to come get you.' It's such a delicate thing. He gave me enough rope to kind of see

what reality was. He also took a gamble letting me do that because I could have—"

"Gone the whole opposite direction?" I say, thinking about
some of the guys we'd grown up with who, despite a middle-
class upbringing, had drifted onto the streets and into drugs.

"Exactly. He really tried and really exposed me to enough.
He and my mom."

Both of Jair's parents are high achievers themselves. Jair's
mother, Martha, is a retired economist who at one time worked
at the World Bank and the Inter-American Development Bank.
Before retiring several years ago, his father, Ackyln, was a highly
regarded professor of political economy and African-American
studies at the University of Maryland. He's written notable
books on African civilization, and lectured extensively on the
African diaspora. They discovered their son's talent through trial
and error. At the local YMCA he tried all of the usual sports—
basketball, softball, soccer: "I just tried different sports and I
think the coaches said something that got my parents' attention
and that got me to go a little further. I think more than anything
I just cut in line. I wanted more 'touches' on the events than
everyone else, so I cut in line and they liked that."

Jair was hungry, and in any field, that is what separates some
individuals from the crowd. That Jair's slight, agile frame fit the
sport's prototype made him all the more attractive to his
coaches. So, starting when Jair was ten, Ackyln came home from
work at four o'clock every afternoon in order to drive his son to
and from practice in Columbia, Maryland, a thirty-mile trip.
Once Jair turned sixteen, however, he was driving himself back
and forth to practice, twice a day.

The sacrifice paid off when Jair was offered a full scholarship
to Stanford. There, the worlds he'd been keeping at arm's
length collided for the first time. His classmates were his fans.
His teammates were his classmates. The adjustment was diffi-

cult for someone who had crafted a compartmentalized existence since childhood. Jair was used to having other worlds he could enter, worlds where the parts of himself that had nothing to do with gymnastics could live. He needed an escape. But it wouldn't be until he decided on a major that things stabilized again.

"I was the only guy on the team who was doing civil engineering, so that kind of took me out of that space. I still had my black friends, and that also took me out of that space. And then traveling took me out of the space."

Meanwhile, Jair continued to excel on the mat. In 1991 he tied a U.S. Olympic Festival gymnastics record by winning five gold medals. A year later he won first place in the parallel bars and high bars at the National Championships in Columbus, Ohio. The same year, at age twenty, he made his first U.S. Olympic Team.

"Ninety-two was overwhelming. I wasn't supposed to make the team. I was at the bottom of the National Team in ninety-one. In ninety, I was still on the Junior National Team. So it was a little overwhelming in Barcelona. I mean, I enjoyed it. I think at that point I thought I was at the top of the game. I didn't realize that the game was bigger because it wasn't just getting there, you had to do well, you had to manage the tickets and the people and the press and the crowd and all the other stuff. I didn't know. When you're young you don't really get that."

Though he hadn't been expected to finish well, Jair nearly medaled, finishing sixth on the parallel bars, and missing bronze by one tenth of a point. Afterward, he returned to Stanford to captain the team to a second straight national championship. In 1994 he graduated from Stanford with academic and athletic honors. Following graduation, he got a job in Silicon Valley. He also continued to compete and train. Three years later he was in Atlanta for the 1996 Olympics.

• • •

I remember watching Jair compete in the Atlanta games. I'd followed the gymnastics competition partly out of interest, but primarily because watching him inspired me. We'd gone to the same schools. We'd grown up in the same neighborhood. If he could make it to that level, I figured I could achieve something special as well. When he overcame a painful callus in his left palm to stick a double front salto with a half twist out for a score of 9.825, good enough for the silver medal in parallel bars, I remember thinking to myself, "He did it. His life will never be the same again. He's suddenly a different person in the eyes of the world." No one had given Jair much of a chance. No other African-American male had ever medaled in Olympic gymnastics competition. In one fell swoop he'd rewritten a piece of history.

"The second [Olympics] I was much more appreciative and much more concentrated on doing well and not just competing. It was a great experience. Actually, I haven't really thought about it in a while. [The Olympics] were humbling. They were euphoric. I felt I was accomplishing something. I'm in a subjective sport and being a black man in that sport means something. It was an interesting growth experience because it wasn't over the top. It wasn't Tracy McGrady famous. It was also small-time enough that people felt like they could have access to me automatically. It was like, 'How could you say no? You're not *that* big.' Coming back to D.C., and there not being a lot of athletes and professional sports being so poor, it was like a double-edged sword."

Parties were thrown in Jair's honor. He shook hands with many of the major politicos in the city. People recognized him wherever he went. He spoke all over town. Jair became the poster boy for everything positive about black America. He came from a stable home. He'd been educated at fine institutions. He'd competed and performed at the highest level in his sport. He had a winning personality. He understood where he came from.

More important, perhaps, he knew who he was and what he was about:

"I knew I had a small window of time. Like a head of lettuce, I knew it would go bad. If you don't know who you are before you get there, then someone else will define you. If you don't know who you are and all of a sudden you end up on television, whoever put you on is going to define who you are and you won't be conscious of it. If people don't have [an identity], then the roar of the crowd, that person interviewing you, the girl screaming—that whole scene becomes who you are. You have to have something to retire to or you will hang on to that one highlight and you'll have nothing else. I had already started working. I was already interested in real estate. So I said, 'You know what, I've gotten where I need to go, I'm not going to try and hold another four years.' I was done. No ifs, ands, or buts about it."

Along with his degree in civil engineering, Jair also received a degree in urban design while at Stanford. Urban design is essentially the conceptualization of a city: How buildings should be organized to facilitate civic life. Where people and their lives will fit into that structure. How human values will be woven into the fabric of the city itself. It isn't as abstract as planning, but it also isn't as concrete as architecture. Urban design is the creative space between, if you will, the demands of the present, the duties to the past, and the expectations of the future.

"I always remember when I was on trips my freshman year. I used to beg my coach, 'Let me have the keys to the van; let me have the keys to the van; let me have the keys to the van.' And he'd be like, 'No. No. No.' Until I started doing good. Then he was like, 'All right.' A friend of mine and I both hated sitting in the hotel room, so if we had an hour or two we'd grab the keys to the van and go drive. We'd drive through neighborhoods in small towns like Columbus, Ohio, or big places like Boston. We'd just go driving. He would drive and I would just look at how the neighborhood moved. We'd go to Houston and see a skyscraper right next to a house and go to Boston and see something totally different. That was helpful for school, but it also helped me relax because it got my mind off the stress of the week or the workout or whatever. We'd just talk and talk. I'd be talking to him and relaxing from the day and looking at buildings all at the same time. There was this kind of layering of life. It's all intertwined."

What is a city? What should it look like? How should a person feel when they walk or drive down an urban block? How does a city's well-being affect the well-being of its citizens? If a community looks downtrodden, won't the people reflect that sense of dejection? And vice versa. These were the kinds of questions running through Jair's mind on those afternoon drives; the kinds of questions that would stay with him as he watched the unprecedented San Francisco Bay Area revival in the mid-nineties. San Francisco, especially, was booming because of the technology blitz rocketing from Silicon Valley. Yuppies with seemingly limitless amounts of money wanted out of the suburbs their parents had reared them in. They wanted the velocity of the big city, its convenience and culture and art and food and leisure. They wanted to be able to walk to work, maybe ride their bike. If they had to drive or take public transportation, they wanted the commute to be as quick as possible. They wanted to walk around the corner to the bookstore, the grocery store, the post office, the new Indian restaurant, the yoga studio, or the local park. Whatever it was this new group of upwardly mobile urban professionals desired, they were willing to pay top dollar to have it at their fingertips. Property values soared. Long-time residents were forced out. New residents were bought in. Overnight, entire communities transformed from gritty and working class to glitzy and leisure class. Jair watched all of this and knew D.C.'s turn was next.

"When I got [back] here it was like *The Matrix*. I could see what was going to happen. I was like, 'Oh yeah, this is going to pop.'"

Just a year after his Olympic triumph, Jair told his parents he was coming home to try his hand in the commercial real estate market. "My dad didn't want me to come back to the city. He said this city is bullshit. It's a bunch of middle-class black people who are pretty apathetic, not politically conscious, not really doing anything." Jair didn't care. He figured D.C. presented a golden opportunity. He knew how to lead and how to succeed. Paying attention to details, pushing himself to the limit, and getting those "extra touches" had taken him to the top in one field, so why not another? Besides, not only was it his hometown, not only was he a hero, D.C. was on the cusp of something big. In California he might've died before he ever got ahead. In D.C., if he just worked harder than everyone else, he could make things happen for himself.

Jair's first development job was, of all things, saving a YMCA.

"The Thurgood Marshall Center on Twelfth and T Streets was the first African-American YMCA. It was shut down by the YMCA in the eighties and a nonprofit bought it for one dollar. The nonprofit struggled for years to try and put a deal together and I volunteered when I came back. I told them I could help them with the deal structure."

Community service was nothing new to Jair. In college, he'd been awarded the Stanford Black Community Service Award twice for volunteer work as a Big Brother. He believed in the karmic effects of good deeds, that if he gave to a worthy cause, it would give back to him. He started with a cell phone, a laptop, and an Internet connection. He didn't have any money. No inheritance. No silver spoon. Not even his own place. All he could bank on was his word, his round-the-clock drive, and his belief that he could make something happen.

"Gymnastics, which had a lot of creativity, spurred my creative juices in terms of how I could make something up," Jair says. Using his creativity, he found the investors. Next, he got them to put up their money. "Once the deal started moving and the deal was bankable, the nonprofit asked me to manage it for them." Jair's next move was forming the Jair Lynch Companies to oversee the rehabilitation of the historic building. Once he got his foot in the door, there was no turning back.

Today, the Thurgood Marshall Center houses learning, heritage, and office facilities; in the meantime, the Jair Lynch Companies have grown from a one-man, one-computer outfit to a seventeen-person operation managing more than $275 million worth of properties in the Washington, D.C., area. A quick look on JLC's Web site shows you just how busy they've been in the past seven years. From consulting to development to direct investment to construction, Jair's fledgling enterprise has its hands in just about every area of real estate development.

"It's amazing," he says of his success. "We have separated ourselves from the typical African-American developer who is a one- or two-person shop, ex–city official. We're not about that. We're about being innovative and having a staff that can actually get things done and not just think of things.

"We have folks from Latin America, we have African-Americans, we have folks of Asian descent. It's a good mix of races, it's a good mix of skill sets, age—everything. It's still small, everyone knows one another, they know if you're having a good day or a bad day, and they help. There are no offices— though there are a couple of conference rooms. It's wide open.

It's just a very good group and the key is we consistently evolve—we're *able* to evolve. We're able to show people the depth, and that's really good. But there's going to be other competitors. There's going to be a two- or three-person shop that's going to be hungry like I was five years ago. We have to continue to move in different directions."

But just as with San Francisco of the mid-nineties, Seattle of the later nineties, and Brooklyn of today, Washington, D.C., has its urban renewal sweepstakes winners and losers. The ugly, inevitable underside of civic "beautification" is the bad taste it tends to leave in the mouths of the lately evicted. Urban renewal projects are sold, essentially, on the basis of city revitalization. A more attractive cityscape attracts higher income taxpayers, who in turn leave a trail for merchants to follow. Cities argue that with the broader tax base they have more dollars to spend on services like health care, policing, education, public housing, waste management—all of the issues that ultimately matter to a community. The 2000 census largely corroborated this theory, revealing a nationwide decline in poverty concentration in metropolitan areas. Washington, D.C., however, is another story. It was one of twenty-nine cities whose poverty concentration levels actually *increased* during that time. Evidence like this begs the question, Is gentrification really benefiting everyone? Is it possible, instead, that rather than diversifying communities, gentrification is isolating and even abandoning pockets of the population?

"There is more poverty in D.C. than there was ten years ago," Jair says. "There's this shift in the population and you have the disenfranchised and, unfortunately, the ultra-enfranchised who think they can call the shots and do what they want. I'm working on this affordable housing project. The south side of the block was a drug area, probably one of the worst. You've got a five-story building, fairly high density. On the north side of the block you've got houses, just regular town houses. The town houses, now, have moved from one hundred thousand dollars to five hundred thousand dollars, but the apartment building hasn't gone up. We're converting them to co-ops for the people who live there to own them, and it's amazing. The people who live in the town houses across the street called the council member—because we got public money. They were upset because there was very little consideration in our plan to work on the exterior of the buildings and renovate the exterior. I couldn't believe these people. We explained that there were three tiers in how we were going to go about construction. The first tier was life-safety issues. There was no fire alarm system, no ADA access. Nothing. Second, because these people are older, we were going to individualize their units so they had their own heating ventilation systems. The third tier was going to be beautification issues, especially on the exterior. They were like, 'Oh no, that can't be on the third tier, you need to put that up higher.'"

While no one group owns a city, it is troubling that what often happens during the gentrification process is that the people who stuck with the city during its lean years, who, for better or worse, helped make it what it is, often don't get to participate in the remaking of the city. Jair agrees. He is particularly fearful for all older working-class people who don't see how the gentrification happening around them will ultimately increase their property's value. "They don't have access to information about how they should protect themselves for the next thirty years. They don't have access to information about how they can actually help their child with college. They sell and they think they're getting the world when someone offers them two hundred thousand dollars. You can't get anything with that."

Jair and I have an honest conversation about his role in all of this at his home one night. Hometown hero or not, he fits the profile of the new class of affluent interlopers. He's educated, young, single, and earns a high income. He even lives on a recently revitalized street in a recently renovated house close to downtown. Inside, walls have been painted, spaces opened, rooms remodeled, floors replaced, and brick exposed. The furniture is sleek and stylish, the art, inconspicuous. In just seven years, Jair, who stays fit by swimming every day after work, has successfully negotiated the divide between one world and the next.

"If you don't recognize you're in the game, then someone's moving you around. You always have to be conscious of what's in front of you, above you, around you. I got that from my dad. Street smarts with intellect in terms of understanding there's a reason why the treasury note goes up and down; there's a reason why OPEC cut back on its number of barrels; there's lots of reasons why things happen, you can't accept them at face value."

Jair also realizes that the reason lots of developers are wealthy now is because they benefited from the privatization of public housing in the 1960s and 1970s. "The housing authority didn't want to deal with poor blacks living in Section Eight housing. [It's] kind of like with prisons in the last ten years. A lot of people got very, very rich taking on hundreds and hundreds of units, taking on the worst of the worst in the worst neighborhoods and having the stomach to do it. And just like in everything, some people did it to help and some people just sucked what they could get out of it."

One situation in particular Jair recalls was when another African-American developer asked him if he was willing to do whatever it took to be financially successful. 'Are you willing to be that man?' the developer challenged. 'Are you going to find the worst of the worst and exploit?'

"I will not lie to you. I'm in, besides finance, the most capitalistic profession there is. And it's about making money. But we don't really think of it that way. We're also not a nonprofit. The way we look at it, we are more sensitive developers because we don't do anything detrimental for the community. We try to empower the communities that we work with. We won't go into a situation and buy a building and kick everyone out just for condos. We try to figure out a way to either not participate or help the residents that are there. Or we'll go into tough neighborhoods.

"We're doing two hundred units of planned housing right near Ballou High School, and one of the things we're doing is that in order to empower the kids, we're going into Ballou and giving the kids an opportunity to name the complex and the community building so they feel connected to the property. We also bring the architects and the contractors out to the site so they see development isn't just hammering nails. We'll do stuff like that. We'll invest in a project like an apartment building, then we'll also do a community center down the street, or we'll help a charter school open up around the corner. It's this concept of wraparound development where you're controlling the destiny of more than just your island, your piece of property.

"I think there has been a systematic disinvestment in these communities and it's not only the physical plan, it's not putting in the windows, it's school systems, it's health care. It's all these things, the whole sense of community. That disinvestment made some people rich, [and] lowered taxes for everyone. It had many, many ripple effects and real estate is just part of it. That disinvestment, more than anything, destroyed hope. And when you destroy hope, you've lost everything, because if I don't give a fuck, then I will kill and I will break and I will loiter or I won't go to school.

"Is there hope for the neighborhoods? I think so. I think the problem is that it's going to be such a long struggle. It's not going to be five years in each neighborhood. It's going to be a generation, it's going to be like ten, twenty years. And there's going to be a lot of people in the middle who are going to say,

'Why isn't this fixed?' Or, 'What are you doing to fix this?' Or, 'You're not doing anything, you're making money.' They're not going to recognize that it's a much bigger problem, that we alone can't fix it, and I'm going to push it from more angles than most people will because I think about it from more angles than most people do. But it's going to take time because right now I've got cranes going up all over the city, but I don't have a vocational program for D.C. public schools, so not enough kids who are graduating can come work at our sites. I would hope that poor kids could come right out of their vocational training in high school and come work on our job sites. On top of that, you have to give them hope that this actually is a good living. You just wish you could do more."

Lord of the Ant-bots

James McLurkin: Scientist/Inventor

"Nothing in the world is accomplished without passion."

If James McLurkin couldn't make his living building robots, he'd probably be an efficiency expert for a company like FedEx or UPS. Never mind that he's considered one of the most promising inventors of his generation, it's *those* guys, people whose entire lives center around optimizing products and services—saving and creating time—whom he holds in the highest regard.

"The only thing that matters is time," James explains the afternoon of our first conversation, one to which I arrived a half-hour late after I got lost on MIT's campus. "I'm obsessed with efficiency. If I wake up and I'm breathing all at the same time, I have twenty-four hours, some I need to spend sleeping."

James turns to his computer, punches a few keys, and on the screen appears a highly organized and intricately detailed "to do" list. "To be honest," he says, scrolling through pages and pages of text, "it goes on for a long time."

Perplexed by the sheer length of his task list I ask, "You keep adding onto that?"

"Let's be honest about this," he replies, scrolling back to the top of page one. "These things on this page I'm actually going to do. These are notes I'm taking about things I'm buying, so I'm looking for a tool chest and a work bench, and these are things maybe I will do at some point in time, there are about two pages of that. Once you get past that, these are things that won't get done. Ever. When I die, these things will still be on this list."

"You're cool with that? You accept that?"

He nods begrudgingly. "It took me a long time to get there, so the things that I do, I try to make them as efficient as possible. That just pervades everything."

James's obsession with efficiency even gnaws at the edges of our conversation. I'd been allotted a certain amount of time, two hours, after which he had other engagements. That I had arrived at the spare office James shares with another doctoral candidate a half hour late was my problem. He couldn't give that time back to me, couldn't spare it. He is, after all, a full-time doctoral candidate, a part-time project director at a robotics company, and an inventor. If I hadn't already been prepared for this I might've been a little annoyed, but his truncated communiqués had already tipped me off. Earlier I had sent him a list of questions to which he simply cut and pasted a series of "yeses" and "nos" capped off by a simple "James" before pressing the send button.

Ten minutes after he shows me his protracted "to do" list (and after I had driven four hours just to see him), we're walking to the elevator, intensely dismantling the meaning (or lack thereof) behind the Grand Architect's speech to Neo in *The Matrix: Reloaded*, and saying our good-byes. After we part ways I feel like kicking myself. I'd driven all that way, and we hadn't even covered much ground in an hour and a half. However, it would only take a cursory review of James's interview tape on my way back to New York for me to discover just how time-efficient he could be.

Born in Long Island, James is an only child. His father is from South Carolina and his mother, the daughter of a Tuskegee Airman, grew up on an air force base in Ohio. They've been divorced since James was four. Mom, a retired speech teacher, still lives in Long Island. Dad, an engineer by trade, is now based in

Los Angeles. According to James—and by way of his wry sense of humor—that's just about the distance they need to be from each other in order to pleasantly coexist. How they ever managed to be in a room long enough to conceive a child, let alone raise him together for four years, remains a mystery to him.

As a kid James preferred small, delicate toys to the clunkier playthings that were the rage in the early eighties. He recalls the serious Legos stage that was followed by an equally intense *Star Wars* phase. Even now he unflinchingly spends hundreds of dollars whenever new sets of *Star Wars* Legos are released.

"You can't help yourself," James says. "You're pulled to these things." After Legos came video games and BMX bicycles. "[Then] somewhere in there I got a computer. I started programming. As opposed to just playing video games, I started trying to write video games. Very, very important. I learned a lot of very palpable programming techniques; I didn't even know what they were called back then. Video games are some of the most challenging pieces of software to write. They're also very challenging to run on your computer. You want to test a system, get a hard-core video game and see how fast it goes. They have to accept input from the user, process it, process their internal stuff, get it on the screen, and they have to do this usually six times a second."

Even as a kid James was attracted to efficiency. Video games taught him how to work within a framework of constraints. You have to make things happen, or appear to happen, in the shortest possible time.

James went on, explaining real-time systems and how they work, and I let him. Not only am I getting a free lesson in computer science, he's on a stream-of-consciousness roll, connecting science with math with engineering. His knowledge is impressive. But then he stops himself:

"I'm getting off on a tangent," he says. "So, there's video

games, there's computers, there's BMX bikes, radio-controlled cars—that got started in high school. I took the first car I had and turned it into a robot."

All along Mom and Dad were supportive. Although he lived with his mother, he spent his weekends with his father. Mom was the creative one, and Dad taught him how to tinker. Where he'd grown up in rural South Carolina the rule was if something broke, you'd better figure out how to fix it, because you weren't getting a new one. Analogously, if you took something apart, you'd better be able to put it back together.

Then came MIT.

"When I came here for college, my parents wouldn't let me bring any of my stuff with me because they wanted me to really focus on my studies. It was very important," he says with more than a slight note of irony, "that I not waste my time with all the robot stuff."

Without really applying himself, he'd finished high school with a 3.8 GPA. His parents thought he could do better if he just tried a little harder, focused a little more. At MIT he was going to major in electrical engineering and graduate from the robot stuff into more estimable scientific endeavors like, for example, electric car power systems, data communication networks, or cell phone antennas. Before that could happen, though, he had to get past the MIT mystique, a major hurdle in and of itself.

"You're with a lot of people who are really smart. The biggest disappointment. Surprise?" As James sometimes does, he stops himself midsentence to make sure he says precisely what he means: "Not so much surprise was that as smart as they are, I'm actually on par with these people. That was good. I remember I was sitting in multivariable calculus. I thought I was really lost, really confused, I didn't know *what* was going on, and this guy in the back asked this question, and I was like, 'Oh man, if you don't understand that then you don't understand this, this, and this.'"

Discovering he belonged had its benefits and its drawbacks. In one sense, realizing he could compete encouraged James; in another, it allowed him to slack off again—something you can't do at a place like MIT and hope to excel. If there were roughly 168 hours in a week, 40 of which were spent sleeping, another 15 eating and showering, an MIT student, James quickly discovered, could be amazingly efficient at converting the remaining 100 hours into work. "They minimize time back and forth to class. They minimize time eating. They can convert all available time into studying and prepping for class. When you get people like that who are also really smart, you will not outperform them. As a matter of fact, you probably won't even be close." So James got mostly Bs, a few hard-earned Cs, and no As; for those were reserved for a particular caliber of genius that even he, as he freely admits, wasn't in the company of.

By second semester James was showing the robots he'd built back in high school to staff members at MIT's Mobot lab. He was offered an unpaid position in exchange for parts. By the next year he was on the payroll and he had built what was at the time the world's smallest robot.

"There's so much more going on here than just academics. There's the lab, there's the people, there's a lot of really powerful stuff. I would have been remiss not to build robots. I'd be remiss not to work in this lab. This would compromise my education almost entirely if I didn't get out of these classrooms and start working on stuff. Now, I should have probably spent more time studying. I didn't realize at the time that when you don't like any of the classes in your major you should probably switch majors, so I got two degrees in electrical engineering before I realized I can't stand electrical engineering. If I have to take another double-e class I will vomit. I got pretty close last year."

• • •

Let's back up for a moment. I'd happened upon James's name late one night while searching the Internet. I was looking for African-American inventors, following whatever leads I came upon, and within a few minutes I was reading about this young guy at MIT who had just won the Lemilson-MIT Student Award for his work in robotics. I'd struck Internet gold. Here was this young man at MIT building, of all things, robots. A few more clicks and I was looking at a picture of James, a good-looking and seemingly normal guy touched prematurely with tufts of distinguishing gray hair, surrounded by a squadron of tiny antlike robots, smiling. These, I would later learn, were his prizewinning Swarm-Robots, a collection of fist-size, and still pretty clunky-looking, automatons that work together to perform various tasks. For instance, in "Follow the Leader" the objective, roughly, is for each scattered robot to read the signals of the ones closest to it in order to fall in a single-file line. Compared to the highly stylized versions of artificial intelligence Hollywood has produced in recent years (*Minority Report, X-Men, I, Robot*), James's robots seemed like crude oddities, but the reality is his work is on the cutting edge of real-world robotic technology. This is the actual building of intelligence, the formulation of autonomous networks of communication that will eventually work independently of humankind.

As I read a news article written about his work, I discovered more. For the last few years James had been studying ants and bees and termites. He believed that nature could provide some of the answers scientists were looking for in artificial intelligence development. He'd taken a course on natural systems at Harvard; he'd spent time at Cornell studying honeybees; I even read something about how he kept pet ants in a drawer at home.

"They're carpenter ants. If they got out it would be bad. I used to live in a concrete apartment building so it didn't matter if they got out. But I moved to a standard, three-story walk-up. There are a lot of scientists working very hard to try and solve the same problems I'm working on, which are, how do they work together? How do they communicate? What are they saying? Because they're not saying much. They have some chemical signals, they have touch signals, they measure certain things about their environment that lets them make decisions, and those decisions then affect the group behaviors. There's a lot of magic going on there and we're trying to demystify the process."

By studying ants, James also learned a valuable lesson: Ants don't care if they run into one another. If they do, they walk over or under one another and keep going. James figured, if nature didn't care about obstacle avoidance, then he shouldn't either. He could just build his robots smart enough and tough enough so that if they ever got stuck in a jam, they could use their sensors to wiggle their way out without causing any damage.

"They're profoundly stupid. You turn them on and they do exactly what you told them to do, which might not be what you want them to do. They run around and when you've decided you've seen enough, you go back and change your software, and you run it again. It's the debugging cycle that any other system has. The only thing that makes this system a little different is that the software I write is individual robot software, but the behaviors I care about are group behaviors and that disconnect between the two."

However terse James is on e-mail, he makes up for it in person. A straight question never warrants a straight answer in his world. Things are far too complex, both on paper and in his mind. Perhaps that's why he prefers to keep his e-mails so brief: The more one writes, the greater the likelihood of misinterpretation.

Even a question as simple as "How does it feel to win a prestigious award for your work?" elicits a protracted balancing act of a reply from James. Is he honored? Certainly. Does he feel better about himself? Yes and no. The validation is nice, but he's the same social outcast who was tinkering with robots back in high school; the same guy who couldn't run with the black crowd because he wasn't cool enough or the white crowd because he wasn't white; the guy who, by default, hung with the bikers, but only by default. In fact, James is a self-professed semi-reformed geek whose mother dressed him in plaid, and who felt every bit of the puerile scorn for getting the 95 percent on the test everyone else scraped by on or failed. His is a classic story, only he's not bitter and trying to compensate for everything he didn't have in high school. As painful as his adolescence might've been, James was fortunate to have people at every turn who led him in the right direction. He had his parents, one or two teachers in high school, and, at MIT and UC–Berkeley, a continuous string of advisers who opened doors for him and gave him what he needed in order to do what he wanted. If anything, finding an encouraging and like-minded community at MIT is what spurred his social development. There he met other African-American students, professors, and administrators with a serious interest in the sciences.

So, no, on the whole, James *doesn't* feel any different because he won an award and he runs his own project at a robotics company and suddenly magazines want to write about him.

Almost a year to the day of our first interview, I find myself standing in front of a hotel just outside of Cambridge when James pulls up on a motorcycle. It's a sleek black Honda and he's got the black leather jacket, black helmet, and even a black backpack to match. He rode it, he says, because he had errands to run in the morning and getting around town, weaving around sluggish Saturday-morning traffic, parking, and whatnot, is just easier—more efficient—on his bike than in his car. The plan for the day is to see the city and go go-carting. Go-carting is a tradition for him, something he's done ten, twelve times a year since the time when, as an undergrad, he made an important self-discovery.

During James's second year of college he noticed that he could work really hard for ten weeks straight; crudely speaking, he could bust his ass day and night. But then, without fail, he'd crash. He wouldn't have any motivation left. The problem was this crash normally took place around the end of the term, so all through finals he'd be listless and unmotivated. Once he figured out what was happening to him, he decided that from then on he was going to take the tenth week of every semester off. If he had homework, it wasn't getting done. If there was a project due, he'd find a way to buy himself some time. No matter what, though, that tenth week was his to do with what he pleased. He'd visit friends, catch movies, eat out, and, of course, drive go-carts.

As James and I ride around the city I ask myself why I felt the need to return to Boston this second time. I wonder what I am trying to get from James that I can't get from a phone interview. While our first interview had been cut short, a thirty-minute phone conversation would have given me enough to piece together a fairly decent profile. In an unusually lengthy e-mail he'd sent the week prior he even wondered what "my goals for the interview" were. There was something else that I wanted to explore, though, some part of his life that I felt I wanted a better, clearer understanding of. Perhaps it was because so much of what he'd explained to me about his work seemed to fly right over my head that I felt in danger of either whittling him down to his science or building him up as this great new African-American innovator, something even he's not comfortable being called. I suppose I had realized that had I gone in either of those directions his story would have suffered. Hanging out with him, having a simple conversation with him, was a way for me to see him outside of the laboratory, away from his robots.

Go-carting turns out to be a thrilling time. I hadn't done it in so long, fifteen years probably. I used to drag my dad to the track nearest my house whenever I could and yet, like so many other things I'd learned to put aside for the sake of adulthood, I hadn't even thought about it since I got my driver's license. I'd forgotten that go-carts were their own experience, something apart from driving a car from A to B for X purpose. On the way to the track I kept asking James why he go-carted, what it did for him, how it figured into his scientific research. But the only response he could give me—the simplest one he'd ever given me in all our talks, long and short—was that it was fun. He likes to drive around in a glorified circle. Granted, he is still obsessive about his driving efficiency—about hitting the curves at the exact angle so he doesn't have to slow down, pulling in tight on the straightaways and stretching out wide on the turns—but the whole time he's on the track he's elated.

After the first race he takes me back inside the dressing room and shows me what I'm doing wrong on a chalkboard replica of the track. I'm hugging the inside of the track when what I need to be doing is loosening up, he says. Whatever I do, he explains, try not to use my brakes, the carts are too slow. Once you've lost ground on your opponent, he adds, it's impossible to make it back up again. After the lesson, we go at it again and again and again, and sure enough by the last race he's only lapping me once.

As we dress in the locker room, something James said in our first conversation crosses my mind again. At the time it sounded like fortune cookie wisdom: "A wise man makes no distinction between work and play," he'd said, after which he explained that, no, there had never been an epiphany or a grand insight that enlightened him on his life's path. He simply likes building robots. In his mind every problem has a certain number of failures attached to it. All you need to do is try once more than you've failed and you suddenly have a success. That success quickly becomes addictive. James had to go through seven years of electrical engineering to figure that out for himself, but eventually he did and that's how and why he landed back at MIT for his Ph.D. in computer science. Like many of us, he'd been pressured to do something he didn't want to do. Just because he was gifted in the sciences didn't exempt him from those societal and interpersonal struggles. The difference is that when he realized what he was doing was wrong for him, he systematically stopped doing it.

For dinner James, his girlfriend, my wife, and I go to a Thai restaurant in downtown Boston. While we're waiting for the main course, James pulls out his ever-present laptop and starts showing us his Swarm-Robots in action. The program he's most excited about is the one-hundred-robot marching band. He looks forward to a day when we see one hundred little robots performing in the Bayou Classic's halftime show. They're not there yet, but they're coming along. Next, James starts showing me the codes he's written for each program. That's when I get lost. I nod and continue following along as best I can, but my brain just can't process what he's saying. Too many variables, too much jargon, too many squiggly lines and charts. At the end of the day James and I will probably never completely understand each other. But then, at the end of dinner, he gets his fortune cookie, opens it, and laughs.

"What does it say?" I ask.

He hands it to me: "Nothing in the world is accomplished without passion," the fortune reads.

What I learned about James McLurkin on my second trip to

Boston is just as valuable as what I learned on the first trip. He's been successful so far because he's figured out how to enjoy his life as often as he can. Of course, he's in the very fortunate position of working in a field that the government and megasized defense contractors find fund-worthy at the moment. Artificial intelligence is clearly the science of the moment, which explains why *Fortune* magazine and *Newsweek* are running stories on him. He's well aware that were it not for this fortuitous confluence of variables, his robot fixation could have easily been relegated to a weekend hobby.

James also knows that in order for his robotics work to remain interesting to him, he has to keep expanding, exploring, and learning. In the year since we first met, he says on the drive back to my hotel, his work has stagnated somewhat. He's ready to get out of Boston, to start a new chapter in his life. There's a scientist in California doing robotics work that he really admires and from whom he could benefit. He'd like to get out there and work with him. That would, as he often says, "be optimal." Besides, he's a little tired of flying around the country to give presentations, writing up project reports, and managing a team of engineers. All of that ends up taking away from the actual work. His plan is to give up the job and focus on finishing his doctorate so he can then devote himself to working full-time on the robots. Technology, as the saying goes, is always changing, and if James wants to stay on the cutting edge, he understands he's got to keep changing with it.

BOHEMIAN BLUES

"At the Crossroads," "Liberation Is a Full-Time Job," "The Bitter and the Sweet," and "It Ain't Over Till It's Over." Each of these stories speaks of the creative creature's struggle in a consumer culture. All of us with a message to share know how it feels to have something important and valuable to say but few who'll listen. It's frustrating. It's lonely. It's financially risky. Indeed, money is undoubtedly the defining theme in all of these stories. With more money, everything gets a little easier. Time loosens up. Doors open up. And people listen up. Without money, everything is a battle.

But it's a battle that's obviously worth fighting. If it weren't, Blake Amos, a musician, wouldn't laugh when he says, "It ain't over till it's over," and W. Ellington Felton, a multitalented performer, wouldn't have seriously contemplated joining the Army Reserves. For reasons that each person makes clear in his or her own way, they've chosen to do whatever it takes to keep their creative aspirations afloat. They'll endure family pressures and financial strains; they'll put up with cramped quarters and they'll bounce back from mental meltdowns. Perhaps it's the struggle that keeps life interesting and the art flowing.

Or maybe just knowing that you've got something all your own makes life livable and each new day tolerable. If there's one thing that none of these people lack it's self-respect. They're able to wake up each morning and honestly say to themselves they're in the fight of their lives. They're not planning to pursue their passion someday, they're doing it. What's really distressing is that so many people don't pursue what they love. We're all guilty of this infraction to some degree. Our society is also partly to blame. So much value is placed on what we do and don't have, what we're missing out on and what's on its way, that there's hardly any time, or reason for that matter, to figure out who we are and what we're about. If the stories in this chapter can help you raise one question, it should be "What am I willing to sing the blues for?"

At the Crossroads

Ellington Robinson: Painter

> "All I want to do is create, but at the same time at whose expense? There comes a time when you want to be self-sufficient and go out there and be able to make decisions for yourself, be able to do whatever it is you want to do."

Ellington Robinson sleeps and works out of the same room on the top floor of his father and stepmother's Washington, D.C., brownstone. His friends sometimes call it the Huxtable house because it reminds everyone who steps inside of the affluent and cultured aesthetic of the old *Cosby Show* set. Each room in the four-story house is its own art gallery. His father and stepmother have traveled all over the world, and each time they return with paintings, sculptures, and exotic pieces of furniture. The floors creak slightly and the house tends toward darkness even during the day, so it feels like you're entering an old Harlem parlor when you cross the threshold. It's a house not unlike one Ellington himself hopes to own one day. For now, though, he's a twenty-seven-year-old artist who's spent the last eighteen months practically in isolation working on a painting he proudly deems an "ambitious piece."

"I've been working since October 2001 in little baby steps, brick by brick. It's been an exercise in discipline for me. It hasn't been easy. You just have to put yourself in a disposition where nothing else matters. I don't spend much time with friends. Sometimes, I don't see my family members for weeks, but it's called sacrifice. I think when you really want something really bad then you're willing to do what it takes to get it done."

Looking at the nearly completed painting that has emerged from the early etchings I saw over a year ago, I find it difficult to believe that Ellington's never taken a class, and that he didn't pick up a paintbrush until four years ago, when, in his words, "I was driving by a Utrecht store and I said, 'You know what, I'm going to pull over and get some paints just to see what I can do with it.'" Back then, he had aspirations of writing and directing films. He'd worked on a couple of film sets back when he was at Morehouse, including one for the Hudlin brothers, directors of the early nineties hip-hop classic *House Party*. After graduation Ellington even spent a summer studying film in Paris; every now and then, he still brings out the short he made while he was there. But no one ever told him he had a gift for painting, much less that he could make his living as an artist. "Just that one day I opened that door and this is what was in that room."

A lamp arches over Ellington's shoulders as his large golden hands painstakingly touch up the smallest details. He's only a shade over six feet tall and of average build, but between the lanky limbs, the heavy voice, the bald head, and the quiet confidence you'd think he was much bigger. Ellington's also a consummate host who likes to make his guests feel at home. By the time I arrive on the night of our first interview, he has a bottle of wine laid out. The comfortable atmosphere he creates allows his guests to let down their guard, feel at home, and say what's on their minds. The conversations that ensue often last into the early hours of the morning and range from art to politics to hip-hop to jazz and back. Ellington laughs more than he talks at these informal gatherings; he prefers watching his friends go at it from the sidelines. Even when the stories told involve him, he speaks up only when the teller strays too far from the truth.

Tonight, however, it's just Ellington and me, and of course his painting, which he talks about like a proud father watching his child grow into something he couldn't have imagined.

"This painting was a grand thought so I needed a grand canvas in order to address all of those ideas, and I've made use of every inch of space. There's no space wasted, no dead space. This is one piece, not several—one. If you want to translate this into literature it's not a novella, it's a novel. It's taken this much space in order to bring together all of my thoughts. It's post–September eleventh, it's pre–September eleventh. It's a juxtaposition between culture and this technological age we're living in. It's bringing those two things together and balancing those two aspects, and it's not easy. It's the biggest project I've ever worked on. I've never put so much energy into anything. I've made this my life."

But by making this single painting the center of his world, Ellington's put the rest of his life on hold. And while his friends have all gone out and gotten jobs that will likely lead them up the corporate ladder, his path is one without similar guarantees. A few of his friends have wondered if he's holding too tightly to this one thing, whether he should just finish it and move on. They don't doubt his abilities; what they fear is that he's setting himself up for a crushing disappointment. Who knows if anyone will buy the painting, much less see it. In the five hundred and some-odd days he's been working on it few people have actually laid eyes on the 72" × 96" rendering of a Manhattanesque skyline. Those who have seen it are friends and family, folks whose opinions, though valued, are rarely trusted by an ambitious artist. Essentially, Ellington has taken a gamble that most of us would just as soon avoid. Not only does his résumé lack significant evidence of ambition (he worked at Borders Books for four years after college), but he's invested his entire identity in a profoundly subjective and fickle enterprise: art.

Despite the odds, however, Ellington shrugs and says, quite

simply, "Whatever happens after this is God's will. Whatever happens, happens. I'm satisfied with it. It's been personally fulfilling." Later, he points out how many people his age often lose sight of the present in their quest for success and stability in the future. "We're at an age right now when so many people are focused on saving. Well, I'm doing something that might not carry me through to tomorrow, but I appreciate the moment. I'm enjoying the process and I think that's most important. If I was to die tomorrow at least I can prove there's something I really enjoyed doing."

Though none of what he says should be taken to mean Ellington is not as interested in making as much money as his college pals, it does indicate that he's looking for something more, something all the money in the world can't give him. While others his age nod their head to the latest pop icon's latest lyrics, he studies the wisdom of his creative ancestors. "I don't look at music videos as someplace I want to be," he says, sluggishly. "I'd rather look up to W. E. B. DuBois or Frederick Douglass or George Jackson, people who are more the intellectual types, than those who let material things speak for them."

In an on-demand society driven by the immediacy and transience of pop culture, Ellington is a throwback to a different time and different frame of mind. Like his namesake, composer Duke Ellington, he's a jazz enthusiast. If you look under his bed you'll discover dozens of shoe boxes filled with records by Charlie Parker, Art Blakey, Lee Morgan, Archie Shepp, Dexter Gordon, and his favorite, Miles Davis. His music collection, along with the stacks of books slouching around his chair, are his only discernible possessions, his faithful companions during the long stretches when he doesn't seek the company of the world. Talking about jazz causes his voice to dip into the rhythmic cadence of an old school aficionado waxing philosophical about its relationship to black culture:

"Think of when King was killed, jazz was there. It was all of the tension that black folks had been going through since slavery. When those riots took place in all of these cities, that was jazz. That was Art Blakey on the drums. That was Charlie Parker on that horn. That was Coltrane when he was so far out there that you can't even understand where he was coming from. These were all of the emotions we were going through. The drugs, the sex, all of it. Jazz is extremely deep. It's beyond music. It's spiritual but it's also intellectual at the same time.

"It's also a record of the feelings of black Americans. When you look at our age now and you look at the civil rights struggle or even as far back as the Civil War, none of that was very long ago. That was basically yesterday, so jazz still applies to today's world. We haven't really moved that much forward. I think more blacks are starting to make more money and more are becoming professionals, but we have more of our people going to jail. With gentrification, communities are being broken up, crack is flooding the neighborhoods. It's the same type of thing that's been going on for some time, but it's changed. Black people are no longer the special minority in this country anymore. You have a lot of other minorities that have come to this country."

As invested as Ellington Robinson is in his art, there is also another dimension to his story, one that plays a significant role in my being in his bedroom/studio tonight. A week ago he called me and said he was seriously considering medical school. After four years as a sales clerk at Borders, and eighteen months holed up in his bedroom, it sounded like his unshakable faith in his craft was beginning to wane. He sounded tense and, for the first time since he and I had known each other, confused about the direction he should head in. The painting was coming to a close and now he would have to return to reality. He still lived at home;

his last steady job was as a sales associate at a bookstore; and several of his closest friends were getting married, having children, buying homes, and making some real money in the real world. I wondered if the pressure was finally beginning to tug at him.

"All I want to do is create," he says in a thoughtful, measured tone when I bring up medical school, "but at the same time at whose expense? There comes a time when you want to be self-sufficient and go out there and be able to make decisions for yourself, be able to do whatever it is you want to do."

When I ask him what it is he wants to do he points to his father, Fletcher Robinson. "He set the blueprint for how I want to live my life."

Ellington's father is a successful dermatologist who splits his time between practices in the Virgin Islands and Washington, D.C. Ellington spent four years of his youth (ages ten to fourteen) in St. Croix living in an old slave owner's house surrounded by six acres of land. "I was just a nature boy, running around wild," he recalls. "Horses and goats would come onto the property. We had five dogs. There were all types of people coming through. [My father] was always the suave, cool-dressing cat. Very friendly, *always* had a lot of friends."

Many of those friends were upper-middle-class professionals.

"I've never really had to go to the other side of the fence in order to find the people that I look up to. That's totally been a blessing. I think my experience has probably been a unique one. There's not too many black people I know who grew up having black doctors. The fact that my father's a doctor, as is my stepmother, and I'm not being pretentious about it, but I grew up around black professionals; blacks who are doing extremely well for themselves."

Ellington sees no contradiction in wanting to pursue a career in medicine, it isn't too far from who he is, he says. "I'm always going to paint," he quickly points out, though. Still, choosing to pursue medicine is no small undertaking, and the chances are he won't be able to dedicate himself to a work of art for a very long time, if ever again. Ellington knows all too well what happens when you "open" a door: life intervenes and leads you in another direction.

As I listen to Ellington make sense of his dilemma for himself I can't help but hear the voice of a young man unsure of his future. He starts to ramble, relating the challenge of medicine to bungee jumping and facing a perfectly white canvas for the first time. Then he begins a jumbled explanation that I have a hard time following. I do, however, realize that he needs to do this, so I sit back, make sure there's plenty of tape left, and listen:

One moment Ellington suggests simply focusing all of his energies on medicine for the next few years. But in the very next breath he says he doesn't want to make too quick a decision. He says he's torn right down the middle. Half of him wants to keep pushing his art; the other half wants to start studying for the entrance examination for medical school, the MCAT. Either way, he needs more time to figure things out. For a couple of years now he's considered moving to New York and seeing what can come of his art. He'd like to give himself a real shot on the big stage. And yet whenever he's been close to making that move, something always manages to hold him back.

"One thing that people find hard to do is change," he says, his voice suddenly taking a coach's affected authority. "They find it hard to pivot midcourse. Or if a plan doesn't work out they feel they've failed. It's not about failure. It's just about changing directions."

This doesn't sound like the same person I'd been speaking with for the last couple of hours, I think; rather, it sounds like someone rationalizing his way out of a quandary. Finally, Ellington lets down his guard, forgets what he should be saying, and speaks from his heart: "This is where the soul-searching takes place," he says, and with that I sense the beginning of a sincere dialogue with himself not only about what he wants to do but about why he wants to do it.

In all that Ellington says never does he talk about medicine as his passion, not even as a noble profession. Never does he drift into syncopated jazz-speak about his desire to help people or to save lives. He certainly can't list off the names of famous physicians the way he can name the artists whose work has influenced his own. In fact, all I really hear is a young man willing himself to take on a challenge in order to perhaps justify his privilege, maybe even his existence. And I hear it partly because that young man was me when, toward the end of college, I willed myself into law school, then through three grueling years (summers included) and a bar exam before finally relenting.

Finally, Ellington pauses. He takes a sip of his wine and collects his thoughts in order to say what he's really wanted to say all along. Sometimes, it takes us talking all the way around an issue to finally get to its core.

"I probably just want to do too much. I want to do everything. I really do. I have a big appetite. I want to get into music, I want to write, I want to direct, I want to paint, I want to do medicine, I want to sail, I want to be a pilot. There's so many things I want to do. Part of my drive is that I've seen people who have done it all. My eyes have just been opened to so much. Why not do it all?"

While his layers intrigue me—as do his sudden doubts—what really interests me about Ellington is how profoundly relevant his rhetorical question "Why not do it all?" is to the wealth of choices available to African-Americans in today's society. In many ways Ellington's appetite mirrors the desires of all those who come to realize how many options there are in life. That realization can be both a blessing and a curse, a motivating force or procrastination's source. While our parents' generation faced a limited number of career paths legitimately open to them, people like Ellington have reaped the benefits of those open doors and are now positioned to take full advantage of the American Dream; yet they feel stifled by a range of emotions that have less to do with the choice itself and more to do with the pressure to perform now that the opportunity is available. The question for them, as it is for Ellington, is which way to go?

All along I feared Ellington was making a decision based on factors that had little to do with who he is as a person. Undoubtedly, he was thinking about upholding a legacy, about keeping up with his peers, and about maintaining the level of comfort he has grown accustomed to. What's troubling is the lengths he seemed willing to go to in order to secure the very creature comforts that could ultimately stand in the way of his passionate commitment.

At the same time I understand where he's coming from. All those hours alone must've given him more than ample time to reflect on the passing of days, weeks, years, without receiving even the slightest recognition. Van Gogh and Degas, two of Ellington's favorite painters, come to mind when I think of all the artists who never reaped the fruits of their labor. The thought alone scares most would-be creators into careers they secretly loathe, which in itself is a bitter irony: While they might gain financial security and social standing, they lose that which they hold in highest regard.

The night wanders into the early-morning hours and my conversation with Ellington loses its focus. When the clock strikes two it's clear that he isn't going to finish the painting tonight. My disappointment, however, is a reflection of my personal desire to have his story end up nice and tidy. The reality is I don't think he's quite ready to let his painting go.

"Do you feel pressure to make a decision?" I ask.

"I do feel pressure to make a decision. I feel like I need to make a decision fast."

Not until I review the tape later do I realize that earlier in the evening Ellington had said that he didn't feel pressured. Maybe he was so tired he forgot what he said earlier. Or maybe he was ready to be completely honest with himself.

I have only one more question: "If you choose to go with medicine, does that mean you're conforming?"

"For me, going into medicine is conforming. I think it's safe to say that the people who aren't conforming are special because shit gets hard, shit gets tough. It's not easy if you don't have a paycheck coming in every two weeks and your work is determining your next decision. That's a lot of pressure. That's why everybody's not cut out to live that way. Those people [who do] definitely deserve that respect. I think the people who have followed their heart and did everything the right way, the universe has rewarded them ten times, a hundred times over. Not everybody can handle that, which is why you see so many talented people in this world lose it. They can't handle it."

Postscript. Two months later Ellington finally finished his painting. Soon thereafter he decided not to apply to medical school. Then he called and said he was painting feverishly. The work, he said, was gushing out of him. I didn't ask where he planned on making his money or how he came to decide against medical school. I just stopped by the house one day and looked at his latest piece.

Liberation Is a Full-Time Job

Marla Moore: Filmmaker

> "You have to find time to be with yourself. You have to do things counter to what society is asking you to do at times. You have to honor yourself. To honor the art is easy."

Marla Moore has a lot on her plate, arguably too much. Besides being a mother of young twin girls and working full-time, she's an inveterate filmmaker. There's the documentary on the growing child-care crisis in the United States, a love story for her Howard University graduate school thesis, another documentary about race entitled, simply, *Black*, and a list of screenplays that are in various stages of production. And that's just what she's producing and directing. Through her production company, Mirrorball Films, she shoots special events, teaches courses in video editing and screenwriting, and freelance edits, all for cut-rate costs. "Say you do music video," Marla proposes, her red wine–tinted dreads draping her round cheeks. "I'll do it for one thousand dollars. *Nobody* will do it for one thousand dollars and have it be broadcast-quality. That means I'll get a good shooter and you'll have a piece that will help you with your Web site, may help you with a record label, and will definitely help you get other gigs. Mirror balls reflect light back to people. I want to help people tell their stories affordably."

One of the films Marla edited was *12 O'Clock Boys,* a documentary about an underground crew of Baltimore stunt-bikers. The crew shot a film about their late-night adventures. "They liberated themselves," she says. "They didn't wait for someone else to tell their story."

Self-liberation, if it isn't already obvious, is Marla's mantra. "I have a home studio. I have editing equipment, a DVD duplicator for copies and dubs. I have an Avid system, Final Cut Pro, Pro Tools up in there." She's also proficient in Adobe Premiere, After-Effects, Photoshop, and Illustrator. In effect, since beginning her film career more than a decade ago as a screenwriter, she's incorporated every major aspect of filmmaking into her repertoire. "I started as a writer and editing is the final polish. Editing is writing, too. You are the magician. Shooting, if you screw up, you screw up. It can be fixed, but not really. But the editor is the one who gets to be like the nurse and say, 'The patient will live. He may be missing a limb, but he'll live.'"

Marla wasn't a natural tech-wiz. She didn't do well in math in school. She didn't even like computers. Like most digitally disinclined people, she only used computers for word processing and e-mail. But then Final Cut hit the market and something told Marla that this was her chance to make her art on her own terms. "When digital first came out, my professors at Howard were like, you need to cut on film, digital video is never going to go anywhere. I said, 'No, that's not true. These cats in Denmark are shooting these movies and winning Cannes.' I was like, I'm going to buy this thing. I'm going to buy a Mac. I'm going to teach myself. When it first came out there wasn't even a class. I got it myself and said, 'I'ma learn.'"

Saying Marla is passionate about filmmaking is a vast understatement. She's more like a creative lightning rod. She sees everything in terms of its artistic potential, looks at everyone as though they were a story waiting to be told. Even my interview with her for my book managed to become her interview with me for her film. Marla's the one who bogarts the Indian restaurant and confiscates their upstairs dining area for three hours; the one who sets up her camera and routinely cuts me short or asks me to repeat myself in order to capture the right angle and sound bite. At times, it's awkward, particularly since her mother sits with us for the entire three hours, but it also helps me to understand Marla on a level that words alone can't fully convey. For three hours, while the camera rolls, and we're rapping back and forth, she's a ball of energy. She's up, she's down. She's checking the lighting, she's ordering food, she's figuring out how she's going to cut my interview, where it will fit into the film, what kind of background she's going to use.

With Marla, I quickly discover, I'm not going to get a linear story; I'm going to have to sift through pages of transcript to find where each story begins and ends. But once I accept her rules of engagement, I find myself observing a woman who is unusually intelligent and brutally candid. Sounding like a character straight out of a Toni Morrison novel, Marla freely revisits the horrors of growing up in Columbia, Maryland, an all-white suburb, in the early and mid-eighties. They were painful, peculiar years, yet oddly fascinating years, too. She was the only African-American in her class, hers was the only African-American family in her neighborhood. Her classmates routinely called her "nigger." Feeling as though she didn't get any positive reinforcement from mainstream media, Marla gave up on being attractive at an early age. She became the girl the guys could be friends with; the girl they would talk about other girls with; the girl who was outwardly funny and smart and creative, and inwardly troubled. In four years of high school, she never went on a date.

"Growing up I always felt out of the pocket," Marla recalls. "I didn't fit in with any of my peers. Either I wasn't cool enough or I didn't think they saw life the way I saw it; except for the punk rock kids. I was really into that. The Smiths, the

Cure, Siouxsie and the Banshees, all that music, and the blues, and certain folk music that has more of a lyrical content about the sadness. I felt like I had more in common with the disenfranchised peoples. Like, if there was a nerd group, a crazy punk rock group, these were *the* people."

Punk-Rasta. That's the name Marla came up with to define the people like her: strange African-American suburbanites with no clear place in America's stubbornly polarized black/white landscape. Marla's prototypical Punk-Rasta is into Gothic's "dark beauty," its "transformative" quality, even the vampirism—all the things punk rock kids were into and about, including the political angst. The Rasta side comes later and stems from an attraction to a nostalgic longing to live naturally and freely. "It's the healing and the anger," she says, "the urban and the organic. It's the reunion of opposites, the yin and the yang. The Rastas say, 'Oh, she's not pure. She's got tattoos. She dye her locks. She not real.' It's just like with punk rock being more serious in Europe with everybody being on welfare, starting with the Sex Pistols. If you trace it in this culture, then the truest thing we have is hip-hop and it's why Public Enemy has punk rock kids at their concerts. They were angry with the way shit was, too. It comes out of a suburban dissatisfaction, an urban dissatisfaction, and somehow the adolescent phase of transformation. You are optimistic, but you're spoiled in the sense that you feel like you should get what you want. That's a bit of a different thing than being a regular Rasta. Punk-Rastas may not be vegetarians. They may smoke cigarettes. They may drink a beer once in a while. They may drink vodka straight. But the roots are still real because there is a spiritual quality."

Because of the racial hostility she encountered, Marla rarely went to school. School was too exhausting, too alienating; not just the other students, but the school itself. The drama club had no use for her. Her voice didn't fit with the choir. Her art was too loopy and pain stricken. Even after scoring sky high on the SATs, her guidance counselor doubted she could make it at the next level. Fortunately, her mother, one of the first ever black Peace Corps members, made her fill out college applications anyway, something for which she's still grateful nearly twenty years later. "That's why the family is so important, because I wouldn't have gone to Howard." That's not to say things got better for her once she stepped on Howard University's campus. The ridicule simply flowed from a different place. Her plaid skirts, tattered dog collar, and Doc Marten boots quickly earned her the title of "campus freak," and instead of being mocked because she was black, she found herself being mocked because she was weird *and* black. Ultimately, and ironically, it would be hip-hop and not punk-rock that helped shape her racial identity during those years.

"Salt-N-Pepa was so revolutionary because they wore Doc Martens. We already had those, the people who were into punk. But for the black girls who were dressing crazy, who saw Salt-N-Pepa out there doing their thing and wearing those clothes we were wearing, but a little different, that made a big difference. They helped us know we were black, too. I know it shouldn't be so much about a pair of boots, but it really was. Because the people who were called to that underground were the people who didn't fit into Jack and Jill (an African-American social organization), who weren't going to be debutante black folks, but who also weren't going to be street. Somewhere there had to be this ground for the disenfranchised."

The trouble with being creative and disenfranchised, Marla points out, is you begin to see yourself exclusively in that light. If you only get love from people when you're performing, if the only time people notice you is when you write something beautiful, if you feel like the whole person you are is unacceptable, then it becomes impossible to think people will want to be around you for any other reason than that "thing" you do. In Marla's case, winning her first poetry competition when she was in her teens gave her the attention she hadn't received before. After that, it was only natural, if not logical, that she continued to write. She'd found something she was good at, something people appreciated her for, so all through high school and college she wrote: plays, poetry, songs, screenplays. Winning the Paramount/Eddie Murphy Screenwriting Fellowship after graduation was the crowning moment of her young life. Marla was flown out to Los Angeles where, for a year, she learned the craft of filmmaking from the ground up. She met producers, actors, directors. She learned about budgets, organization, and management. She witnessed the politics of moviemaking, the good, the bad, and the ugly of it, and it all just fortified her resolve to be a filmmaker.

But time, as the saying goes, crept up on her and before Marla knew it a decade had passed. Despite making important industry inroads, writing, directing, and editing a handful of short films, virtually completing her M.F.A. in film, and having twin daughters, Marla started to feel the pressure most artists eventually feel to put up or shut up. She needed something to show for herself, something tangible and, yes, even profitable. While the drive to succeed is hardly uncommon in our culture, Marla's drive was layered with her continued desire for validation. Between writing, editing, directing, teaching, and making a living, Marla rarely found time for herself, let alone her daughters. Eventually, after years of pushing herself, she suffered a full-on stress attack.

"I was bedridden for two months," she says, offhandedly retelling the ordeal as though it were as common as a stomachache. "I had complete back pain where I was walking and moving with horrible pain. That was really hard. They tested me for lupus, AIDS, cancer. They did MRIs, all kinds of stuff. It was just stress, pure and simple. It was doing too many things."

For years, Marla struggled with symptoms of bipolar disorder. She often experienced periods of intense productivity followed by periods of lethargy acute enough to keep her in bed. But like a lot of artists she was convinced that the power of her art was bound up in her pain. Her poetry had originally been born from the pain of rejection. Her most potent songs often dealt with loss and sorrow. The characters in her scripts were frequently lost or damaged souls searching for redemption. Healing that pain, Marla feared, meant sterilizing her artistic voice. What she needed was a source of vitality independent of pain.

She found two. The first was her family.

Marla has always been close to her parents and sisters, and she'll be the first person to tell you family keeps an artist sane. But she'll also tell you she's taken it for granted that her parents live around the corner and have always been willing to take care of her daughters, Maya and Angelique, if she needed them to. For years that's what they did. If Marla had to work, then the girls stayed with their grandparents. Then, one day, the family found out Angelique was suffering from ADHD and she would have to start following a strict, supervised diet in order to keep her moods in order. That was the moment Marla realized she had to accept responsibility for her own mental and physical health in order to protect her daughter's. "Black people don't talk about mental illness; it's a taboo. What my mom always said is we survived the middle passage. When you're a slave, you can't tell the master, 'I feel I have postslavery stress disorder, I can't get shit done.' What's happened as a result is black people in general have learned to get over their problems rather than confront them. That black people just say 'get over it' has contributed to obesity, it's contributed to alcoholism, all the 'isms.' "

When Marla says African-Americans are often leery of seeking outside help for their inner problems, she's speaking from her own experience. One of her greatest struggles has been with her weight. She knows she needs to take better care of herself, and that the extra size she's carrying around stems from something deep within, namely a lingering sense that she isn't attractive, so why bother. "It's hard for us black women, especially. We don't want to take care of ourselves. We forget to take care of ourselves."

Marla's second source of inspiration came from a woman name Marilyn who spent almost her entire life in a mental institution. "She had no visitors. She was mysterious. But she collected fabrics from sheets, the towels, everything. She stole a needle and made some quilts and coats. It took her thirty years to make five or ten pieces and only two remain."

The one that inspired Marla was a quilt with embroidered images of angels, the ocean, and a Christ figure.

"I wrote a song in one afternoon about it. The whole message of the song is really how we have to make art without ego, if it's really about survival. That woman, nobody encouraged her. Nobody gave her stuff. She made it because God was speaking to her and telling her this is what you have to do. Even when they gave her drugs. Even when she had her lobotomy. Everything they did to her for the thirty years she was there and nothing stopped her from her mission. And the whole thing was she wasn't wondering 'Am I going to hang in a museum one day?' She was doing this because this was her thing; she did it for her whole being.

"The younger you are, the more you are hoping that you will blow up. You're hoping that this special gift that you have will be something you can make a living at and maybe even live large. The older you get, the happier you are every time one person says, 'I like something. It did something to me. That spoke to me because I felt that way.' That's really it. That's really all you can hope for. I never expected to have this kinship and write this song and be that much into that quilt. I never thought about it and she never thought about me. But now we have a connection that's crossed racial and cultural boundaries. It's crossed decades. I've felt that way before. I've had to make something and I didn't know who was going to see it. The ancestors mean a lot to me, my family means a lot to me, but really on my worst day it's all about that woman and that quilt. That crazy woman did her thing and she didn't have any friends, she didn't have any resources, nobody encouraged her, nobody knows where she came from, and when she died they put her into a pine box and threw her into the ground."

Marilyn's quilt and life provoked Marla to ask herself what she really wanted for her art and why. Was she still hoping she'd blow up, make lots of money one day? Certainly. Like any one of us, she has visions of the good life. Hers are set in Jamaica, where she often imagines herself writing screenplays while her daughters ride their horses along the beach. But those visions have nothing to do with why she became a filmmaker. For Marla, film has always been a tool for liberation. "Me doing it and telling my stories and making my movies on whatever level lets other people know that they can do it. I've realized that media is dominated by this so-called industry. But right now there are avenues like film festivals or putting your film on the Internet or like what Haile Gerima does with his films and carries them around from city to city. His company rents theaters. He made a million or so off *Sankofa* and supported his company from his films by taking them around. That's how Oscar Micheaux, the first black director, made his."

Micheaux, the only African-American director to make films in both the "silent" and "talkie" eras, financed his novels and race pictures—films like *Within Our Gates*, the black response to D. W. Griffith's *Birth of a Nation*—by traveling door to door and convincing farmers and other entrepreneurs to invest in his art. Even though his films have been criticized for their shoddy editing and amateurish acting, their overall social and artistic effect was monumental. Micheaux's films have been credited with presenting the perspective of an emerging class of African-Americans in the twenties and thirties known as the "New" Negro. Like Marla's notion of an emerging Punk-Rasta aesthetic, the "New" Negro embodied the conflicting, even contradictory, experience of a particular class of educated and well-to-do blacks who didn't necessarily relate to poor southern or northern blacks *or* to their similarly classed white counterparts.

In light of Marla's regard for Micheaux's visionary work, it's no coincidence that more than three quarters of a century later the movie she wants to make is about the African-American suburban experience—a sepia-tinted version of *The Breakfast Club*. She's already got a plot line sketched out. The film would be set at a class reunion, she explains, plunging into a stream-of-consciousness monologue: "There'd be the fat girl who lost weight and was bitchy and evil and is reunited with the one guy who may have liked her and he's not a nerd anymore. There needs to be an athlete. The problem is, most black people don't go to their high school reunion if they went to a white school. What would make them all go?" Marla rhetorically asks. She quickly logs the as-yet-unanswered question in her mental Palm Pilot and continues: "It would be funny. It would be sad. It would be deep. I look at *Grosse Pointe Blank* and I'm jealous because I listened to that music, too. What about me? Where am I?"

Meeting Marla, talking and listening to her, reminds me that being outside the mainstream is as much a condition of circumstance as it is a choice. She didn't ask to grow up mixed up, it's the hand she was dealt, the hand she'll always be playing one way or the other. The best she can do now is exactly what she's doing: make sense of her life through her art. The least a pluralistic society like ours can do is begin to acknowledge the struggle of the outsider. As her episode of spontaneous creativity concludes, Marla returns to her initial point about *why* she wants to make black films. "In between 'Nine Miles to Slavery' and *Booty Call*," she remarks, facetiously, "there's a whole bunch of stories to tell. That's the goal."

So, what's really changed about Marla since the stress attack and the revelations about family and Marilyn's quilts? How is she any different from who she was before? That's the question I have the hardest time finding an answer to, particularly because in the three hours we spend together she lists no less than ten projects in various stages of production. In reality, her workload hasn't changed. She's still doing way too many things, still slacking about her health, still struggling to balance her life. The best she can say for herself at the moment is that her perceptions and priorities have changed. In other words, she still wants a feature film done A.S.A.P., only now she's not beating herself up about it.

"I realized it's up to me to take the pressure off of myself, because no one's going to do that for me. Sanity and peace are really hard-won. You have to aggressively seek that just like you aggressively seek spirituality. You have to get out there and search for your alternatives. You have to study. You have to find time to be with yourself. You have to do things counter to what society is asking you to do at times. You have to honor yourself. To honor the art is easy. I hardly ever have fun that's not work-related unless I remind myself. If I didn't remind myself to go sit outside and look at a tree I might forget to do that."

These days Marla has grown to accept the nature of her condition: that she is inclined to have her ups and downs, her periods of mania followed by periods of depression. Dietary modifications will help. Self-help and spirituality books will help. Exercise will help. Art, too. But the reality is that she'll probably never shake her demons entirely, and neither does she want to. More important, Marla knows there's nothing to be ashamed of. "If you feel you can't go on, you do need to seek help. It's not a sin to talk to someone. It's not a sin to go to yoga. It's not a sin to do tai chi. Anything that's going to draw you to wholeness."

These days the quest for wholeness includes spending quality time with her two little girls. There are still nights when she has a late shoot and the kids have to stay around the corner with their grandparents. She still stays up all hours of the night polishing screenplays for submissions and editing footage. But all in all, Marla's situation mirrors that of the average working single parent. It's certainly not optimal, but at the moment it's what has to work. In the evenings she's there for dinner and homework and whatever else. Maya's into computers so momma Marla is teaching her how to edit; Angelique is the actress. Weekends are when they get to spend serious time together. Meanwhile, Columbia's seen dramatic changes in the years since Marla was in high school. It's still a suburb, but now it's a diverse one. Maya and Angelique's school is a melting pot of first- and second-generation immigrants from around the world. After school, the girls need not worry about being alienated or insulted. Most of all, they can finally ride their Rollerblades down those smooth, sprawling suburban sidewalks without a care in the world.

The Bitter and the Sweet

W. Ellington Felton: Actor/Poet/Soul Artist

"Destiny is there, it's not going to change. If you have good intent in whatever you're doing and it's really genuinely good intent, then that will manifest itself and nothing else."

Back in high school, W. Ellington Felton's story had Hollywood screenplay written all over it—that or after-school special. He was the inner-city kid who channeled his rage into radical politics. He was charismatic, fearless, and highly vocal, the kind of malcontent you might see organizing school walkouts and spearheading action committees. When teachers asked him what he wanted to do with his life he smugly told them he wanted to inspire a revolution. But as audacious a front as W. Ellington put up, it would only take one of those teachers asking him how he planned on making a living as a professional revolutionary to reel him back into reality's orbit. The chilling truth was that he didn't have a clue about what he wanted to do after high school. The same teacher handed him a copy of Athol Fugard's play *My Children, My Africa*, and told him that if he liked it, they could produce it.

"It was about this student in South Africa who's pretty much the same personality as I was when I was in high school," W. Ellington recalls. "He was very outspoken, very antisystem. I was like, 'This is cool.' I had never heard of a play where they had something of that content. I always thought of theater as pointless or, rather, from the entertainment point of view. I did the piece and I started getting certain reactions from people I knew who would not give me the time of day in terms of speaking to me."

Less than a year later, W. Ellington would apply to one of the country's premier theater conservatories.

"Carnegie Mellon was the only school I applied to. They audition like three thousand kids, but they only accept twenty-six applicants. These were kids who had acted all of their lives, done off-Broadway work. I had never done none of that. It was a thing where I just decided that that was where I was going to go. I wasn't even aware until the closer I got to it and the deeper I got into that system that it was a big-ass deal, globally. They have auditions all over the world to get into this school. There are people who dream and make plans, *like planning their life*, to maybe get into this school one day and have done all kinds of things to prepare for it. They got crucial alumni. Blair Underwood. The entire cast of *Hill Street Blues*. The entire cast of *L.A. Law*. The entire cast of *NYPD Blue*. That's all Carnegie Mellon from producer to director to actors. I had never acted before. Never done no plays, like real plays, never did a monologue. My attitude was always like, 'If I get in cool, if not, oh well.'"

If you can, imagine this as the climactic moment in the screenplay. The angry young revolutionary, through a series of fortuitous events, has dramatically transformed into a budding thespian. We've watched him struggle to channel his rage onto the stage, submerging himself in Shakespeare, committing Chekovian monologues to memory. We've walked with him as he delivers that single application to perhaps the most prestigious theater program in the nation. We stood backstage with him, surrounded by dozens of highly trained actors performing their sacrosanct rituals, waiting for his number to be called. And by the time he walks onto the empty stage and looks into the darkness before him, we're fully engrossed in his story, even rooting for him, the obnoxious rabble-rouser turned poised underdog.

Naturally, as with any Hollywood flick worth its salt, our hero would go on to nail his two monologues and earn a spot at the esteemed institution, at which point the credits would roll. The story, the one Hollywood would tell, would be complete. The inner-city kid would have made it out; what happened once he got to Carnegie Mellon wouldn't be relevant.

"It was deep," W. Ellington says, recalling the Carnegie Mellon experience almost a decade later. "I was the only black male in my class." W. Ellington's slight build stands in stark contrast to his craggy voice and expansive presence. He has the uncommon ability to inhabit more space than he necessarily needs. Maybe it's just his ego, his sense of himself, that confident swagger one needs in order to rise in this world, but maybe it's that he really is totally at ease in the world. He certainly dresses that way. Today, he's wearing a less than pressed green T-shirt, jeans, and a simple pair of sneakers, the only item of clothing he says he ever buys new. Everything else is a thrift-store special.

W. had early success at the school. He was one of the only freshmen ever to be cast in a junior class production. One of his professors asked him to do some voice-over work for a Marvel Comics series he was working on. It looked as though he was on his way.

"They weren't into the concept of individuality, though, and that's what I learned the further I got into it. They wanted conservative actors who would buy into their system. It was crucial. You always have the fear of being cut lingering over your head. It's not like college; it's not grade-based. One day a teacher could just suggest to the rest of the department that they think you should be cut and you could be gone. So you have that stress where everybody in class is always worrying about getting cut, everybody's always kissing ass. Doing whatever they have to do. And me, I wasn't going to do none of that. I wasn't going to stress and be up all night and get no sleep, have no fun because I have a scene to do the next morning. They had issues with that."

W. butted heads with his professors. One day they'd love him, the next they wouldn't. One minute they were telling him how much they thought of his work, casting him in all sorts of productions; the next they were saying he needed to work on his attitude.

"They basically didn't like my method. My method was a laid-back one. I don't have to stress or overrehearse something because I work fine under pressure. I don't break. I don't buckle. Even if five minutes before the curtain goes up I'm shaking like a dog, once the lights come on I'm there, completely there. But they didn't like that because that wasn't the type of actor they were trying to produce."

The situation went from bad to worse. W. Ellington began suffering from episodic emotional breakdowns. He found himself looking for reasons not to return to school whenever he went home for semester breaks. Theater, which had once saved him, was now suffocating him. But he only had a year to go. Conventional wisdom told him to stick it out, to get the piece of paper, then walk. But that didn't jibe with W. Ellington's philosophy. For him, success meant remaining faithful to his art and being confident in his purpose as a creative soul, not relying on an institution's name, its principles, or its legacy to get him in the door. In fact, he ultimately decided to leave, in part, because he wanted to make his name *without* Carnegie Mellon's stamp of approval. Life would play out as it was supposed to. That's how he'd been raised, and that's how he was going to live.

"Basically, it's the idea of not chasing destiny. Most people spend their time running after their destiny. They bite at the first thing given to them because they're trying to get whatever they believe their destiny is quicker. Destiny is there, it's not going to change. If you have good intent in whatever you're doing and it's really genuinely good intent, then that will manifest itself."

But once he was outside the walls of the ivory tower W. quickly discovered how the acting world functioned. While in recent years we've witnessed notable breakthroughs by people of color and women alike, white men still, in large measure, decide who the masses will listen to, watch, emulate, talk about, and even dream about. True, anyone who hopes to make it as an actor must have talent, but a confluence of circumstances must also meet at a precise moment in order for one's star to rise. There are elements of timing, of good fortune, of knowing the right people and, especially with acting, having a certain look. That look is largely dependent upon the tastes of the moment and whether one fits the image a filmmaker or producer hopes to portray. It could be sexy, strong, vulnerable, mysterious, even simple. When it comes to black male actors, however, there is yet another hurdle that must be jumped: authenticity. In order to be cast they have to be *real*, so real, in fact, that it seems as though in recent years casting agents and directors alike have come to conclude that the only place to find an authentic black actor is on the rap stage rather than in the theater. Snoop Dog, Ja-Rule, DMX, L.L. Cool J, Method Man and Redman, Busta Rhymes, Sean Combs, even Will Smith. These are some of the busiest black actors in Hollywood, and they all trace their fame back to hip-hop.

To someone like W. Ellington, who's dedicated his life to acting, this phenomenon is frustrating and insulting. "It's like if a car salesman became a heart surgeon," W. says. "There are way too many talented black actors out here who are really struggling to be able to do their craft and they can't get on because it's set up in such a way that it's all about a name." Since leaving school, W. Ellington has had to battle indifferent casting directors and agents looking for the image rather than the actor. In some respects, W.'s story sounds like a scene from Robert Townsend's late-eighties parody of the black actor's perils, *Hollywood Shuffle,* all over again.

"Some directors will see me come in and if I'm not presenting myself in either the clean-cut or almost passive way to them, then I'm nothing but a young black male. Then they're like 'What I'ma do with him?' They still have the underlying fear of young black males. They tend to relate you to the black male stereotype and they can't look beyond that, so it makes them not even picture you in certain roles. It won't even be an opportunity 'cause they assume what you can and can't do."

W. agreed to meet me inside Studio Stage Theater in Washington, D.C., where he works weekends as a stage manager of sorts. He doesn't have to do much besides make sure the acting troupes who rent the space have the equipment they need. It's a nice gig, he says. It pays pretty decent and it allows him, at least today, to watch basketball, surf the Internet, conduct business on the phone, and even ply his own craft if he feels so inclined. Make no mistake about it, though, it's a struggle. Complex parts written expressly for black men, like the character "Clay" he played in a run of Amiri Baraka's Obie Award–winning *The Dutchman*, don't come every day.

"That's a dream role for a black male actor," he says. "There are very few roles that are written for black males where you're able to show a range of emotions. Black males are [typically cast as] either sexual predators or sexual objects. We're overly aggressive or an athlete. We can shoot and throw your ball."

The $20 million question, then, is how does one not allow stereotypes to defeat one's spirit? It would be easy enough to sit back and criticize the system, to lament the waste, even to become embittered. Many have; we all know at least one. The friend or relative who coulda, shoulda, woulda if only . . . W. Ellington wasn't willing to wait for his time to come, though, so in a gesture characteristic of the hip-hop generation's enterprising designs, he took creative control of his career. Along with a number of other young black actors who were experiencing the same frustrations, W. helped create a genre of stage drama called Hip-Hop Theater.

"Because we're products of the hip-hop generation and we're also reading Chekhov and Shakespeare and know our shit, we're going to create our own genre. We've become a voice for our generation, but still, if a legitimate theater or serious theater person were to come to see what we do, they'd see that it is real theater. We also do it for cats who might not necessarily go to the theater. We present it in a way where they can go to it, too."

One play in particular, *A Rhyme Deferred*, won the company national acclaim and enjoyed a run at the famed Nuyorican Poets Café on New York City's Lower East Side. The play essentially allegorizes the schism between pop hip-hop (or pop-hop) and underground rap to tell a modernized parable of the biblical story of Cain and Abel. W. Ellington played Cain, the successful crossover rapper who ends up stealing his younger brother's book of rhymes in order to remain popular. Since the play's initial run, other companies across the country have produced it as well as other plays the Hip-Hop Theater has introduced to the public.

Of late, however, W. has had to step away from acting in order to focus on his other career. You see, he's also a poet, and a rapper/soul artist with his own record label and, at twenty-six, two albums to his credit. While he was still at Carnegie Mellon he began reading his poetry at open mikes around Pittsburgh. That eventually evolved into rhyming, which in turn has developed into singing.

"I do it all. I like to call myself a Beacon. What I mean by that is being able to basically be a light. You've got ultraviolet lights, black lights, white lights. It's the idea of being whatever kind of light is necessary to communicate to whatever that group of people are or whoever that person is."

A few weeks ago the *Washington Post* ran an article on him, and in a month or two the *City Paper* will do a feature on him in conjunction with the release of his third album, *Blutopia*, a soulful and melodic homage to the old Washington, D.C.

Then there is the song he recently recorded on hip-hop legend Prince Paul's latest album. He can't wait until that one comes out, he says. His already restless nature is heightened by the anticipation. He can hardly sit still. "Prince Paul is basically the father of what we now consider to be neo-soul rap," he says, swirling to meet the computer. He starts to punch the keys. "He's the one who said it was cool to do jazz and fuse it with rock 'n' roll. He was the one who introduced that from the early days of even Stetsasonic and by introducing the world to De La Soul. He's a living testimony of it being okay to be different. This is the guy introducing me to the world now."

For W. Ellington the opportunity couldn't come at a better time. He recently found out his first child is on the way.

Up until now, W. Ellington Felton has fashioned his life so that he can be as creative as possible as often as possible, accepting the financial instability and uncertain future as mere bumps on the road to his destiny. That's fine; far be it from me to judge him. But now with someone new entering the equation it won't just be himself he's looking out for anymore. When I ask him how he's feeling he reacts with a range of emotions. There's the sheer excitement, the wonder, even a bit of wisdom: "I actually have something besides myself to have a purpose for, to work for, to do things for," he says.

But there's also the reality of what it might mean to his own dreams.

"I worry that having a child will put me in the box," he bluntly admits. "I know that eventually I'll have to break down and get another job."

One option he's given some serious consideration to is the U.S. Army Reserves. They offer signing bonuses, a steady paycheck, and only a modest monthly commitment. But with the Iraq War heating up, W. Ellington has had to reconsider that idea. Since high school his life has been a series of odd jobs paying just enough for him to survive and continue doing his art. He can't simply up and say he wants to get an office job. This is the other end of the deal he made when he only applied to one college. He wasn't trained or prepared to do anything but perform. When W. left Carnegie Mellon he made another deal: He wanted to make it on his talent alone. For someone so gifted, that could certainly happen. There's just no telling when.

"I'm very thankful to God that this baby is coming right now. I'm twenty-six. I'm not twenty-one. I'm not fifteen and I'm not forty. I'm at an age where I'll be able to move around with the kid. I'll be able to experience the child. At the same time, I'ma still keep it real. I'm scared to death. I'm *scared* to death. There's a lot of pressure that I think a lot of men don't know how to articulate at this time. What they end up doing is running away or quitting. I don't think any human being regardless of who they are just wants to say fuck a kid. I think they just have emotions they don't know how to deal with." Being the consummate artist he is, W. took what was happening in his life and made it into a song he seamlessly slides into at that exact moment:

"A collaboration of souls all through the night / Somehow I believe has brought forth this life / What's next in God's sight? / You'll be my

wife / But we gonna do it when it's right / Speaking of right your dad called me the other night / All upset like he wanted to fight / I understand his sorrow and pain / If you was my daughter I'd probably feel the same / But if he could see how much I love thee / The beauty of this would outweigh the ugly / Above that there ain't nothin' / Except for that seed that's in your stomach bubbling / Struggling is a part of all mankind / What matters is how man uses man's time / This man's mind is focused on making it work / I don't care who's focused on making it hurt / Because birth is always going to outweigh death / And I don't know how much more time we got left / I'm kind of sad that we're bringing a child into a world full of war / But hey love is something more / Than bombs / And napalms / And baby moms / And dad may be gone."

Summer has come and gone. Now, instead of basketball, football is on inside W. Ellington's glass booth overlooking the theater's backstage changing room. He's as preoccupied as he was six months ago, only now he seems to be bubbling with something new. Things, he says, are falling into place. Seeds he planted years ago have started to bear fruit and it couldn't have come at a better time. His album is in stores. The Prince Paul song created a buzz. A few shows have been lined up, including one at the prestigious Kennedy Center. It's all happening.

I wait a while before asking about his son: "Were you there?" I say.

"I was part of the whole delivery process. We had him in a hospital, but we had a midwife. I was so excited that I didn't even know [the gender], not until the doctor said, 'What do we have?' and it was a boy."

W. Ellington and his lady went back and forth over the names. He lobbied for August, since the baby was born that month and one of W. Ellington's favorite playwrights is August

Wilson. She pushed for Tobias. They finally agreed on Tobias Anthony August Felton.

His goal, especially now that he has a child to raise, is for as many people as possible to be aware of the stuff he creates, be it on stage or page. He wants to make art but he also wants to make money. "If that involves mainstream media then I ain't gonna front, that's a good thing."

So whatever happened to the revolutionary? Has W. Ellington come to terms with the demands of surviving in a capitalist society? In one sense I suppose so; we all do. But, maybe, there's an alternative reading here, one that requires a more subtle appreciation of what it means to be a creator in our sometimes cynical consumer culture. Here and now, under these conditions of possibility, it may just be that believing there's still something worth living passionately for is in and of itself a revolutionary act.

It Ain't Over Till It's Over

Blake Amos: Performance Artist/Musician

"It's about what you settle for, what you want in your life, and how long you're willing to work toward it."

The night I told my father I wanted to be a writer he said something that has stuck with me ever since. It was a quote from Thomas Jefferson. "My father was a farmer so I could be a politician so my son can be a poet." Pop-Pop owned an autobody shop in Richmond, Virginia, that my father grew up working in. After school and in the summer my dad picked up supplies and tinkered with old cars. By the time he was sixteen he'd already rebuilt his first engine. My dad also enjoyed drawing. Privately, he even imagined a career as an artist. And then came the moment he had to choose between a pair of boxes on his college entrance exam. One was marked engineering; the other art. Although he didn't know what engineering meant in terms of a career, that was the profession he had been encouraged to pursue. My dad and my aunt Colleen would be only the second and third Rosses to attend college. He checked the box marked engineering. Pop-Pop's body shop was still around when I was growing up, and in the summers I sometimes spent the day there, but my grandfather never took me aside and showed me the inner workings of an engine; neither did my dad, for that matter. I've often wondered why.

Blake Amos came from a similar background. His grandfather was a prominent Baptist minister whose word was never questioned. Blake's father, meanwhile, came of age on the heels of World War II, and was among a class of African-Americans who, following the war, found steady work at the post office. Where one generation of Amos men found respectable employment only on the pulpit, the next could find it with the government. Then came Blake.

"My earliest memories of my dad are of him listening to jazz at home with scotch and a cigarette, just sittin' there, groovin', boppin', just us in the house on a Sunday and he's obviously in another world 'cause you can see, yeah, he's diggin' the music. I didn't understand it as a young person but I could say later, 'I understand.' It's not just the music and the expression that he was feeling. But his golden moment was leaving New Orleans and going to school in California for a while, and being a witness to a lot of the birth of bebop, and seeing Miles and talking to Miles after the gig in the fifties, and seeing Coltrane. He's somebody who got glimpses of other horizons by leaving New Orleans. New Orleans is really a small town; as much as it's international, at the root of it it's a small southern town. For a black man, at his age, he's seen a lot with segregation and the whole struggle."

As important as it had been for Blake's father to get out of New Orleans for a few years and see a different lifestyle and be a part of a seminal musical moment, he discouraged Blake from getting involved with the business of music.

"He saw a lot of people with heroin habits; people that were actually good musicians and never made it. Being good doesn't necessarily make you successful. He played music, he sang in the choir, there was a piano at my grandmother's house growing up and we eventually got one. He would always play. He could really play, some classical stuff, some jazz—whatever. I grew up with an outburst of singing in the house, so it became clear he enjoyed music, enjoyed being given an opportunity to do stuff. But life didn't present that opportunity for him to really pursue it. Considering the circumstances, he just put it on the back burner, but he used to always say, 'Make sure you do something that you enjoy because that's what you're going to have to spend your time doing.'

"[My father's] been a postman as long as I can remember. He would get up at five, be to work by six, and walk his route. He enjoyed certain aspects of it; it was a good deal for what it was. But he could have done something else. I think he just didn't believe it enough. He stayed learn*ed*, and kept educating himself, but he never pushed further into something where he would have felt more realized, although he raised a family, bought a house, has a relatively comfortable retirement and life now. That's the hugest thing you can do: have a kid. I learned a lot of things from him, about society. He loved to critique society, what people really want and their real motivations, you know, break things apart. And it made me think about a lot of things and question a lot of things. It made me really stick to my guns and not just give in to the system."

At thirty-seven, Blake Amos decided he had finished another chapter in his life and that it was time to move on. The decision wasn't an easy one to come to. He had a decent life in New Orleans. He was near his son. He and his wife were happy there. And after sixteen years and countless bands it looked like he'd found a sound people were digging. What had begun as a three-hour set paying a modest hundred dollars a week had grown into something of a success story. At first it had been just Blake and two other guys: a percussionist and a saxophonist. He played the guitar and sang lead vocals. They blended elements of jazz and funk and Brazilian samba and it sounded pretty good. People heard about happy hour at Jimmy Buffett's Margaritaville. They gigged around New Orleans, played in all the festivals that came to town, even performed on a local morning show. They were a serious band on the New Orleans music circuit. Over time, Blake added a pair of conga players, a bass drum player, a new sax player, and they each brought their own style and sound with them.

"The band evolved from a trio to a five-piece band that could appeal to anybody, from middle-aged, middle-America people to young people who didn't know anything about Brazil but they could feel that rhythm. I eventually had three percussionists, one cat on bass drum, electric guitar behind me to make my guitar sound that much sweeter because we interlaced and we turned out to be basically a pop Brazilian jazz band."

Building a following felt good. Blake appreciated the fans, and gained confidence in his musical vision. The band's modest success showed him a broader range of possibility, how far he could go; also how far he still *had* to go, literally. New Orleans was, and probably always will be, a jazz town. And a Brazilian pop band, no matter how good they were, could only hope to go so far or touch so many.

"I could see the ceiling from where I was sitting," Blake says. Instead of waiting for the band to max out, he decided he needed to be where pop music could reach its widest audience. "I'm going for the middle, and to go to the middle, you've got to go where the middle is."

The "middle" was New York City, and it wouldn't be the first time Blake moved there with big-time aspirations. In the nineties he'd spent some time living in Brooklyn. He'd moved back to New Orleans partly because he wanted to be closer to his son and partly because he needed to regroup. This time around things would be different; Blake was different, clearer. In his twenties and early thirties he'd overthought the music. He got caught up in playing what people wanted to hear and not what was closest to his heart and soul. Blake had grown up on Parliament-Funkadelic. P-Funk wasn't rock, soul, or r&b, and its place in the African-American musical canon remains a peculiar one, but that was exactly what Blake found inspiring about the group. They were original, and for a moment in time they were outrageously popular. "They were creating a whole new world around an album and slipping in their different statements and different attitudes about things, but it was their own reality. You've got to admire something like that."

Blake wanted to apply an aesthetic similar to P-Funk's to his own sound.

In the year since Blake left New Orleans for New York things haven't come easy. Finding work, holding down an apartment, keeping a marriage together, finding gigs, being available to his son, and making an album every free moment in between has taken its toll both physically and mentally. He's not twenty-five anymore, not even thirty-five, and while he looks like he probably hasn't gained a pound since high school, the heavy eyelids and the forehead wrinkles are starting to betray him. Lately, it seems like every week something new is coming up. Last week his wife got laid off. This week they found out they have to move from their apartment. Summer will be here soon and that means his son's going to be looking to go to camp. He's trying to pick up more hours at one of his three jobs.

Then there's the music. During times like these, when nothing seems to be going right, any one of us in Blake's shoes would wonder if we made the right choice by leaving something steady for something unknown. New York challenges people. The city takes people's hopes and dreams and puts them to the test. Despite the setbacks, though, Blake remains clear about what he's doing and where he's headed.

"It's about what you settle for, what you want in your life and how long you're willing to work toward it. It's not our first time together seeing hard times, not my first time seeing hard times alone, and all in the name of having some integrity. It's always that same battle with jobs and looking at the big picture. To a lot of people it seemed like a weird time to leave, but the fact is I had other plans on the back burner that pertained to coming up here."

While Blake's decision to relocate might not have made sense to people on the outside, those who knew him well weren't surprised by his decision. After his freshman year of college he'd dropped out to take an extended trip to Brazil because he felt he could learn more outside the classroom than inside. To his classmates, most of whom were studying business administration ("even though they didn't know why," adds Blake), it seemed like he was making a huge mistake. Blake didn't agree. For him, it made perfect sense. Instead of sitting in a classroom and studying cultural anthropology out of a textbook, why not become an anthropologist and learn through doing? At the time he was already working in a kitchen alongside Cuban dishwashers and French and Ukrainian chefs. He was learning as much from them as he was in school, maybe more.

After Blake left school he spent a year working and saving. He got connected with an overseas travel organization, and took a few introductory Portuguese courses. He read up on the history and culture of Brazil. By then he was already a budding musician, so part of the draw was bossa nova and samba.

"What did your parents have to say about it at the time?"

"I guess they thought it was ambitious, but they thought it was dangerous and they wished I was back in school. I think once I did it, once I was there and in touch with them, they saw that it was going fine. It is a respectable thing for a young man to do, especially since I went with the mission that I would learn the language if nothing else."

Blake took a pocket dictionary everywhere he went. That and a notepad. Whenever he was out, even when he was partying and drinking, and he heard a word or phrase he didn't understand, he'd stop whatever he was doing and pull it out. He did that for eight months straight, until he had command of the language. After the first three months, he moved to a hostel in Bahia, where he wound up living two doors down from a percussion shop and school. As soon he moved in he went to meet the owner. They got to talking and the next thing Blake knew he had an apprenticeship. In the beginning, he watched; then he started doing sales; later he learned how to make instruments himself. Ultimately, he ended up performing with his instructor. At the same time he found his way to capoeira.

"That was a big thing [self-] esteem-wise: finding an African martial art that had kind of a spiritual, physical system that I could understand partially just by my heritage. It's something that was developed by slaves, developed in chains, and it's this motion that incorporates rhythm with acrobatics. It's a really thorough system."

A year passed idyllically, but when his plane ticket was about to expire Blake knew it was time to go. He didn't have the money to pay for another ticket and the minimum wage he was making selling instruments to tourists would never amount to enough for him to purchase another.

"So I came back. Started having my own projects music-wise. Started writing my songs more seriously. I had been writing for a few years but, you know, started *really* formulating some things. Started my band and joined the samba school that was just starting at the same time. That was just coincidental. New Orleans has never had a big Brazilian representation going on before. I played bass drum and marched in a lot of parades and Mardi Gras."

Two years later Blake moved to Thailand to work in a refugee camp with his then girlfriend. He taught children how to play instruments and she taught English. On the weekends he took a two-hour bus ride to Bangkok to play in a jazz band.

"They used to call me Brazil," he says, chuckling at the irony. "I'm in Thailand playing with a jazz band with Louis Armstrong on the wall and *I'm* Brazil. I sang a little bit with them and played percussion. Saw a lot of beautiful things. Did a meditation retreat for five days where we didn't talk at all."

A year later Blake was once again back in New Orleans, playing music on the underground circuit, when he heard about a performance art competition. He'd never acted before, but he decided to put a monologue together anyway: a piece about a guy chasing himself. He wound up winning the first of two major artistic grants. This one took him on tour with three other artists. The other, a Fulbright, led him back to Brazil.

"For the tour I did a piece called 'Am I a Monkey? The Black Man in the Concrete Jungle,' incorporating capoeira, Buddhism, and P-Funk into the monkey comparisons and the monkey attributes and monklike, too. I was a jester. I made myself as a monkey and I did this tour. And that was really successful and well received and got good reviews. I did that and really enjoyed it and then I just kind of left that alone."

"A couple of years later I found out about the artists' Fulbright Award, so I put together a proposal to do a show, a performance for kids, dealing with the similarities between Brazilian culture, particularly Salvador, and New Orleans. I applied for the grant and got it, so then I went back to Brazil to study historical folklore to gather information for this performance piece back in New Orleans."

Being awarded a Fulbright is a big deal for an artist. Professional distinction aside, the living stipend pays for a year of immersion in a culture outside the United States for the purpose of personal enrichment and societal advancement. Thousands of talented, brilliant, and accomplished people apply for only a handful of grants each year. That Blake won one without having studied drama, and with barely any formal training in cul-

tural anthropology, says a bundle about his talents; in fact, I wondered if perhaps he was one of those rare people who are gifted
in so many areas that they have a harder time choosing a path
than the rest of us. Whatever Blake tried, artistically at least, he
found success in. Wherever he traveled, he was able to carve out
a niche for himself with relative ease. The question was, What
was his passion? What did he really want his life to be about?
And more important, What didn't he want his life to be about?

Back when Blake was studying capoeira, he learned a valuable lesson. The more time he spent studying the martial art
form, the more he realized its depth and the more he appreciated the people who were at the top. They didn't just dabble in
capoeira, it defined their lives. They ate, drank, and slept their
craft. Seeing them, their intensity and focus and discipline,
helped him better understand himself. By watching the best
capoeira artists perform daily, Blake knew that he loved music
more than anything else. In addition, he realized that if he was
ever going to make it as a musician, music was going to have to
be his focus.

Another few years, and several more detours, sharpened those
early realizations. Within the realm of music, Blake decided, he
wanted to sing and play the guitar. Percussion wasn't going to
be his specialty. There were still several gray areas, though. Blake
still had to find his voice, his sound, the right place, space,
time—the list goes on. And it all took patience, which is something Blake has always struggled with. Part of the reason he
went to Brazil in the first place was impatience. He couldn't
wait to get out into the world and see it for himself. That was a
choice he made and, though much good has come his way, he's
also had to bear the burden of his restlessness in times of uncertainty, like now.

The flip side of Blake's impatience, however, is his decisive-
ness. Whether or not you agree with them, there's something to

be said for people who set a goal and won't stop until they achieve it. Where most of us have reconciled our youthful aspirations by our late thirties, Blake, for better or worse, is still pursuing his daily. Inside the one-bedroom apartment from which he and his wife just learned they have to move, he's built a small studio by the front door. The space is little more than a cordoned-off area behind a curtain, approximately five feet by five feet, but it's where he's spent the better part of the last year. There's a sound board, a receiver, an amp, mike stands, headphones, a few drums, and his guitar—everything he needs to finish his album. Once he has a product in hand he'll look for some gigs and, later, a record deal. For now, though, he's happy enough to pull out his guitar and play for an audience of one—his wife.

"Everybody's got some kind of struggle they've got to deal with. Thinking outside the box takes courage. But it gives you fruits only you are gonna know how good; it's what you're getting from being true to yourself. Because you're gonna face a lot of obstacles, you're gonna face people seeing you with that courage and not wanting you to have it, not wanting you to find out what's in store for you. It's not a coincidence that everybody just kind of goes with the flow. There are obstacles out there that you are not even aware of until you challenge them. Then they become clear to you. Eventually, you realize what it takes to just be different."

Postscript. I lost touch with Blake shortly after that afternoon in his apartment. I didn't find out where he moved or what happened with his wife's job situation. Summer came and went. So did fall. Then I found out through a friend that Blake was performing on the trains. He had quit one of his day jobs and started playing his guitar for dollars. It didn't surprise me. He hadn't played for an audience in almost a year when I'd seen him last. After I learned this, I found his number and gave him a call. He confirmed the rumor and said it had actually opened some things up. On a good day he could pull in $300. He had used that money to bring his son up for the summer. He'd also found a weekly gig at a Chelsea dinner club that doubled as a nursery during the day, and in a month he was playing at S.O.B.'s, a well-known venue in Tribeca. The dinner club gig didn't pay much, the crowd was touch and go, and he wasn't playing his own stuff, but he seemed not to mind. He got a free meal out of the deal, he said. He and his wife had someplace to hang out with their friends. Then he leveled with me. "Dax," he said, "it's just good to be playing again."

THE DAY EVERYTHING CHANGED

Sometimes it takes a triggering event for us recognize that the direction we've been heading in isn't leading us where we'd like to be going. We might have sensed that something was wrong all along, but we've tried to make things work anyway because we've invested so much time and energy that a change of direction would be like an admission of failure. Then again, we might honestly believe that we're doing precisely what we planned to do, and leading the life we'd always wanted. A third scenario finds us settled comfortably into something that's no longer a challenge, something that's secure. The three stories that follow show us what happens when people suddenly find their way in life.

Twenty-seven-year-old Stacey Barney had just finished another exhausting teaching day at a high school outside of Boston when she realized that she was unusually interested in a book publishing class she was only taking to complete her M.F.A. requisites. For thirty-three-year-old Kymone Freeman, change came the day he was suspended from his job at a Washington, D.C., post office after a customer overheard a disparaging remark he'd made about President Bush, and reported him to his boss. Stacey and Kymone were working in two primary professions in which African-Americans of generations past had found economic stability and social status. At the outset of their careers, they found a similar sort of security—they bought their first car, they rented their first apartment. In short, they got their first taste of independence. But over time they began feeling the impulse to travel beyond those traditional territories. While Stacey was somewhere in Boston discovering that she enjoyed the book business far more than correcting English papers, Kymone was finding out that maybe his calling wasn't distributing stamps and money orders, but using his activism to change his community. These traditional institutions serve specific social functions, which means the people who choose to work within them must either accept those restraints or find other lines of work.

Keith Norris, a fifty-year-old medical scientist from Los Angeles, may have the most compelling story of the bunch. Not only is he the only M.D. I interviewed, but his story isn't so much about a career conversion as it is about a radical transformation.

While in law school I clerked at a construction firm three days a week. I wrote complaints, filed briefs, and issued memos. I sat in on client phone calls, took long lunches, and came in late on Fridays. I remember thinking the lifestyle of an in-house attorney wasn't bad. The pay was fair, the hours were as close to nine to five as any lawyer can expect, and I didn't have to pay for parking.

Then one Friday morning when I was sitting in my cubicle reading the *Washington Post* I came across an article about a young law student who had been killed by a drunk driver the night after he'd finished his last exam. I sat up at my desk and read the article straight through. The reporter talked about him being an only child, a well-liked student, a handsome young man, a fellow with a bright future. I hadn't noticed his name right away, but when I did it rang a bell. He was a classmate of mine. We weren't friends, but we were friendly. He was a nice guy, a handsome guy—he did have his whole life in front of him. What was more, I remembered seeing him just hours before the reporter had said the accident occurred. I was leaving the law school, he was heading back in. We'd both just finished our last exam of the semester, and we both couldn't wait to celebrate. We gave each other a quick "five," I told him to take care of himself, and he said he'd see me in January. Then we went our separate ways.

I replayed that exchange at my desk. He and I had owned the same wool coat, and whenever one of us saw the other wearing it we'd say something smart like, "Nice jacket, where'd you get it?"

There I was in my cubicle, the fluorescent track lighting buzzing down on me, and a memo I'd written on mold growth at a construction site with my boss's red-ink comments slathered all over it awaiting me. In the cubicle next door sat a guy who ordered the same sub from the same deli every Friday night. Beside him sat a woman whose exact occupation—outside of resident gossiper—had remained a mystery to me for more than a year. If there was ever a moment when everything suddenly changed for me, it was then, it was there.

I had no idea if Seth—that was the young man's name—really wanted to practice law or not, but what I realized at that moment was that I didn't know what I wanted, and that if I didn't at least test the waters, I might wake up one day and find that I'd missed an opportunity to find out. Within the hour I'd written my letter of resignation.

One in a Million

Kymone Freeman: Activist and Artist

"It was a beautiful day. The sun was shinin'. We're having little drinks, a little Remy. And this brother just came by and said, 'Brothers, we're not niggas today. Just for today.'"

The post office is probably the last plantation on the planet," says Kymone Freeman. He should know. For nine years, Kymone was the guy behind that bulletproof glass passing stamps and money orders. For the last half-hour—as long as I've known him—we've been reliving his time as a postal service employee over a game of pool. Where others I've interviewed have taken their time warming up to me, Kymone has been perfectly, disarmingly, candid from the moment he opened the door.

"It's a whole other universe," he adds, lining up his next shot. He's solids, I'm stripes, and neither of us is very good. "For one, you've got the highest concentration of ex-military people. Because you've got to take an exam to get into the post office and they get preferential points for having military experience. That's why you hear about people going postal, because you've got a system where people who are doing the work may have had combat training, or [they may] have been in combat situations. And this guy that's coming from school, going straight to management, never carried mail, never sweated, never been out there in the elements, is telling him how long it's going to take him to carry this much mail, and when he should be back. Then they're penalizing you if do come back late.

"This is a good example, this actually happened. A summer day. Guys have been carrying mail ten or twelve hours. They get back, it's rush hour, so they typically sit in the parking lot and wait a little while for the traffic to die down. They buy a few beers, they're sitting in their cars, having a few drinks before they go home, they're off the clock, outside of the building, in their cars, and this guy comes out, skinny dude, with a shirt and tie, thumb up his ass, goes out there, says, 'Y'all fired, you're drinking on postal property, I'm writing all of you up.' This man is telling men twice his age that he's going to threaten their livelihood, and they got mortgages, kids in college, and you threaten their livelihood? They been working here for twenty-five years, they don't know nothing else. It's not like it's a marketable skill you're learning working in the post office, you can't take that nowhere. So, if you take somebody's livelihood, especially someone who's been in combat situations . . ." Here Kymone momentarily pauses as if to let the facts speak for themselves before he does. "You see what I'm sayin'? Their mind is fragile anyway, because part of the military training is programming. We're all programmed to an extent but we're talking about a life and death situation, so that's why they typically react violently. That's a broad generalization of what's really happening in situations when we have a loss of life in the post office."

Talk to him long enough and you'll find Kymone has an opinion on every subject in the news, from the war on drugs to the war on terror to the war in Iraq. He prides himself as an informed and outspoken member of a democracy that protects its citizens' speech rights. He takes seriously the notion of the people's right to express dissenting points of view. The only caveat is that the right to speak freely isn't automatically protected. There are certain exclusions to the free speech doctrine, and as it turns out working at a post-9/11 post office in Washington,

D.C., gave rise to one in particular for Kymone. As a condition of employment with the federal government, employees take an oath to uphold the Constitution. Article VI, cl. 3, of the U.S. Constitution provides that all federal and state officers shall be bound by an oath "to support this constitution." While on its face the First Amendment seems to provide blanket protection to all citizens to speak their mind, courts have construed this apparent conflict of law by assuming that the same framers who had penned the Constitution certainly wouldn't have contradicted their own intentions in the amendments.* Since courts later found that the language of the oath need not follow the language of the Constitution to the letter, the word "support" in the phrase "support this constitution" has come to mean anything from "uphold and defend" to "oppose the overthrow of the government of the United States of America . . . by force, violence or by any illegal or unconstitutional method."[†]

Of course, not everyone agrees with this reading of the Constitution. That a citizen's right to speak freely and openly can be compromised merely by virtue of his employment with the government raises serious questions about the future of speech. That a court made up of nine justices with a history of political motivation[††] interpreted the law on this matter without any

---

*Bond v. Floyd, 385 U.S. 116 (1966)

[†]Cole v. Richardson, 405 U.S. 676 (1972)

[††]In 1937, President Franklin Delano Roosevelt threatened to have Congress pass a law expanding the size of the Supreme Court, and to allow Congress to appoint a new justice for every current justice over the age of seventy. The purpose of the legislation was to thwart the largely Republican Court's continued and repeated blocking of Roosevelt's New Deal reforms on the grounds that the Commerce Clause did not extend the federal government's power to include virtually anything Congress might choose to do with regard to interstate commerce. After the threat was issued, the Supreme Court changed its voting patterns in order to suit Roosevelt's plan and to protect the number of seats on the Court. The change is now referred to as "the switch in time that saved nine."

clear indication from the Constitution's framers is even more troubling. As it stands, the Supreme Court's interpretations are so vague and broad that practically anything a government employee says against U.S. policy can land him or her in its net. Or in Kymone's case, out of a job.

The story goes something like this. A couple of weeks after 9/11, a customer walked up to Kymone's window. She was a regular and sometimes they chatted about the day's news. Chatting made the day go by a little faster—it helped humanize the mundane exchange of one form of currency for another. Plus, customers liked stopping by Kymone's window. He always had a joke to tell or something deep on his mind and he never shied from speaking his thoughts. The customer asked him his opinion about the government's response to 9/11. A deep breath followed the question. "Instead of giving her the X-rated version, I gave her the PG-thirteen version," says Kymone. "I simply said that if George Bush is our only hope to guide us through this crisis, then God help us. And she was cool with that. But somebody else overheard it and felt offended that I would criticize the president. Come to find out, it was some congressman's wife. She wrote a letter to the postmaster, the manager, my supervisor, Jesus and his twelve disciples."

A few days later Kymone discovered he was under investigation.

This all occurred in the immediate wake of the towers collapsing, and in the midst of the anthrax-by-mail scare that ultimately left one postal employee dead. The economy was sputtering, flags were waving, and war was bubbling. This was also the beginning of tense times for people who held dissident views. The Patriot Act had passed practically overnight and, as we now know, without any meaningful congressional review. Men who fit the general terrorist profile were being rounded up by the hundreds and thrown into jails without due process. For months they went without access to lawyers, the courts, or their families. Kymone found himself, his livelihood, caught up in the hysteria.

The postal service took almost a year to shore up its case against Kymone. But once it did, he was suspended without pay or benefits. He was unpatriotic, un-American, and, therefore, unfit to work for the federal government, especially as a mail handler. He lost nine years for less than twenty words. His one saving grace was the union attorney assigned to his case. With his attorney's guidance, Kymone filed a counterclaim against the postal service for back pay and for reinstatement to his old position. The postal service balked on both counts, so the suits went ahead.

At first, Kymone saw losing his job as a blessing. "I was never scared to get fired," he says. "I was just too chickenshit to quit. I thought I needed this job to pay my rent and maintain my apartment and my car, not realizing my possessions were enslaving me. The post office is the only full-time job I ever had and it didn't require any thought. I was making enough money to get my first apartment and my first car, all those things." For the first four years, says Kymone, he allowed himself to be complacent. "And then I realized, 'Wait a minute, what do I want with my life? I'm living check to check. Only two weeks out of the year do I get to go and do what I want to do? And I'm free? For two weeks out of the year?' "

If Kymone wins his case, he'll get a lump-sum payment in the range of $25,000 to $30,000. That's roughly how much money he's lost since he was suspended. He won't be set for life, but he won't be living hand to mouth, as he is now. Despite his calm, cool air, it's clear that Kymone is banking on that money. He mentions it too many times in the few hours we spend together. The money has even begun taking on political connotations as he refers to it as his "reciprocity." While I believe in his cause, I worry about the faith he's putting into the very system of which he is critical. But I also don't think it's my place to serve as a reality check. Not when the money symbolizes a new chapter in his life, not while he's musing on a range of possibilities. Maybe he'll leave the country for a while, finish his book, the screenplay he's been working on, or start the garment enterprise he's been considering for a couple of years. He's thirty-two now. At the end of the month, the same day he's to learn his financial fate, he'll turn thirty-three, which, as he jokingly reminds me, is the same age Jesus was when he made his great sacrifice.

Kymone has an uncommonly strong sense that he's here to fulfill a mission. In his view, everything that's happened in his life so far has happened for a reason. He was supposed to lose his job. He's destined to do something important for his people. I'm not surprised when he tells me *The Matrix* is his favorite film. "It should be used in workshops or any discussions about freeing your mind, opening your awareness," he says after accidentally hitting the red ball rather than the white one during one of our lackluster pool games. He smiles and shrugs, then says he was thinking of the moment in the film when Morpheus offered Neo a choice between the red and blue pills. The red pill would open the door to freedom and everything that came with it. The blue pill would send him back inside the Matrix.

Kymone can trace the awakening of his consciousness back to the day ex–Black Panther Huey P. Newton died in a drug deal gone bad. At the time he was working for CMP Telephone, which became Bell Atlantic, and which is now Verizon.

"I was a 'scab' employee. They had a strike going on outside, so to make it comfortable for the 'scab' employees, they had free catering, and a big TV. I was four-one-one directory assistance, so on one of many breaks—because I'm having breakfast, lunch, and dinner in this mutha—the TV comes on. They don't say Black Panther, because that would have red flagged it for me; they say something like, 'Controversial black civil rights leader Huey P. Newton was murdered today in Oakland' and this sister sittin' there just starts cryin'. And I'm like, 'Who is Huey P. Newton?' This is eighty-nine, this is Public Enemy days. I got the leather African medallions goin' on, and she said, 'You're wearing this and you don't know who Huey P. Newton is?!!' And she snatched the medallion off my neck, threw it on the floor, stomped the joint out, and said, 'You don't know shit! You need to get the hell outa here! You need to go to somebody's school, read a goddamn book or something, 'cause you don't know shit if you don't know who Huey P. Newton is! You don't deserve to call yourself black!' And she stormed out of the room. There was white people around. I felt like a midget, on my knees, sittin' on the curb. I just stood there dumbfounded.

"So, that's when I started reading. That's when I started educating myself, when I realized there's three educations. You've got the education that they give you, you've got the education that you can pay for, then you've got the education that you give yourself, through experiences, through associations with other people. I think that's the ultimate in education: life lessons. When I started educating myself, acknowledging that I had to unlearn and start to relearn, I was deprogramming myself to re-program myself."

Deprogramming himself meant Kymone had to take a long, hard look at his past. There was a time in his life when he sold drugs, when he stole cars, when he had a hot head and was quick to throw up his hands. He put his life at risk on more than one occasion, running from cops or other crews. He stood trial for grand theft auto. Even as he adamantly maintains his innocence, were it not for an overaggressive prosecutor, a pair of favorable witnesses, and a sympathetic jury, he likely would've spent five years behind bars. Kymone grew up in Washington, D.C., when it was the murder capital of America. The value of life was so diminished that people actually took pride in an otherwise disgraceful distinction. "I thought I was *supposed* to get shot. I was *supposed* to get locked up. These are normal things. Going to funerals at seventeen or eighteen was a normal thing. Somebody got killed every two or three months. I'm *supposed* to be running from the police. I'm *supposed* to be out there sellin' drugs, callin' these women bitches all the time, smokin' dope. This was presented to me as true and I accepted it as true. I see now that whole scenario was put in place for us. Self-destruction was put in place for us."

Kymone's next big step was attending the Million Man March. "When the Million Man March got here, I had already had some knowledge and understanding. I was there in the morning and I convinced some of my boys to come. It was a beautiful day. The sun was shinin'. We're having little drinks, a little Remy. And this brother just came by and said, 'Brothers, we're not niggas today. Just for today.' We kind of looked at each other. He was an older cat, and we had to respect him. We poured our drinks out, straightened up, and got into the spirit of the day. I hugged more men in that one day than I have in my entire life altogether. I felt the love and the energy. I was at CVS and two cats was arguing over who was going to go through the door first. They were like, 'After you, brother.'

" 'No, you.'

" 'After you, sir.'

" 'No, I insist, I live here.'

"That's when I started believing in unity, the possibility that we could actually come together and do something. That's when I started believing that there is some power within us to overcome. Specifically when the Minister [Farrakhan] said, 'Go back to your communities and if you feel this love out here today, if you feel this and you believe this, take this back to your communities and do something.' That rung in my head for a long time. I didn't know what I was going to do. But that just convinced me that I was going to do something because I was part of this. I was one in a million."

Like all of us who were in Washington, D.C., on October 16, 1995, Kymone went back to his life. For him that meant working at the post office during the day and promoting cabarets on the weekends. Then, one night about two months after the march, his cousin stumbled into his arms at the end of a party he had promoted. "I'm thinking he was drunk and I'm like 'Why don't you sit your drunk-ass down?' When he let me go my shirt was all wet and I see blood everywhere." Kymone's cousin had been stabbed in the parking lot. He later died. "So, I've got this march on one hand, I'm seeing the best about people, then I've got this murder and I've seen the worst about people. I had this little hurricane inside." The following summer he found himself in Jamaica standing on a cliff overlooking the ocean. Kymone was deathly afraid of heights, but he jumped anyway. "That's when I started to do my fear exercises, facing my fears because it wasn't a question of what can't I do, but what am I prepared to do."

Back home, Kymone quit the cabarets and the clubs. Later on, while at work one day, he met a poet who was sending off a copy of his book. They got to talking and instead of sending the book off, the poet gave the copy to Kymone. After that, he started going to readings and poetry slams. Next thing he knew he was meeting artists and activists who shared similar ideas about the need for unity in the community. This was all new to him and right away people were trying to get him to join their organizations. From the beginning, though, Kymone knew he wanted to be the one who transformed the talk into action, so in 1997 he organized the first annual Blackluvfest in Washington's Fort Dupont Park.

"It wasn't but three hundred people and it wasn't professionally done. I had artists, activists, dancers. I thought that was all I needed to do. Then, the next year, people were like, you gonna have another Blackluvfest, so I did it again. I never intended to do an annual thing, but it has grown. What made it so beautiful was the first time I didn't know nuthin'. I never really organized anything."

What Kymone did was go to the National Park Service office where he was told to write up a proposal. He didn't know exactly what a proposal was or how much it would all cost. When he returned for a meeting with the fire chief, the head of the park police, and a park ranger, he thought for sure they'd send him on his way. The fire and police chief were both white and the ranger, though black, didn't appear as though he would be sympathetic to Kymone's cause. The man was exceedingly fair-skinned, therefore Kymone automatically thought he would be against him. Kymone had a choice: let his personal prejudices defeat him before he even began, or make them believers. He chose the latter. Not only did the park ranger like his idea, he offered Kymone a better-equipped facility and arranged to have the event labeled as a demonstration rather than a special event. Demonstrations, the ranger told Kymone, didn't require bonds or insurance or extended police security.

"He could have turned me down, threw me out of that office, and I probably would have never came back to them again. I would have just left defeated and humiliated, but he encouraged me and made it happen for me. I go back to *The Matrix*. People can show you the door, but you have to walk through it.

He didn't come get me. I came to his office and I sat down. I took that first step. I did that and that sent me on a whole path because the Blackluvfest has created other opportunities. Every time I step out on stage, it has created other opportunities. The nature of life requires you to start doing what you want to do and figure out how to do it afterward. You learn by doing. There's no other way."

The life lessons Kymone learned from organizing Blackluvfest were put to a series of tests once he lost his job at the post office and he could no longer afford his apartment or his car note. Expecting he'd find work somewhere, he moved in with a friend who agreed to take him in on the strength of his word. But as the months passed without an interview or a call back, Kymone's confidence waned. Maybe he should have kept his mouth shut. Maybe he should have finished college. Maybe. Maybe. Maybe. He missed meals, shut himself up in his room for days, and stopped answering the phone. Finally, after four rent-free months, Kymone's friend had to ask him to leave. He simply couldn't afford to support them both. Before Kymone left, though, his friend reminded him of one thing: that this was what he asked for. Consciously or not, he'd chosen this path and now he had to walk it.

Kymone moved into his sister's basement and eventually started tutoring kids after school. In the midst of this, he was invited to speak at a drug policy conference in Los Angeles, where he met community activists who'd heard about his work in D.C. By then not only had the Blackluvfest been going strong for five years, but Kymone had also formed a truth-telling collective. The collective's purpose was to bring like-minded people together for political dialogue about improving their community. Through that L.A. experience he was also able to land work on an election campaign. Slowly, he started rebuilding his life. Kymone even started working on his manuscript, *One Love from the*

Bottom Up, again. The book is a series of essays about his own transformation. The way he sees it, he's the latest addition to the history of African-Americans who evolved from petty criminals into radical thinkers—a history that includes Malcolm X and George Jackson. Once the book is finished, he'd like to take it into prisons and juvenile detention centers and halfway houses. Although some of the essays date back as far as 1992, something had kept him from completing the book. Now he understands. He had to live his own liberation before he could write about it truthfully.

"They said it took Thomas Edison two thousand experiments before he got the lightbulb right. A reporter asked him how did he feel about all those failures and he said, 'Failure? I never failed. I invented the lightbulb. It just so happens it was a two-thousand-step process.' Fear is part of the process. I was scared to let my possessions go. I thought, 'I have to have that job because I have to have this apartment, because I have to have that car. That's me. If I lose those things, I've lost.' And when I lost them, I thought that I was lost. Until I realized, wait a minute, I'm still here. That was my lesson. You can take all of that and I'm still here."

The other lesson Kymone learned was that even the post office served an important purpose in his life. The job gave him the stability he needed in his life at that particular time. That steady check meant he didn't have to worry about his next meal or the roof over his head; he could focus his energies on learning.

"Everything is a process. Once I understood that, things got better for me. You have to go through the process. If I hadn't been at the post office, I wouldn't have met some of the people who inadvertently introduced me to some other people that inspired me to do something else with my life. Nine years and every year after the fourth I said, 'This is my last.' I didn't know what I was going to do, now I've realized it. I'm not doing anything anymore that doesn't represent or reflect some aspect of my being."

On the morning of the sixth annual Blackluvfest I'm one of the first people to arrive at Malcolm X Park near the Adams Morgan section of Washington, D.C. Malcolm X is the name the people of Washington have given the park, though its formal name is Fort Dupont Park. The grass runs the length of a football field and the gravelly track surrounding it is lined with sturdy trees that are starting to show signs of fall. At the south side of the park sits a stage behind which lies a fountain, a garden, and an impressive view of the city's sudden downtown descent.

When I spoke to Kymone last night he said he'd meet me early, that way we could talk before things got too hectic. A vendor setting up tells me I just missed him. The vendors are the only people in the park this early. I talk to some of them—a guy selling his own line of skin cream and a young designer with her own signature handbags. They're both from the metropolitan area, but many others have traveled from different sections of the country. When I ask why, they tell me there aren't that many events geared specifically toward African-Americans, let alone in the name of love. Hearing all this I think back to the night Kymone and I shot pool, nearly two seasons ago. He'd deliberately chosen the name "Blackluvfest" because he knew it would make some people uncomfortable. Some wondered why he didn't just call it "Luvfest," criticized the name for sounding exclusionary. None of that concerned Kymone. He didn't start the event because he wanted to throw the biggest party in town; he wanted people to come to a peaceful event that was about black love. The festival is political, social, artistic, cultural, and grass roots.

And while it sounds so simple, no one else is doing anything quite like it.

When Kymone does arrive he's already in "go" mode. We talk briefly. He hasn't been to sleep yet and they're behind schedule. I offer to help and he hands me a box of trash bags. The park needs to be cleaned up before people arrive. Then he's off again. There's a problem with the sound and the DJ isn't answering his cell phone. When I finally do have a moment with Kymone later that morning, I ask him if his money came through. I'd been thinking about it off and on the last few months and while my gut instinct told me his would be a tough case to win, I had hoped the best for him. Kymone looks straight ahead and lets me read the outcome in his expression.

The postal service ruled that he hadn't been unlawfully discharged. He was a loudmouth and he'd broken an oath, therefore he could be fired summarily and without further remuneration. I consider offering my condolences, then stop myself. This is what he asked for. For years he'd wanted to get out of the post office. If Kymone has one regret, it's this: that since he lost his job anyway, he might as well have really let loose and said everything that was on his mind when the customer asked his opinion. But nevertheless, this is what he wanted. The money would have just been the cherry on top. Besides, he has the Blackluvfest, an idea he made real, an event that's bigger than him now. Though it isn't flawlessly orchestrated, it is a success.

A host of local artists and activists, even old school rap duo Black Sheep, take the stage over the course of the afternoon. The day's mood and tone are celebratory and yet there's an urgency that each speaker brings to the stage. There's a war going on both here and abroad and that message is just as important as the dancing and the socializing.

Somewhere around dusk, I spot an old law professor of mine standing in the crowd. This, with Kymone's lost legal battle still fresh on my mind, throws me back to my first year of law school. I was so eager and excited to be in that world. I couldn't wait to be a lawyer. Even nowadays I sometimes ask myself why I didn't just practice law like the rest of my classmates. Then I meet someone like Kymone and I remember the disillusionment that quickly followed those first weeks of school, when I learned that the law isn't about right and wrong, it's about winning and losing. Law school taught me that the law comes down to who's slicker, richer, and better-connected. And somewhere in that ugly mess justice, ethics, and plain humanity have to exist. Kymone's case reminds me of that all over again.

What has to be changed now is people's hearts and minds, and if that's going to happen it'll be because of what we do for ourselves, not because of what's done for us. This was the message that more than a million men who converged on the Capitol on October 16, 1995 (which, as Kymone points out, was also the day he was officially dismissed, as well as the same date abolitionist John Brown led the Harper's Ferry slave revolt) walked away with. Critics belittled the march because of Minister Farrakhan's involvement. Watchdog groups demanded an immediate accounting of the money that had been collected that day. Detractors from all sides diminished the turn-out numbers, chided the "men only" directive, and otherwise looked for any and every reason to diminish the meaning of the day. Meanwhile, people like Kymone Freeman were literally being transformed.

In a very real and meaningful way, Blackluvfest is an extension of the Million Man March. The event is about unity, self-determination, transformation, inspiration, and most of all love. And as long as we live in a society that's obsessively divided into haves and have nots, it's necessary. As for Kymone, the last time I see him he's standing on the stage, holding a microphone and leading a crowd of more than a thousand in a chant. The sun has nearly gone and my bus back to New York leaves in less than an hour, so I let that be my last image: Kymone exhausted. Kymone free. Kymone just as he shoots his last ball, the red one, into the side pocket, proudly announcing, "I came from a car thief to a person who has the audacity to think he can change the world."

A (Would-Be) Martyr

Stacey Barney: Book Editor

"I love books. That's the heart of it."

At twenty, Stacey Barney was majoring in literature and African-American studies at Temple University when she walked into Sonya Sanches's poetry class eager to begin her own writing career under the tutelage of one of the foremost poets of the generation that came out of the sixties. Sanches is the godmother of the staccato-steeped, coffee-shop poetry media mogul Russell Simmons brought to all of America via his Def Poetry Jam series on HBO. She is a small, white-haired lady with a gutsy voice, an imposing scowl, and a warm heart.

"She had a habit of taking her class out into the school system in West Philadelphia and having her students talk to middle schoolers and high schoolers," Stacey says. "I did a presentation and I was like, 'Oh my God, I can't do this, I can't do this,' but I pulled it off. Afterward Sonya said to me, 'Sister, you really did that well. You should consider joining the education program here and being a teacher.' "

Temple had a fast-track master's in education program that would allow Stacey to begin taking graduate classes before she even finished her undergraduate work. She figured she could still write in the summers and on the side. She'd be doing important, necessary work in a blighted Philadelphia school system, not to mention following the direction of a woman she idolized. That she wasn't cut out for teaching never crossed her mind. She was passionate about literature and she enjoyed sharing that passion with others. She was a positve role model. The students she'd already met saw her as cool and interesting and young.

But it's one thing to go into someone else's classroom two or three days a week, maybe teach a lesson, maybe not; it's something else entirely to be in charge of that classroom, those kids, their learning.

After an initial three-month stint at a small church school in Philadelphia that quickly soured, Stacey went to the board of education where, after being given a list of available positions, she chose one in what was then reputed as the worst school in all of Philadelphia: Olmey High.

Hers was a cautionary tale in the making, a headline that could easily read "Young, Gutsy Martyr Walks Directly into Pit of Fire." As an early July sun warmly rises on our backs outside a Brooklyn café, and the surrounding sidewalks thicken with leisurely paced weekend traffic, the soon-to-be twenty-eight-year-old laughs at her naïveté before continuing with her story:

"I thought being black and being from Brooklyn was enough. It's not, and I discovered very quickly that it's not so much about race as it is about class. I grew up in a household where I had both my parents. I didn't have to worry about where my next meal was coming from, I didn't have to worry about the phone being turned off, I didn't have to worry about anything other than going to school and getting good grades. And I had my chores, which I reluctantly did. I had *nothing* to worry about. I didn't live in a neighborhood where safety was an issue. I had extracurricular activities. I had the sort of structure that these kids I was encountering in my class just did not have. And I couldn't connect with kids who thought it was okay to come to school and curse their teacher out. Understandably, you can't really concentrate on school when you're pregnant, but I was just like, 'This was not like when I was growing up.' And they looked at me—I might as well have been white. I was proper-talking, I placed a value on reading. It was clear to me that their view of me was not what I thought it would be. They thought of me as an outsider coming in, not really understanding what they were going through, and they were right. They were absolutely right."

In Stacey's mind being a teacher meant examining literature from a critical perspective, and teaching her students how to express themselves through the written word. What she hadn't expected was being a confidante, a best friend, a priest, and a psychologist. She didn't foresee weekends she wouldn't be able to get out of bed because she was still recovering from one week and dreading the next. She was partly to blame for this exhaustion. No one told her to give out her home phone number. But there were also administrative issues she couldn't be blamed for: kids who were supposed to be in her class roaming the halls, even stopping by to say hello; security guards who were nowhere to be found when she needed students removed from the class; and a principal she had "knock-down, drag-out fights with" about student attendance.

Stacey still gets worked up when she thinks about that year. The year was a nightmare she had barely survived. She even recalls an unsettling feeling that, perhaps, she didn't want to be a teacher. Determined to give teaching another chance, Stacey moved to Boston, where she took a position as a humanities teacher in a pilot school. She also enrolled in an M.F.A. program. "If you're a Type-A personality overachiever and something's suddenly not working, you just want to pile more on and do more stuff." Stacey figured that if she taught, got back to her writing, and worked toward her M.F.A., she'd be happy again. Piling on more work was the way she'd learned to rise above her problems in college, so that's what she resorted to once again. "Going to get my M.F.A. and going to class, and having my teachers tell me, 'Oh, you're really a great writer,' sort of helped me deal with what I was doing in the daytime."

I find myself nodding more than usual, listening even more intently than I normally listen to my interviewees. This is the end of my first year of teaching and all year I've struggled with some of the same challenges Stacey had faced in her first year. Also, I've been taking evening classes, and from my professors I, too, receive the validation that allows me to approach my day job with a little less anxiety and uncertainty. Stacey, I come to realize, is holding up a mirror for me to see my own situation more clearly.

For Stacey, the job in Roxbury was as disastrous as the job in Philadelphia. The school was supposed to be a new age, alternative school where the students called their teachers by their first names and didn't get letter grades but progress reports that read "Beneath Expectations," "Meets Expectations," and "Exceeds Expectations." The premise was laudable. But schools don't exist in a vacuum. You can't hope to create a school life that isn't mirrored in the child's home or community life. There needs to be a conjoining of all three. Even freedom needs structure, otherwise it's just chaos. At the end of that year Stacey and sixteen other teachers left the school.

But the move to Boston wasn't all in vain. The M.F.A. program turned out to be a turning point in her life. "When you go to grad school you don't necessarily get the courses you want the first time around," she explains. "You sort of have to build up the requisite credits and I did that in book publishing classes." The plan, as she'd worked it out in her mind at least, was to get off work, dash to class, sit in the back with her hat tipped over her eyes, maybe take a nap or prepare the next day's lesson—just stay out of the instructor's purview. She was going to be the one writing the books, not the editor, so what did she care about the business of books? But then Stacey came to a startling realization.

"There was a point in class where I was like, 'Wait a minute, I'm listening, I feel good, I feel okay, I feel normal, how did this happen?' That's when I realized: This is what I want to be doing. Then I started doing all this research on book publishing and editing and how you get started in a career and asking my professors questions. That energized me in a way because I knew I still had to teach."

This go round, however, her last, was at a public school in suburban Concord, Massachusetts. Concord is one of the richest communities in the state. Stacey knew she didn't want to teach anymore, but for her own peace of mind she needed to understand what it would have been like to teach in a setting where the kids came from stable backgrounds and the school provided its teachers with a wealth of resources. Though the year went well, it didn't go well enough to make her want to stay. Stacey still couldn't quite draw the necessary boundaries. The lives of her students still intersected with hers. The kids themselves still had issues, like drugs and underage drinking, anxiety about getting into the best colleges, and fitting in with the right crowd.

School finished on June twenty-second. By June twenty-third she was back in New York, where she found a job interning at a children's book publisher first, then landed an editorial position at one of the most prestigious houses in the country: Farrar, Straus and Giroux. After the struggles she'd encountered in teaching, she'd expected finding an editing job in New York to be yet another grueling ordeal, only it wasn't that way at all. In fact, it was almost as though it was meant to happen.

• • •

Stacey and I have an interesting history. A year before I interviewed her, she wanted to buy this book for her publishing house. She was the first editor who saw the proposal and the first person outside of my agent who was in any way excited about it, which obviously gave me a much-needed jolt of confidence. Together, the three of us devised a plan to prepare the book for formal submission, and for the next three months she and I worked together to get it in top form. For the most part, we got along well. I wrote drafts, she shredded them, and my agent helped me see the bright side of things when it came time for rewrites. In the end, after months of working together as if we were already bound by contract, she wasn't able to buy the book. We were both bummed out, but I think, more important, just having an African-American editor take such a keen interest in the book kept it alive when it could have easily died. This isn't to say white editors couldn't grasp the book's concept. If anything, I'd have to say the opposite is true. White editors, perhaps more so than black editors, were willing to give it a shot. Ultimately, a white editor bought the book. Notwithstanding that, there aren't many African-American editors at the handful of mainstream publishing houses that comprise the lion's share of the book publishing market. What that means is that while book editors aren't paid like Wall Street brokers, they do wield a considerable amount of power when it comes to deciding who gets published, how much they get paid, and to whom the book is ultimately marketed. The "race" question, then, is clearly one Stacey and I needed to discuss. In particular, I wondered how she had negotiated issues of race in an overwhelmingly white, and arguably elitist, profession like publishing.

"I don't think about it," says Stacey. "I actually got into an argument with this woman who wants to get into publishing, a young black woman, about my age. She's been looking for a job for about two years." The woman on the outside looking in saw her inability to get a job as clear and convincing evidence of discrimination. In her mind at least, she had the skills, she had a considerable background in editing and writing, she was willing to work hard, and she loved books: What else could explain her not being able to find a job in two years other than her skin color?

Says Stacey, "Sure, there's discrimination. There's discrimination in any industry you go into. You must remember we're still the minority in this country. There's always going to be more white people in whatever industry you're in than there are black people. It's just numbers."

Also, an industry like book publishing doesn't have governmental hiring quotas it has to meet, and since, according to Stacey, there are no set prerequisites for being a good editor, people tend to hire who they like: "It's not just about if [someone] can do the job. You want to be able to get along with that person. You want to be able to feel that you have something in common with that person whether you're black or white. Look at me, I'm a black chick with dreads. I don't wear shoes around the office and it was fine. Why was it fine? Because these people felt they had something in common with me. In publishing you're not just in your office editing all day long. There's a lot of socializing, you get somewhere because somebody likes you."

There's also the very real issue of pay. A 2002 report issued by the State PIRG's Higher Education Project found that while overall 64 percent of students took out loans for college in 2000, 84 percent of African-American students took out loans. Fifty-five percent of those African-American students then left school saddled with what the report called "unmanageable" levels of debt,★ as compared to an overall percentage of 39 percent. The average African-American student coming out of college is saddled with so much debt that it simply isn't possible for them to afford to live in New York City on an editorial assistant's salary of $30,000 a year or less. Even Stacey has to deal with it. Her loans have been in deferment for a couple of years now, and come next year she's going to have to start paying. Between now and next year, she says, she's got to start making some *real* money. So, yes, there is discrimination, a version of it at least, in that the people who tend to be able to take these jobs usually need outside support in order to supplement the high cost of living in a city like New York.

Stacey is also uncomfortable with her de facto position as "resident black person." "I don't like that I'm the go-to black girl. At FSG, I was that with this book *Graceland*. The first cover that they came up with was this cartoon of a black person and I was the trump card. My boss said, 'Well, Stacey doesn't like it either.' Then it was, 'Okay, we have to go back to the drawing board.' I was the black person who understands the black stuff. That bothers me."

At the same time, Stacey recognizes that being black and in her position allows her to wield her own kind of power. People don't come to her simply because she's African-American, they come to her because they respect her ideas *and* because she's African-American. It's a tricky situation for everyone involved—one that gets to the heart of the dilemmas still surrounding touchy race issues: How to act and how not to act. What's right and what's wrong. What's really racism and what's simply favoritism.

★The State PIRG's Higher Education Project. 2002. *The Burden of Borrowing: A Report on the Rising Rates of Student Loan Debt* (Washington, D.C.). The report calculates an unmanageable debt as that which exceeds 8 percent of the person's monthly income.

• • •

Considering the amount of time she spends poring through manuscripts and keeping abreast of the work by authors whom she admires, Stacey's still very much down to earth. She's wearing a floppy, though chic, straw fisherman's hat and a stylish sleeveless top. Somewhere beneath the hat's broad, bending shadow, her eyes hide. We talk about the books she's working on, others she's acquired, even a couple of beauties that got away. At the moment she's trying to get Henry Louis Gates to write the introduction to a reprint of the underground classic *The Life and Times of Mr. Jive Ass Nigger*.

"So what is it about publishing?" I ask.

"I love books. That's the heart of it. I love working with writers on their material. That feeling when the finished book comes into the office and you see them on the shelves at Barnes & Noble, it's like nothing else in the world. I always compare it to teaching because I never got to see the finished product. You don't see the impact. When you're feeling ineffective, people who have been teachers for twenty-five years say, 'Oh, they come back and tell you.' I don't know if I want to wait ten years for the payoff. In book publishing there is a payoff and you see it. When you find the nugget, you say, 'Oh my God, this is really good. Could it really be as good as I think it is?' Then you send it to other readers and then your marketing director comes along and says, 'Oh my God, this is really good' and someone else comes back and says, 'Oh my God' and you have the support. Then doing the whole negotiation with the agent and bidding against other houses and then the agent calls you and says it's yours. Then it's getting the manuscript down, editing, seeing it go through production, actually becoming a book, actually becoming something. It really is like giving birth to something, and when the book finally comes in, I get high off of it. I can't explain it."

In just three years Stacey has managed to turn her life around, to make it what she wants it to be. A few months ago she started a new job at Amistad Books, a black imprint of HarperCollins, and since then she's been working around the clock. Meetings with agents, bids for books, piles of manuscripts to tear through just to find that one that arrests her. Her boss, the woman who hired her, has been out on maternity leave since before she arrived, so the load has been dropped at Stacey's feet. She doesn't mind; in fact, after our interview, she'll hop on a train and head into work for the rest of the day, happily, I might add.

"Truth Is a Pathless Land"

Keith Norris: Scientist/Metaphysician

> "I think the most important aspects of life, in many respects, are those things that can't be measured."

For the better part of the last quarter-century, Dr. Keith Norris has studied, practiced, researched, taught, and written about kidney disease and other health disparities among minorities, particularly African-Americans. Nephrology, the science of the kidney and its diseases, is his area of expertise, what he knows and cares about most. Of the roughly fifteen professional organizations he belongs to, no less than half are centered on kidney disease. Keith is editor in chief of the International Society on Hypertension in Blacks' official journal, *Ethnicity & Disease*, his community outreach and education record is as long as it is impeccable, and he regularly travels the country speaking about health disparities. As a matter of fact, the day before he and I met in Manhattan he had given a talk in Chicago. He's only in town for the day to visit family and attend his niece's thesis presentation at Columbia, then he's heading back home to Los Angeles.

Back in L.A., Keith directs Drew University's Clinical Research Center, and teaches second- and third-year courses in medicine. "Being able to do something is good," says the athletic-looking fifty-year-old, "being able to teach others how to do it for themselves is so much more." In Keith's family, education and medicine have always loomed large. His father was a veterinarian, his uncle and paternal grandfather were dentists, his grandfather on his mother's side was the first black school superintendent in New York City, and his paternal great-grandfather was the first black chairman of surgery at Howard University. He didn't discover this last piece of family history until years after he'd graduated from Howard Medical School himself, at age twenty-three. Keith entered Cornell at sixteen, and after gaining early admission left for Howard at nineteen. Curiously, Keith never actually graduated from Cornell. He simply scored so high on the MCAT that Howard offered him immediate enrollment.

"I felt blessed that I had the opportunity to go to Howard to get my degree," Keith says. "A lot of people leave places and feel people didn't treat them right; I never felt that. I felt I had an opportunity and it's given me an opportunity to do a lot more. Giving back to historically black colleges has given me a way to more dramatically have an impact."

As the chief resident of internal medicine during his tenure at Howard, Keith had originally been interested in hypertension, a disease blacks have historically suffered from disproportionately. He later chose to focus his research on one of the key specialties dealing with hypertension, kidney stress. Blacks are about four times more likely to be on dialysis than whites, so he figured that would be a more critical area for him to focus his energies.

"In general, if you look at health in the United States, there's a difference in health outcomes by gender, but also by race," says Keith. "Certain differences may be just things we can't control, but a lot of differences that exist were [due to] sociocultural factors, so blacks have the worst health outcomes, they die younger from most everything, they have higher rates of most bad stuff. The question is, Why? There's more and more evidence that a lot of it is due to less access to health care. But also, a lot is due to interactions both at the health-care level and the health-system level. People see [these patients] as black and as inferior, and as people who *should* have problems. They're not accepted the same way. They're not treated the same way. They're not given the same recommendations. It's something that does not have to be, but people have chosen to believe it and hold on to it and perpetuate it. Just transforming that could have a substantial effect.

"At other levels, particularly for blacks in America, but for any minority society in postcolonial civilization, the minority community not only suffers from discrimination, you have high levels of stress because everywhere along the system you're discriminated against. The system was set up to discriminate and the system teaches people to discriminate. Yeah, discrimination goes both ways, but it's much more structured against someone who's not in a position of power than it is for a person who *is* in a position of power. All of those systems contribute to adverse health outcomes."

Until five years ago Keith was a staunch believer in access, education, and understanding as the keys to shrinking the health disparities African-Americans face. He thought that by alerting people to the obstacles blacks encounter, be they stress or insitutional discrimination, he could effect change within the healthcare system. He wrote articles about the problems, he spoke about them to other professionals, he dialogued with community leaders. Then, in 1999, Keith had what can only be described as a spiritual experience that fundamentally transformed the way he saw the world.

Explaining exactly what happened isn't easy for Keith, though not for the reasons one might think, such as not wanting to sound foolish or fanatical. From the moment I met him it was obvious that he's perfectly comfortable with what happened— that no matter what I or anyone else thinks, he knows what he knows. What's difficult is putting the experience in the appropriate words. Nevertheless, Keith tries his best to put the puzzle of his experience together. For as long as he can remember, Keith's world has almost exclusively been numbers and calculations. One of the main reasons he chose nephrology in the first place was because he'd excelled in math in school, and it was an area of medicine that involved facts and figures. Then one morning Keith felt the beginnings of a series of unusual spiritual sensations. Over the course of the next two weeks Keith says he experienced unusually high levels of energy, an unconscious awareness of time, an unconditioned appreciation for life itself, and spontaneous emotional outpourings that brought forth tears of joy. His work life improved, his outlook brightened, and for the first time in the forty-plus years he'd been living, he felt inspired to write poetry. What really grabs me is Keith's intensity, his conviction, and the remarkable sense of gratification in his voice when he speaks of "a lifting of the clouds," "periods of extreme clarity of the interconnectedness of life," "an awareness of life," an "understanding of where one fits in the puzzle of life," and the fresh feeling of being "free of the conditioning of society."

Since that initial two-week "high," Keith has frequently experienced these periods of clarity. "I don't always have it and I usually know the difference," he says. "I know when I'm functioning more to my conditioned mind as sort of the primary level of energy in me versus when the primary level of energy in me is an awareness of an interconnectedness of life and my conditioned thoughts are secondary."

Because he came from a science background, Keith hungered for a rational explanation, so he began searching for answers in an ever-widening range of religious and philosophical writings. However, the common roadblock he encountered was the spiritual guru who insisted he or she had found enlightenment, and alone could lead him if he only devoted himself to their path. Not until he came upon the writings of Krishnamurti—and his idea of "choiceless awareness" in particular—did Keith begin to feel as though he'd at last found something worth holding on to.

At birth, Krishnamurti (1895–1986) was proclaimed the future spiritual leader and religious savior of theosophy, an ancient religious order founded in India. But after several years of leading the order, and while still a young man, Krishnamurti dissolved the organization, proclaiming that all forms of organized religion hindered the free and independent development of human awareness by mediating humankind's relationship with the divine spirit. "Truth is a pathless land," Krishnamurti declared in the speech that effectively ended his tenure as the leader of the order. Afterward, and for the rest of his long life, Krishnamurti traveled the world speaking only for himself as himself.

To be "choicelessly aware" means to withhold judgment or the making of decisions about one thing or another that one is presented with. For example, instead of judging an image based on its appearance, a "choicelessly aware" person merely observes it, thereby reaching a more profound understanding of its nature and the nature of life itself.

"By being aware of life and spending more energy on being aware of life without choosing, just observing, it tends to quiet down the energy of thought that's usually choosing and judging and everything else," Keith says. "If that quiets down, then the other energy has an opportunity to rise up and predominate. This allows one to be aware of the life functioning energy that might be considered the soul or the spirit, and yet still be engaged with life day to day, which is different than going off by yourself and creating a stupor to feel some sense of awareness. In my mind, the true beauty of life is to be engaged with life yet to feel the interconnectivity of life."

In the weeks following our conversation I listened to Keith's tape several times. And the more I did this, the more the groundbreaking work of psychologist Abraham Maslow kept popping into my mind. In particular I was reminded of a book-length essay Maslow wrote called *Religions, Values and Peak Experiences,* wherein he coined the phrase "peak experience." Subsequent to surveying hundreds of subjects and compiling the "religious experiences" of still hundreds more, Dr. Maslow concluded that a significant number of normal everyday people were capable of experiencing heightened states of awareness. The experiences that Maslow documented and drew from shared several common features, such as a "clear perception that the universe is all of a piece and that one has his place in it,"[*] a "very characteristic disorientation in time and space, or even the lack of consciousness of time and space,"[†] a "perception of unity and integration in the world,"[††] and a "loss, even though transient, of fear, anxiety, inhibition, of defense and control, of perplexity, confusion, conflict, of delay and restraint."[§]

The similarities between what Keith was explaining to me and what Maslow had observed were uncanny. What was more, Keith had never read any of Maslow's work, never heard of the term "peak experience," and he only knew of Maslow's name in passing. Yet his experiences mirror what Maslow described more than forty years ago. Even beyond their list of striking similarities, however, stands what is perhaps their most significant commonality: what followed the "peak experience." According to Maslow, "peak experiences sometimes have immediate effects or aftereffects upon the person. Sometimes their aftereffects are so profound and so great as to remind us of

[*]A. H. Maslow, *Religions, Values and Peak Experiences* (New York: Penguin Compass, 1970), p. 59.
[†]Ibid., p. 63.
[††]Ibid., p. 66.
[§]Ibid.

the profound religious conversions which forever after changed the person."★

In Keith's case a professional crisis ensued.

"One of the hardest challenges of my life when I first had this sort of clarity was to continue to do what I do," Keith says. He wondered whether he could continue with his research, or, alternatively, how he could make his work fit with his new awareness. "In [the medical] profession it's easy to be selfish and narrow-minded and not really give much attribution to anything else that goes on, yet the reality is it is just another piece of the puzzle here on the physical plane. It was clear to me that, while relevant and important, helping improve some of the physical manifestations of disease was truly limited in the scope of what life has to offer."

At the same time that Keith was grappling with the limits of Western science and medicine, his readings and experiences began leading him toward the bold realization of his role as a healer not just of the body, or even the mind, but of the spirit as well. At that point Keith decided he wanted to dedicate the next stage of his career to reconnecting science with the soul:

"Our practice here in the United States comes out of the dark ages in Europe. The church actually allowed science to be involved in medicine under the premise that the soul and the spirit remain the purview of the church. It was one of the only healing practices that emerged with a wide divide between physical and spiritual. Most other indigenous practices have a combination of the two. We do a good job of addressing physical manifestations of disease states, but somehow we feel like once we've addressed that, it's over, and there's so much more.

"Say ten people come into the office with pneumonia, and I

★Ibid.

say, 'It's raining outside, so the tendency is to catch pneumonia.' There's a million other people outside, they didn't all catch pneumonia. You give them an antibiotic and they may get better, but there's a reason why they developed pneumonia. When we give the antibiotic that person may have gotten better, but what's going on in their body at a variety of different levels that predisposed them to develop whatever that is? That's what we don't address. Disease is just that: *dis*-ease, lack of ease. It could be stress or conflict on a psychosocial/spiritual level. That conflict is disease. It leads to physiological imbalances, certain physical manifestations that try to tell the person to wake up. This is a message you need to do something. A lot of people have headaches and backaches, all sorts of pains, those are all manifestations of the spiritual energy trying to wake us up.

"But we don't put those things first. We just want to go to the doctor to get that fixed and the doctor obliges and supports everybody by saying, 'You're fine, the problem is this. You have this here.' That's where we miss out on the opportunity to really be healers; we chastise many indigenous practices of healing, but that's really what they embrace."

Everything that Keith has to say relates directly to the health status of minorities in general, and African-Americans in particular. If blacks are encouraged not only to seek relief from physical illness, but to free themselves of the conditioned thoughts that lead to illness, then there is a distinct possibility that many of the sicknesses that have disproportionately plagued African-Americans for generations may begin to dissipate. Put another way, if more black people were mentally free of the *double* conditioning society sends about (1) what it means to be black and (2) American, then perhaps the nearly four-to-one ratio between blacks and whites who develop kidney disease would begin to balance out. Even better, we might one day see the elimination of certain diseases from the human species not by new drugs but by new mind-sets.

Forty years ago Abraham Maslow was writing about the need to reintegrate science and spirituality in the treatment of human beings. As the leading humanistic psychologist of his day, Maslow, like Keith and many others in the alternative health-care field, saw how by dichotomizing science and the soul humans were being fragmented and stunted. Just as Krishnamurti worried that organized religion would only stand in the way of one's own path to enlightenment, the exclusionary emphasis we in the West have placed on science and medicine as the lone source of hope also runs the disastrous risk of creating an irreversible dependency on drugs. As it stands, hospitals and doctors' offices are like islands unto themselves. They are imposing and intimidating and they rarely inspire hope or joy. We enter them because we must and because society offers no alternative. We put our faith in physicians because we have been conditioned to accept their diagnoses and prognoses, and because we have been equally conditioned to accept our own ignorance.

But imagine an alternative future where hospitals housed both hospital beds and yoga mats, where macrobiotic menus were offered, and daily hikes through nearby woodlands were part of a daily recovery regimen. Imagine the hospitals themselves being transformed into wellness centers where music flooded the hallways, and practitioners led their patients through morning tai chi. Imagine if instead of the out-of-date magazines lying around the dull waiting rooms, an anxiety-ridden patient or loved one could pick up something like one of Krishnamurti's dialogues and experience a deep insight. Imagine if health-care coverage included an annual spa treatment. Finally, imagine an army of physicians like Keith: competent, compassionate, creative, and courageous.

I ask Keith why this isn't the case.

"A lot of people are very conditioned to think that things should be the way they are, that's all they want to talk about. That's all they want to address. If you can't measure it, it's meaningless. I think the most important aspects of life are those things that can't be measured. There are many people in health care who have approached this, [and] who are trying to add to the field and open people's minds to integrating combinations of different approaches to health care. I want to make sure I have as clear an understanding as possible, particularly with the way to articulate it in a rational manner to someone who is very wed to the classic scientific approach to medicine. To people who are open to it, it's not a big deal, but to be able to articulate it to someone who is not open to it forces me to understand it on a different level. It's hard to tell people who are in the matrix that they are in the matrix, and what it's like to be outside of it."

Inside a cab weaving its way through Midtown traffic en route to a lunch date Keith has with his cousin Jan, who's also in town for the day, he happens to mention that he's working toward his doctorate in metaphysics. He's been in the program for more than a year. All of his classes are online, he has an adviser he communicates with, a list of courses he has to take before he graduates, and a dissertation to write. When I ask where he finds the time, his reply is that most of the books he's reading for his classes are books he'd be reading on his own anyway. That being the case, he figured why not write a paper now and then and get credit for it. Furthermore, he recognizes that the letters "Ph.D." after his name will give his atypical ideas the credibility they might otherwise lack. As an M.D. he's licensed and qualified to talk about traditional medicine. As an M.D., Ph.D., he'll be able to hold court with anyone, anytime.

Over lunch I get to see another side of Keith. In his attractive older cousin's company, he suddenly becomes younger, shyer, and wittier. Jan lives in North Carolina, where she home-schools her twelve-year-old daughter. She went to the University of Pennsylvania Law School, but quit practicing after a year in which she rarely spent any time with her son. He's studying abroad now, his junior year at the University of North Carolina. According to Jan, he bears some striking similarities to his uncle Keith. For one, they're both tall, both bright, and both good basketball players. Jan's son plays for the junior varsity team at UNC. Keith, she tells me, was a heckuva ballplayer himself in his day. Discovering that someone as devoted to his work as Keith is has other worlds where his "work" is irrelevant is refreshing. Modest and tight-lipped about his basketball prowess at first, Keith's braggadocio side finally reveals itself when I tell them about my hoop days. While he never had time to play for Cornell or Howard, when he moved to Los Angeles he played semi-pro ball in one of the city's storied summer leagues. He even goes so far as to boast a bit about playing in the legendary pickup games at UCLA's Wooden Arena with some of the old L.A. Lakers. Unfortunately, bad knees and old age have conspired against him of late, and he hasn't played seriously in several years.

Sensing her cousin had left out anything having to do with his stature in the scientific community, Jan also tells me that just a few months ago Keith was inducted into the National Black College Alumni Hall of Fame. A combination of research, writing, speaking, and teaching earned him the distinction. The award, she proudly adds, is only given to one scientist each year. Former surgeon general Dr. David Hatcher was one of the award's previous recipients. An induction ceremony complete with formal attire, laudatory speeches, and fine dining was staged in Keith's honor.

In the midst of his cousin's recollection of the events, I glance over in Keith's direction. I wonder how we'd spent three hours talking about his most intimate spiritual experiences and he'd never mentioned the award. Then I notice the glazed-over look on his face and I remember something he said earlier in the day. "Anything else in my life, no matter how great, no matter how wonderful, no matter how thrilling, no matter how enjoyable pales by so many magnitudes to the feeling that I have in that space," Keith had said, reflecting on his moments of transcendence. I realized then that the award hadn't come up because it wasn't relevant to our conversation, and because he didn't feel the need to impress me with a list of credentials.

As the sun dims over the Manhattan skyline I make my way farther uptown to Columbia University, where Keith's niece Leah is presenting her thesis. After lunch I had gone back downtown to run some errands, and to give Keith some private time with the cousin with whom he shares his experiences. Once inside a third-floor room in Barnard Hall, I find Keith and the open seat he has saved for me. The performance has already started and the crowd of about fifty is glued to the fiery young woman with narrow hips, wild hair, and a magical voice. Leah's thesis is everything you'd expect from a brilliant twenty-two-year-old ready to take on the world: angry, joyous, bluesy, hopeful. It's an homage to revolutionary black art and music, a retrospective tribute to the creative voices that shaped twentieth-century African-American consciousness. At the conclusion of the performance, Leah asks us all to create a mental picture of our "Freedom Song." Then she hands out pencils for us to write with. Afterward, she invites the audience to share. After a number of others share their thoughts, I watch Keith's arm slowly rise. His niece offers him a smile and a nod, followed by Keith standing and clearing his throat:

"I once felt the weight of the world sat and watched my every word,
Waiting to fall on me should I utter that which was mine.
Now that I am free, no one and no thing can stop my song but me.
For now I know it was always only me who could stop my song.
I watch myself each day hoping I am no longer in my way.
In that awareness I became free.
Not because I choose to be free,
But because I could no longer choose not to be."

THE TIES THAT BIND

I interviewed Kimson Albert and his mother, Barbara Summers, separately; I never even sat with them together. Actually, come to think of it, the only reason I wound up interviewing Barbara was because of the scattered references Kimson made to his mother during one of our conversations. At the time, I'd already considered including an intergenerational chapter. I was hoping to find a set of stories about parents and children who had both chosen to walk unconventional paths. The initial idea was to link the courageous choices of one generation with the expanded opportunities of the next. That is and isn't what I wound up with. Barbara, who came of age in the sixties, has more formal education than her son, who came of age in the late eighties and early nineties. When I first met Barbara she was trying to sell a book and pay her mortgage, while her son was trying to find a job in animation and pay his rent. Kimson is a devout Buddhist, while his mother is skeptical of all organized religion. My whole evolutionary theory would have been out the window if I was concerned with the standard benchmarks of generational progress like education and income; instead, I looked at the values Kimson and Barbara shared. They are both generous and compassionate. They are both candid and lucid and, at times, highly opinionated. They are both engaging conversationalists.

Barbara's life has been defined by the unexpected. Her careers in particular were not the ones she set out to pursue when she was an undergraduate at the University of Pennsylvania. But for her, life has always been about setting herself apart, so when uncommon opportunities arose, she sensed and seized them. On the other hand, Kimson has been focused on his goals since as far back as he can remember. For him, life has always been about being naturally different from everyone around him. As his mother joked one afternoon, he was born half-Jewish, has always been short, and has a funny name. Kimson never had a choice about whether he was going to fit in or not, so from an early age he had to define himself.

But individuality is exactly what Barbara had always intended for her only child. More than anything else, she wanted him to embrace the world and make of himself what he wished. That's how he was raised; that's also how she lived her own life. As a younger woman Barbara did what others couldn't have expected, and now, as she gracefully approaches sixty, she's doing precisely what she *hadn't* planned to be doing at this stage of her life.

An Unexpected Life

Barbara Summers: Fashion Model/Author

"I'm always called a sellout. Well, in order to be a sellout, you have to have something to sell."

The first place Barbara Summers shows me when we enter her home one mid-summer afternoon is her workroom. This is where she spends most of her time these days. There's a desk by the window where she can savor the sunlight and let her mind wander. There are stacks of books, many of which she's using for a four-volume anthology of African-American literature she's putting together, and a wall full of photos of glamorous women, mostly models, many of whom she interviewed for *Skin Deep,* a book she wrote several years ago about black models. Barbara points out supermodels like Iman, Naomi Campbell, Karen Alexander, Beverly Johnson, and others whom I've seen but whose names I've never heard before. There's also a copy of the first book she edited, *I Dream a World,* a best-seller and coffee table staple in many African-American homes, including my own growing up. Like *Skin Deep,* it focuses on the lives of black women. In fact, one of Barbara's missions as an author has been to rewrite the story of black women. "So much of what's known about black women on paper has to do with clichés and stereotypes and unrealistic images," she says. Not until we are on our way out of the workroom, however, do I notice what looks to be a storyboard hanging from the wall. Within its margins are dozens of small slips of paper on which she's written notes for a novel.

"This is one example of how I work," Barbara says, pausing by the doorway. She's tall and slim and, even dressed down for the day, graceful. "This is sort of like a scene breakdown. This book is called *Razzmatazz*. It takes place in the summer of 1926. This is just to help me keep in mind the different beats of the story. A friend of mine uses this flat, black paint—she has a wonderful wall—and she paints that wall black and uses colored chalk to outline her story. I don't have a wall, I just break down the story this way. So instead of having to go through the entire manuscript to find a scene, generally I can just pick it out from here and remember what happened in it to keep things in order."

The main characters in Barbara's novel are Zora Neale Hurston, Langston Hughes (whom she met on her sixteenth birthday), and Wallace Thurman, three of the Harlem Renaissance's foremost personalities. *Razzmatazz* captures them in their twenties (although Zora is believed to have been passing for twenty-five when she was actually thirty-five) and at, arguably, the genesis of black literature as a coherent literary form outside of the slave narratives that preceded it.

"Black folks are still new as originators of literature, as the source of characters and life experiences, as well as the artists, interpreters, re-creators, and visionaries. We don't have novels from the eighteenth century to build on. Since we don't, we have a lot to make up for in rewriting our past. But we also have a tremendous amount of freedom in writing our present and future."

Which is why, perhaps, the Harlem Renaissance is such a fascinating and desirable subject for Barbara. Why she envies it, too. She loves the story, she says, because writing it has allowed her to, as she describes it, "move into their world through their writings and pictures" and because she's not just telling a story—she's reinventing language. "The Renaissance was nothing if not a total upheaval of what black culture, especially in the

United States, was about. They were reinventing literature and language, attitudes, mores, dress codes."

But as high as Barbara's hopes are for this novel, and despite her passionate and pure pursuit of high-quality literature, there's also a pragmatic side to her that fifty plus years of living can't negate. Barbara understands the nature of the publishing industry, who's in charge, how it works. A simple stroll down the fiction aisle at your local bookstore will tell you how interested publishers are in books by and about African-Americans that don't fit within the parameters that purportedly comprise the black experience, if such a term even still means anything. What sells in terms of fiction, irrespective of race, often has less to do with thought-provoking dialogue, masterful narrative structure, and credible characterization—literary craftsmanship, that is—than it does with duplicating a daytime soap opera.

That people simply don't read literature like they used to is equally evident. Television and film have usurped the medium as our primary means of knowing the world. They are easier to consume, more visually stimulating, and, of course, less time-consuming. The writer, therefore, is left in a precarious position. If they want a family, a home, an education, and all of the other American accoutrements, they either need to be wildly successful or connected to some regular kind of income, which for most professional writers these days means a professorship at a university. Where it gets tricky is when it comes to balancing the creative urge and the practical necessities. Writing, working, and carrying on some semblance of a life ain't easy. After a long day of work, the last thing most of us have is the energy to conjure some imaginative universe, especially when so many are readily available on television.

"I bitch and complain and moan and groan every single day," Barbara says, "but I'm at home doing it, I'm not working for somebody else. Whatever I'm doing to make the *zero* money that I make, I'm doing it from my house. I'm not having to deal in some situation that's going to make me terribly unhappy. I don't know how long this is going to last, because it can't. But it is a privilege to be a writer."

Barbara is startlingly candid about her own financial state. Despite her beautiful, though modest, suburban home and the classy ride parked in the driveway, she's recently had to consider selling pieces of her art collection to pay bills. Already, she's stopped buying books, something anyone who loves the feel of a new book in hand knows is nearly impossible to do. At one point, she even seriously considered writing a beach blanket paperback. Something unabashedly topical that could make her enough money to write the novels she cared about without the stress of wondering where her next dollar was coming from. That didn't work out so well. Barbara couldn't escape her literary leanings, her Ivy League education, her race-conscious upbringing, her years in Paris. Hers is the curse of acculturation. For Barbara, to know great literature and not strive for it every time she sits down is to betray the essence of the craft.

Well into her fifties, Barbara is the picture of the writer. She appreciates the way a book looks and feels, understands that a story is invaluable, that it can change a life, open up a world. She laments the fact that young people aren't reading. If African-American kids aren't reading, she says, then her purpose as a writer isn't being served.

Curiously, Barbara didn't set out to be a fiction writer when she enrolled at the University of Pennsylvania in the fall of 1961. Back then, she was one of only a handful of black women in her class, one of no more than two dozen in the whole school. As she recalls it, theirs was an isolated world. They were among the social elite, blue-bloods, old money people from Manhattan and Long Island, from around the country. This was before affirmative action and they were there. Because they belonged there. Because they deserved to be there. Not because, in today's idiom, they were "trying to be white," a phrase that infuriates Barbara to no end:

"Frederick Douglass, W. E. B. DuBois, Alaine Locke—all those people were the most genius people this country has ever produced, and they never had any kind of question about whether they were trying to be white or not, or what was wrong with them because they were super-genius."

"Bell Hooks actually writes about that in her book *Rock My Soul*," I add. "She writes about how African-American kids at Ivy League schools are psychologically troubled because they question whether they're worthy."

"We were spared it. [Penn] was a strange world because while things were changing in the South for example, and in the North—I graduated from Penn in sixty-five—it did not really touch campus. Malcolm X came to speak on campus and it was cool, but it was no big deal. We were so isolated, in a cocoon, at least I was."

After Penn, Barbara went directly to Yale for her doctorate in French literature. That a young African-American woman whose parents were both educators and what was then termed "race" people—meaning they were active in the civil rights movement—chose French literature as her course of study struck me as not only unique, but gutsy. To her it made sense, though. Her whole family was in education, either as teachers, principals, or superintendents. Barbara wanted to be different, so different that no one would be able to understand her, literally. Her plan was to have her Ph.D. by twenty-five, after which she would proceed to, in her words, "smoke the Ivy League and just be this brilliant black woman, redefining the canon and bringing all these West Indian and African writers into the French canon." At that stage of her life she wasn't concerned with American literature, not even African-American literature.

Then came the "little" year in Paris at the Sorbonne. Barbara had been to Paris once before, when she was nineteen, with $300 and a backpack. She and a friend hitchhiked throughout Europe. They had the time of their lives, she recalls. This second trip, however, was supposed to be for a year of serious study. It was supposed to be a stepping-stone toward a stellar career as a scholar. By the time she left the United States she'd completed her course work. All that loomed was the dissertation and then an associate professorship and then . . . Well, the year passed and Barbara, after all of the "neat preparation," never returned to the Ivy League. Instead, she discovered a new life in Paris. She won a grant and began writing her own stories. During that year, Barbara says, she discovered her "blackness."

"There, not only was I one of very few [African-Americans], but I was speaking another language in another culture, and I could be so many different things that I ended up choosing to be who I am, who I was. I was in Paris when Martin Luther King was assassinated. That same year, sixty-eight, they had these huge riots in Paris—the French kids were rebelling against the school system. It seemed like the world was just on fire, and so being black was a part of a worldwide revolution. It was an amazing time."

Even after Barbara returned to America in the early seventies in order to have her son, Kimson, her life didn't stop taking detours. She and two friends who also had small children moved to an unused parcel of land in Puerto Rico for a time. They lived off the land, picking oranges and bananas from the groves, and driving into town once a week for other essentials like milk and eggs. Later, in New York, she opened Barbara's Backyard Café. She hired a cook who prepared a vegetarian menu, and she opened up the backyard of her ground-floor apartment

Thursdays to Sundays for business. In one sense it was a crazy way to live, but it was also fun, and it was fearless.

From the outside looking in it might've seemed like Barbara was deliberately attempting to sabotage her life. But for Barbara the choices she was making were not only logical, they were authentic. She wasn't forcing anything to happen. Her experiences, her son, the general turbulence in her life, reflected the upheaval of the times. She was simply living in that moment, walking through the doors opening before her. Naturally, one of those doors would lead to a career she never envisioned.

"I had a sister who was working for *Mademoiselle* magazine. She was an associate editor, one of the very few African-Americans in an editorial position at Condé Nast. I had just come back from spending years abroad in Paris, and in Puerto Rico and Haiti, and I had taken a teaching job over at Medgar Evers College, which was brand new at the time. I was teaching French and journalism. They were doing a story on 'real' people and I was a real person. I was a vegetarian and had no hair and I was rail thin."

Barbara went for an interview, shot some photos, and before she knew it she was in a meeting with Eileen Ford of the famed Ford Modeling Agency. After giving Barbara a spiel about there being no work for African-American models, Ford tested Barbara on her French. "I zapped back at her showing her I spoke better than she did," she says. Barbara was signed to a modeling contract on the spot.

"I had a very interesting career with them, not one I expected at all, and not one that I was prepared for because I knew nothing about makeup or hairstyling and clothes and all this kind of stuff. That's what you see happens much more often than not. The girls that really do well in fashion and modeling, they're not trained in it. These unfortunates that go through the training process never make it because they're too slickafied, they're not naïve anymore, they're not natural anymore. What the camera really wants is a truly fresh face. It doesn't matter really the age. I mean, now you *have* to be fifteen. If you're over that, you might as well apply for social security. There's got to be some innocence, some curiosity, something naturally elegant and fine, and then they'll put you through their makeup, their hair and styling, and find out what kind of clothing they want you in. That's where all the other upkeep comes in, the fabulous hairdressers. But if you're too well schooled, too prepped, it's not gonna work, it's overdone, and the camera sees that and people aren't really going to buy it."

That someone who had spent her life cultivating her mind, particularly at a time when "women's lib" was at its height, would choose a career that many consider hostile to the struggle for gender equity struck me as strange. But for Barbara that was all beside the point. Modeling was a means to an end more than it was a source of validation. She hadn't sought out a career in front of the camera. If anything, she wanted a life behind the printed word. Barbara isn't shy about assessing the situation at the time. She had a son to raise. Modeling gave her a good income for a number of years, more than even she expected. Modeling allowed her to be there for Kimson. She could be the mom who drove the car pool. She could be the mom who was home in the afternoon. She could be the mom her parents were afraid she couldn't possibly be.

Before Kimson was even born Barbara decided he was going to be bilingual and bicultural. If that meant she'd have to forgo her summers with him so he could know his family in Paris, then so be it. If it meant he needed to spend a couple years in school abroad, then that's what had to be done. She was adamant about Kimson being an international person, someone who wasn't afraid to move around in the world, someone who could find his way without her, or anyone else for that matter, having to push him in a certain direction. Barbara's own mother sometimes criticized her for treating Kimson as if he was a grown-up, but she wanted him to be responsible for himself. Drawing those lines wasn't easy for her, but she did it for him, and for herself because quite often her career demanded it.

Despite the benefits Barbara drew from her modeling career, there is still a broad cultural perception that modeling isn't an intellectual profession, that it exploits beautiful brainless women and discards them when their looks fade. "There was never an issue of 'this isn't an intellectual profession'?" I ask Barbara.

"No. I'm always called a sellout. Well, in order to be a sellout, you have to have something to sell. If money is time, [and] time equals money, what is it that you're going to sell to make money with your time? They use up your hands. They use up your brain. They use up your butt."

In Barbara's eyes beauty is political. When you see a dark-skinned woman with short hair and broad features gracing the cover of a fashion magazine, that says something about the evolution of consciousness as well as about the demands women of color are placing on the industry as a whole. Now, we can certainly debate whether that image of an African woman is more a matter of fetishizing the "other" than rendering a beautiful image. We can also ask ourselves why we don't see more images of African-American women on the covers of high-profile fashion magazines. One of the reasons Barbara wrote *Skin Deep* (a book for which she received a great deal of criticism within the modeling world) was precisely because she wanted to interrogate the inherent racial inequities of the modeling industry; more important, she gave these women a voice.

"What is the big cliché about models? Models are dumb. Listen to these girls and they're brilliant. There's no black woman in fashion today who is successful who is a dummy. It's just impossible. You can't be stupid. You'd never survive. Everyone's out there to shoot you down and not give you a chance to be successful. If you're successful, you're close to genius. On the basis of my research these are smart women out there." A great example of this was when she went to Japan in 1976 with designer Issey Miyake as part of a group he put together called 12 Black Girls, one of whom was Grace Jones ("She's everything you heard about her," Barbara reverently recalls). They were mobbed wherever they went. They didn't all know one another and, with all the publicity, egos could have easily gotten in the way. But they managed to keep the show together and when the organizers tried tacking on a series of additional shoots they hadn't been told about or paid for, Barbara was the one who organized them for a strike. If they didn't get paid more money, they weren't going to do the extra shoots. Ultimately, their demands were met. While the money has long since been spent, the principle on which the twelve women stood remains a defining moment in a career Barbara is both proud of and happy with.

"I have no idea how I did it. I have no idea where the energy came from. To do the shoots, the traveling, to have the energy to interact with total strangers on a daily basis, on an hourly basis, to be totally naked in front of half a dozen to two dozen people in a room for hours on end. It's amazing. It's like I was a star."

The Faith Factor

Kimson Albert: Animator/Producer

> "I wasn't going to be a dentist and then animate on the side.
> I made a determination in college never to do what I didn't
> want to do outside of my field."

Kimson Albert and I met through Buddhism. When I was just beginning this book and my Buddhist practice, he and I chanted together. At the time, *Beat of a Different Drum* was just an idea that I was tinkering with. Meeting Kimson turned out to be one of the many divine interventions that helped me stick with the project. He saw the vision and he encouraged me to carry it forward because, as he would say time and time again, it had value.

Still, when it came time to write Kimson's story I hesitated. I wondered if there might be a way to write around Buddhism, shroud it like a patch of missing hair or a stain. At the heart of my dilemma lingered an ingrained idea that the religious and the secular are separate conversations, never to be mixed. I also didn't know how people would react to a conversation about Buddhism in a largely Christian society. Many people still see Buddhism as a form of mysticism. They associate it with aesthetic practices, fortune cookies bearing Confucian maxims, Tina Turner's "What's Love Got to Do with It," and kung-fu flicks. I wanted to avoid those stereotypes if at all possible. But it wasn't. Kimson's story is bound to his Buddhism. As he says himself, Buddhism, getting into film school, telling stories, and drawing were all "one big thing."

• • •

When Kimson was sixteen his dream was to become a film director. He also wanted to be an animation director because he loved drawing, loved comic books, figurines, cartoons—anything that had anything to do with visual storytelling. Unlike his parents, who were both writers, he knew he didn't have the patience or temperament to tell a story on the page, nor did he think the written medium could fully render his vision. In order to make his dreams coalesce into a lifestyle, he decided he needed to go to film school. The only catch was he'd never made a film before, nor had he ever taken a drawing class in his life.

"I was not an artist," Kimson says. "I drew, but I just wanted to go to film school." Not just any film school, though, N.Y.U.'s Tisch, the best film school in the country at the time.

By his own admission Kimson has always been unusual. His name is Vietnamese, his father is French—Parisian, rather—and his father's family is Jewish. The elder Albert grew up amid Europe's Resistance Movement during World War II. His grandfather, who was wanted by the Nazis for helping English soldiers get passports, had to flee the country at one point. Other family members were sent to concentration camps.

Kimson's mother, Barbara, grew up during the civil rights movement. Her father was a "Morehouse Man." She went to the University of Pennsylvania in the 1960s and later to Yale for her graduate work before moving to Paris for a number of years.

Kimson's formative years were spent between continents, cultures, and languages. "I'd be spending my summers in Europe and then come back to Teaneck," he recalls. "I was climbing the Pyrenees when everybody else went to camp. Not to judge or anything, but I was on the beach in the South of France, taking trips to Spain, and my friends were like, 'I made it with so and so.' I was always the outcast growing up. I never fit in, even if it was just being short. Even in France, when I went to school there, they wouldn't believe I was American because I looked Arabic. They wanted a tall, blond kid."

To compensate for his outsiderness Kimson did what most youthful outcasts do: He conjured up his own interior world. He collected action figures and used them to tell stories he created. He watched films obsessively. He pored through countless comic books.

"I don't know why, but I always thought film and animation was something I could do. Sometimes I'd even know what an artist was trying to say, but also that they didn't say it right. I wanted to find out how they tried to say it so I could say it better than them. It was a competition thing for me, too. Growing up on hip-hop, that's part of the culture: 'He did that? Oh, I gotta better that.' When you're thirteen, fourteen, you're breakin', and it's who rhymes better and who can do graffiti better. Battles were it! Everything became a battle."

Kimson came of age during what many consider hip-hop's golden era. The music was still being formed, and large corporations hadn't yet figured out how to package and market the music as a pop product. At that point, there was still space for niche groups like 2Live Crew, conscious groups like Public Enemy, party groups like Kid n' Play, avant-garde groups like the Beastie Boys, and hard-core MCs like Rakim and Big Daddy Kane. Today's pop-hop landscape doesn't lend itself to the same kind of deviation, exploration, or innovation. While there are more songs on mainstream radio than ever before, the true seeker of hip-hop must dig deeper and deeper underground to find satisfying, stimulating content. That being said, Kimson's teenage years, roughly 1984 to 1988, were an age when hip-hop still belonged to the artists, dancers, and writers who were creating the culture the rappers then rhymed about.

"What I really liked about what we had was that it was ours, completely ours," he says. "Our parents would be like, 'What is that?' We'd be thirteen, fourteen, talking for hours about who's better, Kane or Rakim."

Then, along came Spike Lee. He released *She's Gotta Have It,* then *School Daze,* followed by *Do the Right Thing.* Spike's early films wrestled with what were quintessentially American problems from a decidedly African-American perspective, one that allowed for celebration, appreciation, and consideration of an unmediated black experience. Kimson had his own stories to tell and Spike, a successful African-American director, was actually doing it.

"The way Spike introduced himself had a pretty big impact on me. He went to film school and did it all on his own. That to me was pretty encouraging to see. I think people underestimate Spike's impact. He was determined and he wasn't going to work on anybody else's film."

Against this backdrop Kimson decided he wanted to go to the same film school that had nurtured Spike's talents. The bigger question was how was he going to make that happen without any experience, and without any money.

Enter Buddhism.

At fifteen, Kimson sought out the Buddhism of Nichiren Daishonin, a thirteenth-century Buddha. He was told that if he simply chanted the words "Nam-myoho-renge-kyo," he could attain enlightenment and fulfill his dreams. For a year he chanted to his wall. He didn't join the organization, nor did he receive his Gohonzon, the object of devotion in Nichiren Buddhism.

"I started practicing Buddhism because I felt like I needed a certain rhythm to my life," he says, explaining his adolescent conversion. "That's a nice way of putting [I wanted] girls to like me, get a job, have money, and do good in school."

The following summer Kimson read *The Human Revolution,* a novelization of the history of Nichiren Buddhism in Japan during and after World War II. He began to understand and value the principles upon which Buddhism stood. When Kimson returned to the United States he received his Gohonzon. He chanted more than ever. He applied to film school, went for an interview, and in February of his senior year he received a letter in the mail informing him that he'd been granted early acceptance. Everything was shaping up nicely. The only question that remained was how he was going to pay his tuition.

Winter became spring, which rolled into summer, and on the day before the first semester's payment was due, Kimson still didn't have the money he needed for school. He called his father, who told him to think about a cheaper school. That wasn't in the plan. Kimson was determined to go to Tisch. This was to be his life's work. Nothing could stand in his way. Once again, he turned to Buddhism, chanting on his situation for nearly two hours that day. The following morning he received a phone call from an aunt who asked him how much money he needed.

Cut to the second week of school. After all of the effort Kimson put into getting in to Tisch, his very first professor told his class that they didn't need a film degree in order to become great directors. Kimson wasn't shaken to his core, but the professor's warning changed him, modified his outlook on school, and granted him a deep and personal understanding of life's perpetual dichotomy. "That was my wake-up call to understanding the way life moves," Kimson says. "There's a contradictory aspect for everything you think is one way, the only way."

To help pay his way through school Kimson was assigned a work-study job in the cinema studies department. He ran a sixteen-millimeter projector for classes; he also taped movies onto VHS. At first, it was just a job, a fairly mindless one at that. Then he saw the job's value. He was being paid to watch movies. "I'd be in this little room and be surrounded by VHS tapes with numbers on them and a title. If I was watching something I didn't like, I'd just pop in another tape and watch a movie. I could always watch movies that way." Over the four years he worked in the library Kimson developed what he calls a "library of imagery."

By the time Kimson graduated from film school he knew where he wanted to make his mark. He was going to direct animation. He would have his own show, something edgy and high-tech, something aimed at adult audiences. He'd grown up watching movies like *Heavy Metal,* shows like *Heavy Traffic* and *Fritz the Cat,* and that was what he was going to do. But he struggled through a year without much luck before landing his first paying gig as a layout artist on *Beavis and Butt-head.*

In the beginning he wasn't too keen on the show. Technically, it was disastrous. *Beavis and Butt-head* wasn't cool like other animated shows. The animation was rudimentary. The main characters were a pair of middle-America burnouts. There wasn't any flash. Yet, amazingly, the show was a hit.

"I got hired in May. I thought we would work until September. We ended up working four years. That was the beginning of my career in animation."

I ask Kimson what it was like being a young black kid raised on hip-hop, working on a show about two white kids obsessed with Metallica and AC/DC.

"That's when I became fully aware of blacks in the industry because there were only like—" He stops to count them on his hand, then gives up. "The lady who hired me had a thing for black dudes. She always had black boyfriends. She really was like 'Free Mumia.' She hired a bunch of black people on purpose and was always very clear about that. For whatever reason, her fetish for whatever was black at the time maybe, she understood that black people need breaks and she hired me and a bunch of other black dudes. We were seven black people working on a show that was lily white in its expression, whose creator, Mike

Judge, only loves James Brown, Dr. Dre, and Bootsie Collins." As an ironic homage to their revolutionary predecessors, Kimson and the other artists cut out the head on the Black Panther logo, replaced it with Butt-head's, and stuck it on the wall in their office. "We called ourselves the Butt-head Panthers," he says, laughing. That no one would have guessed seven black kids worked on a show like *Beavis and Butt-head* is exactly why Kimson has always wanted to work behind the camera.

"It's important to have a variety of people who control the image. We need to have a variety of voices and people in positions. One thing that was a letdown was seeing the subliminal limits that people in positions of power put on black folks just because they're not trained to see us in a certain light. Since they don't see it, they don't promote it. Casting people don't see how variety and diversity can empower them and again that transcends race, too. That's *Hollywood Shuffle* all over again. It's the tradition of the black thespian in American culture. It affects everybody, not just black people. That's why I have to give credit to the lady who promoted me because maybe that's the kind of energy you need to reverse the subtle . . . I guess it's racism."

As an animator, Kimson's life is consumed by "process." Process is in his work, his faith, he even jokes about how it has seeped into the most mundane aspects of his life. He uses words like "amazing" and "fantastic," and phrases like "turn on" to describe all of the elements that go into making an animated character's eye blink or its arm swing, the number of frames that go into a slouch, the musicality of animation itself. "Timing is everything in animation. You can make a hand move left to right. If you space the framing evenly it'll look like a robot, but if you space it out, and this is where it gets musical, then it becomes a shuffle. You have two notes and in between the notes or

extremes you fill in those poses. As a viewer this all appears natural to you. Human beings move in this way. It's very nonro-
botic. Robots move in a very even way. Human beings move
with swings."

In many ways, the process of creating a cartoon mirrors that
of creating a product on an assembly line. Everything moves in
stages, and at every stage a different department has its role. In
this way, one can easily become a cog in the wheel, a mere func-
tionary, performing a job instead of pursuing a passion. Kimson
recognized this early on when he was still working at MTV, and
he made a private pact never to take a job unless he was attached
to the creative source. Since then he's produced with the likes of
P-Funk legends Bootsie Collins and Overton Lloyd, Russell
Simmons, and adult film maven Heather Hunter.

Kimson also made a pact to invest in himself. His subter-
ranean dwelling in a burgeoning Brooklyn neighborhood dou-
bles as his private studio. Alongside stacks of DVDs, CDs, and a
shelf full of collectible figurines, sits a professional-grade Mac
complete with mike and keyboards.

"I wasn't going to be a dentist and then animate on the side.
I made a determination in college never to do what I didn't
want to do outside of my field. I've done graphic design. I
taught myself about the computer and Photoshop. I have everything I need. The only thing I'm missing, which is just a funds
thing, is a digital camera."

These tools are particularly handy during the intermittent
dry spells. When you decide to live by your own set of rules,
you accept the bitter with the sweet. A show that captures the
attention of the nation and runs for four years like *Beavis and
Butt-head* is a once-in-a-lifetime thing for even a fortunate animator. In animation the greater likelihood is that you'll work some
and then you won't. Therefore, you learn to save up during the

good times and to keep your overhead low at all times. During the rough times, you hope you qualify for unemployment.

When Kimson and I first met we were both out of work. I'd been on the dole for almost six months, he'd been on it for roughly four. Unlike me, though, he wasn't consumed by the impending end of unemployment. Whereas I had the date marked off on my calender, he was never quite sure when his funds were set to run out. He just figured when the checks stopped, they stopped. Over a period of months I watched the way he used his time to work on his personal projects rather than worry about where his next check was coming from, how he was going to eat the next day. That's not to say he didn't think about his future. He simply didn't allow that which he couldn't control to stand in the way of what he could.

"I've been through this so many times that this is where my Buddhist practice really comes into play. I'm still living my dream and I'm not trying to compromise, and with my practice I'm able to not compromise, and I'm able to use wisdom. I'm not going to go get a clerical job because that wasn't part of my initial determination. My determination is to stay on track.

"Buddhist practice for me is all based on the self-revolution or what we call the human revolution. It's that your individual change affects the larger society. That said, my not compromising my dream is connected to the betterment of society. For me to compromise my vision would be defeating that whole process. My personal determination was a spiritual one. I'm dedicated to my dream spiritually and physically on a real, fundamental level, and I can't waver from that. My practice has enabled me to fulfill that vision. Actually, sometimes I wonder if I should be more committed to that. Maybe I'm not doing enough toward my dream and that's even better. It's not so much, 'I'm living my dream, it's all good, it comes with its bumps.' Dude, if there's bumps work even harder."

Postscript. Almost a year after our last conversation Kimson and I finally hooked up again. By then he'd been working as an animation director on a series called The Venture Brothers *that came on the Cartoon Network's Adult Swim. He seemed happy with his work.* The Venture Brothers *was more in line with what he'd always wanted to do, edgier. He liked the group of people he worked with, many of whom he'd started with back at MTV more than a decade before. He was heavily involved in the creative process, from scheduling to the scriptwriting, which meant he wasn't just a cog. More than anything he was happy to have steady income from doing what he loved.*

That wasn't all, though. Kimson had finally found the right ingredients for a show he'd been thinking about for years. He and a friend had been working furiously on the pilot in their free time for a couple of months. The following week, he said, they had their first pitch meeting with a studio.

WHERE A WILL
MEETS ITS WAY

Although St. Louis is known in the business world as a major connecting point between east and west, it is not known as a mecca for business. Travelers pass through. They stop in to see the Arch, the riverboats along the Mississippi, and the Budweiser plant. Then they move on. St. Louis's struggles are partly due to Chicago's reign as the central commercial city in the Midwest. But they're also the result of the city's enduring image. Interspersed between the city's pockets of prosperity, the "blues" that birthed William Christopher Handy's classic "St. Louis Blues" still linger. The city ranks above the national average in almost every quantifiable crime category, and a simple drive down the streets of many of its seventy neighborhoods reveals a tale of two cities: one black, one white. One downtrodden, one prosperous. While almost half of the population is African-American, all observable evidence points to an overwhelming majority of blacks dwelling near the bottom of the socioeconomic ladder. Considering their dismal state, it's no wonder that between 1950 and 1995 nearly half a million residents, many of them African-Amercans, "fled" north, east, west, and all points in between. Some left with the major companies like Southwestern Bell, others because they knew St. Louisians weren't ready to alter their attitudes toward race with the changing times.

Perhaps St. Louis's troubled history explains why the city came to figure into *Beat of a Different Drum* the way it did. I certainly hadn't planned on visiting the city, not until Ray Hill contacted me and invited me out for a week. He said there were some things happening in his hometown that I needed to see. Even though I was still skeptical about what the city had to offer, by the time I left, I knew I had seen something special.

The stories in this chapter speak of a new kind of entrepreneur. They are linked as much by proximity as they are by philosophy. Alvin, Matt, and Ray are all making serious strides in their fields because they have the drive not only to do something unique, but to do it on their own terms, using their own means, and while creating their own standards of success. They aren't all college graduates, and not one of them has his M.B.A., or any other advanced degree for that matter. But that's part of what I was attracted by. Whatever they'd learned about their fields— and they all knew plenty—they'd taught themselves. Whatever success they'd had, they made for themselves, and in spite of the "Show Me" state's enduring opposition. At the same time, I'm willing to bet that the very opposition they faced, racial and otherwise, is what has made them sharp, appreciative, and committed to opening doors for others.

Starting from Scratch

Ray Hill: Brewmeister/Entrepreneur

> "People love beer. Whether I come out with a company or not, people are going to drink it."

When Ray Hill first contacted me saying he was a young entrepreneur and that his story belonged in *Beat of a Different Drum,* I hesitated to write him back right away. I wasn't particularly interested in "business" people, not for this book. I figured there were already plenty of stories about African-American entrepreneurs who've made millions in the public domain. What we—as in not only black America, but America—have a shortage of are stories about African-Americans who break even the traditional "success story" mold, stories that actually challenge and in some instances subvert that mold. Not everyone comes into this world wired with the same moneymaking gene. Some of us have other aspirations, follow different paths.

And yet in the days that followed Ray's e-mail, I couldn't stop thinking about the black brewer from St. Louis, home of the King of Beers—Budweiser—who was convinced he belonged in this book. Why? What made his story unique? That he brewed his own beer? That he was African-American? That there aren't any African-American-owned beer companies on the market?*

---

*Back in the late sixties, a brand called Black Pride Beers, purported to be black-owned, tried its hand in Chicago but failed within three years. Another, Brothers Beer, a premium brand based out of Oakland, has yet to make its way East.

Well, yes. I didn't see it right away, but Ray was right. I needed people like him in this book as much as I needed people like Sariya Wilkens, a young woman who needed to be convinced that she had a story that belonged in here. Just as I had to pursue and persuade Sariya, I, too, had to be open to persuasion and pursuit.

When I wrote Ray back I asked him to tell me a little more about himself. I also asked whether, if I did come all the way to St. Louis (the "Hub of Business," as it heralds itself on its official visitors Web site), he knew of any other people I might be able to interview while I was in town. Within a day, Ray sent me a reply e-mail that listed the names and occupations of people he could put me in contact with in St. Louis, along with a sketch of his backstory:

Ray grew up poor in a semirural suburb outside of the city of St. Louis. Directly out of high school he enlisted in the navy, where he spent three and a half years studying electronics. After his discharge in 1993, he looked for work in computers because "that's where the money was." Ray found an entry-level job working with the Department of Interior's Office of Surface Mining (OSM). He worked hard, moved up the ranks, and by the time he was twenty-eight, was the lead network engineer for the southeast region of the United States, designing and implementing computer networks in large-scale government offices all over Alabama, Oklahoma, and Kansas City. Even without a college degree, Ray was making in excess of $72,000 a year, a figure all the more impressive when you consider he was able to buy his first home, a "fixer-upper," in one of St. Louis County's premier communities, Creve Coeur, for less than $120,000. He'd made it. He had the big office with the leather couch. He'd paid off all of his debt. He'd bought a nice home. The only job left in his office was his boss's, a big shot in the field, a guy who had the letters "OSM" tagged to his license plates, a guy who wasn't going anywhere any time soon.

That's when Ray, who'd been brewing his own beer in his basement for three years by then (he got the idea after traveling to different cities for work and stopping in the local microbreweries, chatting it up with bartenders—usually the brewers as well—and marveling at the beer-making process, how pure and simple and gratifying it was) decided to do what every one of us has spent many a Monday morning dreaming about. After much deliberation, he walked into his boss's office à la Kevin Spacey in *American Beauty,* and handed in his resignation. Mr. OSM was stunned. Ray remembered closing his boss's office door on his way out that day. He also recalled catching a glimpse of him leaning back in his swivel chair, staring out of the window, his mouth slightly askew, and his eyes lost in the distance.

Two months after his initial e-mail, Ray pulls up to the lower-level arrival terminal outside Lambert–St. Louis Airport. He meets me at the trunk with a hearty, wholesome handshake and says in his jolly yet earnest tone, "Welcome to St. Louis." Ray, squeaky clean head and all, stands a notch or two below five-ten. The extra bulk around the middle makes him look a few years older than thirty-one, particularly when he's sitting behind the wheel of his '91 Crown Victoria. He bought it on eBay a week ago for $1,000, he tells me. A grandfather who recently passed away had been the car's only owner. The car was a steal, he says. It needs a paint job. The odometer isn't working properly. One of the windows won't go up. But it's reliable. The sedan gets him to Reuters where he works nights as a network engineer and to his meetings during the day. Aside from having his salary reduced by more than half what it was two years ago, the only other difference is that Ray rarely sleeps more than two or three hours a night. But for the sake of his company, he feels it's worth it.

Over breakfast Ray tells me the unabridged story of how he became an entrepreneur. He was like most twenty-somethings with disposable income for the first time in their lives. He bought what he could and couldn't afford. Racked up credit card debt. Spent his money in clubs. Worked just to stay afloat. But when an older colleague took him aside and explained what an entrepreneur was, he began reading up on the subject.

"You hadn't even thought about it prior to that?"

"I guess not seriously. Everybody says, 'Oh, I'd like to do this or I'd like to do that.' He was the one who really pushed me in that direction. Not pushed, informed me. A lot of people don't even hear about being an entrepreneur and the different ways you can do it. What really drew me to beer is that a lot of people are thinking right now: Entrepreneur means starting a record label or getting a new clothing line out. That's a problem, we're still thinking in that kind of box. This is thinking out of it. People drink beer. People love beer. Whether I come out with a company or not, people are going to drink it."

Even though it sometimes sounds as though Ray has practiced this speech over countless sales pitch meetings, what's clear is his determination. He knows the beer industry, his specific market, the competition, the niche he's filling, and why, as he says with uncommon poise, "the sky's the limit" now that he has a marketing team, St. Louis–based Schmoo, on board. They've agreed to invest a quarter of a million dollars in in-kind services, including photos, design, distribution, and ad campaigns. Ray has invested over $12,000 of his own money in the company. Based on his estimates, numbers dutifully calculated and recorded in a thickly bound business plan/prospectus bearing the company's logo, he needs slightly more than $1.2 million to get things rolling on a national level. You see, Ray Hill isn't thinking microbrewery. He's thinking major industry player.

Ray is also encouraged by the notoriety rappers like Nelly and Chingy have brought to St. Louis in the last few years. He figures that if he can link his product to a city on the rise, then his business, combined with hard work on his part, will expand. The plan is to start in St. Louis and then move on to Kansas City, then Chicago, then New York. Ray sees his Ray Hill's Premium Beer in stores across America right next to Corona, Heineken, and, of course, Budweiser. Everything is in place, ready to go. He's got a major brewing company on board. He's got his attorneys and accountants. He's got a line of beer from the signature brand to a new low-calorie sports brew. All Ray needs now is the venture capital to flow through. All he needs is $1.2 million.

Don't we all.

But Ray isn't like everyone else. Ray Hill's Premium Beer will be in stores, if you ask him. He will make a fortune from his ideas. He's been successful before, so he figures there's nothing standing in the way of continued success in the future. The kind of doubt that most people deal with, struggle with, and often succumb to, Ray doesn't allow himself to even entertain. As for anyone who expresses their doubts about his vision, he doesn't want them around.

"I totally separated myself from the self-doubter," Ray says. "People with self-doubt don't understand that I'm on a mission. I want to surround myself with positive people who are going somewhere, people who are doing something."

Ray is an avid reader of entrepreneurs' stories. Anytime he has a question or even the slightest doubt, he picks up entrepreneurial books like *Rich Dad, Poor Dad,* which he paraphrases from more than once over breakfast; or he finds an article by another entrepreneur who was also struggling before they had a breakthrough. Take the guy who started making pies but who couldn't afford to pay the baker. When faced with the prospect of going out of business, he came up with a solution: open his own bakery and do it himself. These kinds of stories are the grist for the entrepreneur's mill.

As the morning wears on it becomes clear to me that my initial ambivalence toward Ray Hill had more to do with me than with him. While he's perfectly comfortable saying he wants to make millions off his beer, I feel a twinge of shame whenever the thought of penning a best-seller even crosses my mind. The only suitable explanation I arrive at is that somewhere along the way I bought into the idea that writing is supposed to be a purer pursuit than other occupations. Ultimately, talking to Ray motivates me to ask myself whether I doubt my ability to earn a living as a writer.

"Why is money so important for you?" I ask Ray later.

"It's power. When you're wealthy you're not forced to do anything, you're free to do whatever you want, you have a whole lot more opportunity to develop wealth. It has a lot to do with how I grew up and not having anything. I think that's why money is so important."

Ray then takes me through the outskirts of his old neighborhood, past the Boeing plant that used to be a McDonnell-Douglas plant ten or so years ago. When he was growing up, he says, laughing at it now, the people in his neighborhood considered the factory workers at McDonnell-Douglas rich.

"We were like, 'When I grow up that's what I want to do.' My brother worked for Boeing. His whole lifetime goal was to work for Boeing. It was like, 'That's where the rich people are.' Now I look at it and laugh. We had no clue."

Ray drives by his old high school next, a banal brick schoolhouse standing by itself along a shoddy-looking road. He blew off school, he says, but he's trying to teach his own son, "Little Ray," whom he's raised on his own since the age of two, differently. As we turn into his old neighborhood our conversation delves further into Ray's relationship with his son. Ray bought the house he now lives in because Creve Coeur has one of the best school districts in the county. He wants Little Ray to have the best. When I ask him how his son's doing in school, though, Ray shakes his head and dons the confounded look of parenthood. He sits with him, reads with him, buys him educational programs for his computer, monitors and limits the time he can play video games and surf the Net, and still Little Ray's grades remain flat at best. He's a smart kid, Ray insists, he's just not applying himself.

"Everyone sees he's more capable of doing it and when he doesn't, I feel that does reflect on me."

Like any parent, Ray sometimes wonders if he's failing his son by putting so much of himself into his business. When Little Ray is going to school in the morning, Ray is just getting in from work. When Little Ray gets home from school, Ray is either sleeping or at a meeting. Maybe he shouldn't have given up the job at OSM. Maybe he needs to just concentrate on working at Reuters and being the best father he can, at least until Little Ray heads to college five years from now. But Ray feels there's a bigger purpose at work. He's showing his son how to create wealth. Once his business does hit—once Ray Hill's Premium Beer is in stores all across the country—Little Ray will be able to say he can do anything he wants to do.

As we pass through his old neighborhood, Ray points out two of the homes in which he spent time growing up. One is little more than a shack sitting on the side of the road, the other, an old wooden two-story, sits on a hill, abandoned and eroding. Here I begin to understand that Ray Hill comes from a place that more closely resembles a rural plantation than an urbanized project. While modest homes line a few streets here and there, most sit out in open fields of grass like vacant relics from the early twentieth century. Streets are cluttered with rubbish, old mattresses, box springs, tattered-looking couches, even a bombed-out car or two. Packs of young men wander aimlessly. There is a convenience store and some recently developed public housing, but the general tenor of the place is one of desolation and despair. I consider asking Ray if he's ever brought his son here so he can see where his father came from, how he grew up, but then I realize just how difficult it is for Ray to come here himself. He doesn't seem to have a lot of fond memories of this place. Even people he knows, has known all his life, he'd rather not stop and chat with. Instead, he honks his horn, waves a civil hand, and keeps his foot on the gas. It makes sense that Ray blew off school. He just wanted to be free of this place, to breathe a different kind of air first. Everything else had to wait until he could get a footing in the world, until he could make some money.

Back at Ray's house later that afternoon, I get a chance to meet Little Ray. The resemblance is obvious. They have the same dark eyebrows and high-yellow skin. Little Ray's not so little, though. After his birthday three days from now he'll only be thirteen, but he's already threatening to surpass his father in height. He's got huge hands, too. When I tell Little Ray I hear he's a budding football and basketball star he doesn't hesitate to corroborate his father's claims. Confident, just like his dad, I think. Then, without the slightest provocation, he offers me his room for the next few days.

"I can sleep on the couch," he says.

"No. I'm fine downstairs. Everything's already in place."

Later, while I'm watching television, I see the younger Ray outside raking and bagging leaves. Ray Sr. has been in his bedroom sleeping for the past two hours so I know he wasn't told, or reminded, to finish his chores. I remember a story Ray told me at the restaurant that morning about how he paid his son and stepson twenty dollars each to rake the leaves. When they were done, he offered them ten dollars, but with a caveat. Either they could take the ten dollars, he said, or get a lesson in wealth management. His stepson took the money; Little Ray didn't.

Before I go to bed that night I read the book *Rich Dad, Poor Dad,* which is where Ray borrowed his little scenario from. In the book the story plays out differently. Both boys, one of whom is the author, agree not to take the money in exchange for the father's lesson and both end up as wealthy men. *Rich Dad, Poor Dad* is the first book I've read that is purely about creating wealth; it's also the first time I seriously consider the kind of values regarding money I was instilled with.

The truth is that while I was always the kid who mowed the lawns and raked the leaves and shoveled the snow, I only did those jobs so I could have some spending money of my own. Granted, I was only a kid, but reading *Rich Dad, Poor Dad* helps me realize that I had never really learned to value money outside of what it could do for me immediately. After my parents divorced, there was always an impending sense of dread around the Ross household when it came to money. My mother was always worried about paying the mortgage, while my father cringed and sighed whenever I asked for the monthly child-support check. There was even a stretch when I was so concerned we would be evicted from our home that my heart beat frantically each time I rounded the bend to my house. And how can I forget the time in high school I was pulled out of class and told I couldn't come back to school until the tuition was paid.

Eventually I quit recalling my stories of fiscal dread and put myself to bed. My childhood woes are too deep and dense for me to process them in one sitting; nonetheless, I feel as though, thanks to Ray, I've begun to unearth some of my anxieties about money, where they came from, and how they can be overcome.

The next day Ray and I set out to make a batch of beer. We go to a local supply store and buy all of the ingredients from the hops to the malt to the yeast. Once we're back at the house we brew, drink, and talk about beer. The first batch Ray ever made was undrinkable. He'd thought if he just followed the instructions he'd been given the beer would come out fine. What he didn't realize at the time is that if anything goes wrong at any point in time, an entire batch is ruined. It took Ray three more tries, almost four months of close and constant monitoring, before he finally made a batch he could tolerate. After that, he set out to create his own recipe. Ray knew that if anyone was going to buy his beer, it would be because it had its own distinctive taste. Naturally, that involved many more batches of beer, as well as trips to microbreweries, local and otherwise. Once Ray finally got the taste down, he started looking for places to test the market. He rented a van and took five cases to the Black Beach Party in Galveston, Texas. He went to the Kentucky Derby (which, unbeknownst to me, is a fairly large African-American event). He rented a U-Haul and designed his own float for the annual May Day Parade in St. Louis. Everywhere he went people enjoyed Ray Hill's, wanted to know where they could find it, and said they would certainly buy it over other brands if it was in stores

Once the boiling water has reached its ideal temperature, Ray drops in a chalky mineral called gypsum. Gypsum isn't required, but it adds to the flavor, he says. The difference, though subtle, is discernible to the seasoned drinker. He's learned some of his tactics from a local brewmeister's club he joined some time ago. At meetings and online, home brewers and microbrewers alike give talks and tips to one another; members go on trips to breweries; and home brewers bring their latest batches to meetings for taste tests. Ray's the only African-American in the group, but he doesn't mind. They're all interested in the beer, the camaraderie, and learning. For most of us beer is part of the scenery of a party, but for these guys, beer is the guest of honor.

After the gypsum has settled Ray drops in the aroma hops and steps back to take it all in. "That's what I enjoy, smelling it," he says, closing his eyes and discharging that jolly, endearing smile he greeted me with what seems like ages ago already. "A lot of times while I'm making it, I'll drink some I've brewed and I think, 'Wow, I created this.'"

Just then Little Ray comes into the house. "What are you doing?" he asks.

"Making some beer," Ray casually replies, still stirring the hops and enjoying the aroma.

"Have you ever seen him go through the process?"

"Yeah," Little Ray says.

"He helps me bottle sometimes and do the labels. The wood crates, he did all those. I pay him two dollars a box," says Ray. "He made his own root beer one time."

"Orange and cream," says Little Ray, grinning.

While standing in the kitchen with a father and his son I discover the story I want to write about Ray. By now, we've spent hours talking about his marketing plans, his distribution plans, and every other plan that goes into selling a product in a consumer society. Ray knows what he's doing. He's done his homework, he's made the hard decisions, and he's put himself in a position to succeed. Everything he can possibly do to make his business work, he's either done it or he's willing to do it.

Even my being in his kitchen is part of the master plan. I know enough now to say that while Ray doesn't have a malicious bone in his body—in fact, he's a decent human being with a generous heart—he's a capitalist through and through. He sees every meeting, every networking event, every simple drive in his car as an opportunity to promote his business. But whether or not Ray gets the million he needs to get the business off the ground, whether or not Ray Hill's is the next Sam Adams, doesn't matter nearly as much as the bond I see between a father and his son. I am deeply moved and impressed by what I see happening in the Hill house. Whether he knows it, whether or not anyone even bothers to tell him, Ray Hill Sr. is a damn good father who takes his charge of single parenthood seriously. In the mornings, after a ten-hour shift at Reuters, he makes sure to check his son's homework before school. In the evenings, after Little Ray gets home, he makes sure he gets a decent meal in his stomach. Any time there's work to do around the house, whether it's knocking down a wall, raking the leaves, or sanding down the old Crown Vic for a new paint job, they do it together. Having Little Ray around is like having a little roommate, he says.

Nevertheless, Ray is also sensitive to the needs of a boy. On Saturday, just hours before I leave, we head to the supermarket to buy Little Ray's birthday cake. Between shuttling me around St. Louis for three days of interviews, arranging a small gathering of St. Louis entrepreneurs for me to meet, and carrying on his own affairs, Ray also finds time to plan a party for his son's thirteenth birthday. Sure, he wishes he could do more for his son, be there for him more often. But he's only thirty-one, and he's been a responsible father all of his adult life. He's taught his son respect. He's taught him hard work. He's taught him the value of a dollar. But most of all, he's teaching him not to let go of his dreams.

Food for Thought

Alvin Morrow: Holistic Healer/Author

> "People [here] have to see things because it's a material city. That's why they call it the 'Show Me' state. If you're in the process of manifesting an idea from the mind to reality—to the material—you're gonna have a real difficult time in this part of the country."

If by chance you ever find yourself heading south on Airport Road in St. Louis County, I recommend you stop by the nutrition store in the strip mall on your left. The atmosphere is inviting, and if you have time the store's owner, Alvin Morrow, will gladly sit down with you. Alvin prides himself on knowing his business, and he can tell you things about your body that you never thought you'd know, or need to know. Most first-timers won't even make it past the first two shelves where he keeps his colon cleansing agents. "All good health and bad health starts and ends in the colon," he'll say, pointing to the two shelves nearest the front door. "Once you clean a person's colon out, then their body can start to utilize all of the other nutrients. A lot of health problems leave once you start cleaning the person up." In Alvin's opinion the key to good health is as simple as basic math. If a person's body isn't functioning properly that can only mean something needs to be added or subtracted. Figuring out exactly what that "something" is is Alvin's area of expertise.

At this point, when you think he's told you all you need to know, the thirty-two-year-old Alvin will say that life abides by the same set of principles. Then he'll proceed to show you how the moral, psychological, social, and economic wellness of black

America is all linked to physical wellness. Alvin does this because he believes that once he's helped you heal your body, he
can help you elevate your life. Just as Day Light Nutrition isn't
your run-of-the-mill strip mall health food store, Alvin isn't
your everyday nutritionist. As a matter of fact, he'd prefer you
refer to what he does as healing, since, in his opinion, the health
problems African-Americans suffer from disproportionately—
heart disease, liver disease, various forms of cancer, diabetes,
obesity—are all just the physical manifestations of generations
of trauma.

Taking a moment to bring me up to speed, the sleepy-eyed
Alvin explains why his store is so significant to this community.
"This is pretty much my neighborhood," he says, glancing toward the window. "I grew up in this neighborhood. Everybody
knew me already from running track—I was a big track guy."
Back when Alvin was a nineteen-year-old, six-foot-two, rail-
thin 158 pounds, he ran the 800-meter race in 1:46, less than
five seconds off the world record time. His coaches thought he
had a shot to make it to the Olympics. But then he went and
shocked everyone by joining the Nation of Islam, and starting
the first ever African-American organization at the Baptist college where he'd earned a track scholarship only a year earlier.
Alvin didn't like the fact that the only black students on campus
were, like him, athletes. He felt it was his responsibility to challenge the administration to recruit more African-American students. The situation turned ugly when local media caught wind
of the campus discord. Ultimately, then nineteen-year-old Alvin
wound up expelled from school, homeless, and in need of a way
to make money.

"I ended up washing windows in the wintertime in the middle of St. Louis. [I was] on foot with a bucket. Fortunately, I
ended up moving in next to a strip mall, so I got quite a bit of
business that way and I was able to eat."

Although Alvin was eventually able to buy a car and expand his fledgling enterprise, that early experience humbled him. He hardly had enough money to put gas in his tank or food in his belly, and for the most part he and his squeegee slept on floors. But Alvin was also learning something invaluable about his personal resolve, and about persistence. As far as he was concerned, he was moving forward with his life. What surprised him, however, was that the very people who'd admired his athletic accomplishments suddenly looked down on him. "Everybody thought I was crazy," he recalls. "Everybody thought I was nuts. They had this image of me as an Olympian, a great runner, but nothing as a man, outside of sports." For the first time in his life Alvin had a real glimpse into what he was up against in his hometown. "People [here] have to see things because it's a material city. That's why they call it the 'Show Me' state. People have to see things. If you're in the process of manifesting an idea from the mind to reality, you're gonna have a real difficult time in this part of the country."

What folks on the outside didn't understand was that Alvin had been interested in health since his first trip to the St. Louis Mosque. He'd had a temper growing up, but once he converted to Islam and gave up meat as well as dairy products, he says he experienced a significant change in his disposition. He was more tranquil, more focused, and more productive. Alvin's new religious faith also gave him discipline, so that in between work and a rigorous religious practice, he began setting aside six to seven hours each day for reading and writing. He developed serious interests in history and economics to go along with health and religion. Soon, his curiosities led him to his life mission. Alvin wanted to teach African-American people how to live richer, fuller lives, and he wanted to begin with wellness.

"You're not going to be understanding about your social environment unless you really understand what's going on with your personal environment in terms of your health," he says. "That makes you concerned about the air and the environment and what's going on in society."

One night shortly after Alvin came to this realization, he ran into one of his window-cleaning customers at a Kinko's. Along with several others, Alvin's acquaintance owned a local health food store that Alvin thought was being mismanaged; he didn't hesitate to share his views. "I saw some flaws in how the business was going. It had too many partners, the space was too big, and I knew they couldn't afford it."

Alvin's acquaintance listened intently to the twenty-three-year-old's ideas, then he suggested they go into business together. At the same time, a family friend, also one of Alvin's customers, was looking to lease a space in a strip mall. The building was moderately spacious, the rent was reasonable, and it was located in Alvin's old neighborhood. His partner signed the lease and within three months Day Light was open for business. While Alvin was a skilled nutritionist, he knew next to nothing about running a business, so for the first few years of operations he watched and learned as his partner handled the finances. Alvin didn't entirely understand or agree with the arrangement, but when his partner offered to sell him the business outright so that he could open another store on the other side of town, it dawned on Alvin that he'd be taking over the business debt-free.

"You have to divide to multiply," Alvin says, adding, "A lot of people looked at my partner and me in this business when we divided, but he always told me that black people have no plans for expansion when we do a business. He was teaching me all along the way by watching his mistakes."

Alvin believes in showing people how to be successful. When people see success, they become hopeful, and hope is the missing ingredient in many communities. By operating a positive community "institution" for the last nine years, Alvin has been able to help, by his count, close to thirty small businesses get started. In the relatively short time we spend talking, a handful of customers who've each left jobs to become entrepreneurs stop by to chat, or to use the computer he has stowed away in a backroom. One man runs a trucking business, another buys condemned homes and refurbishes them, and a handsome couple in their early forties tells me they both recently quit their jobs to pursue commodity trading full-time. They each have a story about how Alvin inspired them.

"Part of my life purpose is teaching people. That's what helps them live their dreams and manifest their ideas. I gain strength from that. I gain energy from it as well. That's my exchange: My joy at seeing something blow up in the 'hood, seeing things blossom. The key is just initiating the process. Most people want to go from A to Z. We really don't understand all the middle intermediary details that are involved in creating something. And we all are creative, because we have that in our nature. A lot of us are like roses that never blossom. We live and we die, we just never blossom in between. And that, for me, is a really painful reality. That is really my key motive in seeing people live their dreams. Because I'm a dreamer. And my father was a dreamer. And I refuse not to live all of my dreams. And that's the child in me. And I think people don't take the risks necessary to see their ideas materialize. They may have the knowledge. But we know the wisdom is the application. The key thing is being youthful-minded enough; not being too serious about life will allow you to take the childish risks that will bring you fortune in time."

Had Alvin Morrow's against-the-odds story plateaued with his "Health Food in the 'Hood" success story, I would have been content to stop the tape, shake his hand, and be on my way. I would have thought about Alvin fondly as the positive brother in St. Louis trying to single-handedly undo the physical damage alcohol, drugs, fast food, and stress have done to ghetto people the world over; I would have written a brief profile about him and moved on. The thing is, the store's success is just the beginning of Alvin's story. On the coffee table stationed between us sits Alvin's first book, *Killing in the Name of Love,* while in a box beside his feet the final proofs for his second book, *Breaking the Curse of Willie Lynch,* await his approval.

Alvin was inspired to begin penning his thoughts after he discovered a series of books that gave him a different version of black history than the standard "slaves to civil rights" saga high school textbooks tend to regurgitate. He questioned the education he'd received growing up, and wondered whether the reason he never took an interest in school was because education never gave him knowledge about himself. Like many African-American students who learn what they know about slavery in school, Alvin was too ashamed to want to explore it, understand it, or learn from it. Slavery was something he'd just as well not think about.

Alvin became particularly interested in families. He figured that if healthy communities begin with healthy families, then the only way to begin the healing process for struggling African-Americans was by restoring the relationships between black men and women. However, Alvin believed that could only begin once people came to grips with slavery. With that as his thesis, Alvin got to work. He wrote most of the book in a three-month, round-the-clock flurry. But then he got married, had a child, and of course there was the store. He put the book aside so he could make his own family work. Then one night he came home to find that his wife had taken their daughter and moved out. Alvin was devastated; he couldn't eat or sleep for days. Akil

Clopton, author of the popular underground book *From Niggas to Gods,* and a friend of Alvin's, came to his aid.

"They say when the student is ready, the teacher will appear. Along the way I've had many people teach, [and] share with me—give me what I was crying out to the universe for. That brother kept me afloat. He had been through the same exact circumstances, so his life served as a model of what to do and not to do. He's pretty much focused. That's one of the things I learned from him: regardless of the outside appearances, stay focused on reality because reality is what you project. If you can hold on to your vision eventually it will materialize."

Using the store's storage room as his writing quarters, Alvin threw himself back into his book. Once the manuscript was complete, he incorporated his publishing company, designed a cover, arranged for an author photo, and sought out blurbs from other authors in his field. On the eve of publication Alvin went on a weeklong fast in order to, in his words, "be in the zone" when the book came out. As soon as the books arrived from his distributor, he hit flea markets, book conventions, and sent postcards to every African-American bookseller in America. That hard work paid off, and in the first year alone Alvin cleared $34,000.

What I admire most about Alvin is his audacity. He doesn't have a Ph.D., nor has he been anointed the next African-American leader, but that didn't stop him from putting his own thoughts on the state of black America out into the world. Alvin feels he has an important message to share and he isn't waiting for a publisher to give him its stamp of approval. Meeting Alvin is a reminder that the only authority people have is the authority they are given by others. According to the statistics, Alvin isn't "supposed" to be where he is right now. His father died when he was young. He never finished college. He's not an athlete or an entertainer. He's never even filled out a job application. But Alvin has started two businesses, and published two books with a third, devoted to black community health, forthcoming; in addition, he's been trying his hand in the alternative medicine industry, developing his own colon-cleansing product as well as a home remedy for herpes.

"We put twelve women that we worked with over the past year and a half on it, and they only had to take it for the first three months before they stopped having outbreaks cold. It's been a year and a half since any of them have had an outbreak."

Alvin also offers accounts of customers with cancer and HIV that he's been able to help. But I'd be lying if I said I wasn't skeptical about the whole alternative medicine phenomenon. Although holistic treatment has become a popular trend in the past decade, listening to Alvin shows me that deep down I still subscribe to the status quo notion that traditional medicine is more effective than its alternative counterpart. Perhaps I have a certain nostalgia for the conventional wisdom of a family physician who cures our stomach ailments with ginger ale and chicken soup, predicts our height by looking at a chart, and doles out lollipops at the end of each visit.

Despite my skepticism, when Alvin says black America is experiencing a health crisis with which conventional medicine evidently isn't prepared to deal, I have to acknowledge the validity of his point of view. African-Americans die younger and at higher rates than their white counterparts; African-Americans suffer disproportionately from fatal diseases like HIV, heart disease, diabetes, and various forms of cancer; and far too many African-Americans lack access to quality health care, education, or the kinds of foods that promote healthy lifestyles. That there don't appear to be any signs of relief for these ills on the horizon makes it all the more difficult for me or anyone else to argue with Alvin's alternative approach, particularly when, nearing the end of our conversation, he compassionately declares his mission: "I want to show people alternatives. I have a very unorthodox approach to life, and I think that is what people need right now. In order to get different results, you gotta do something different."

Mind to Market

Matt Walker: Inventor/Entrepreneur

> "I'm past doubt and disbelief. I can do what I want. I can dream into existence anything I want. There's nothing nobody can do to stop me. All I have to do is sit down and think about it and develop a plan."

Long before Matt Walker ever heard the word "entrepreneur," he knew that was what he wanted to be. Not only did he have ideas for inventions, Matt wanted to be in charge of the company that produced and sold them. What Matt didn't have was someone in his life who could show him how to make all of that happen. Mom, a nurse, and dad, a bus driver, were both too busy just getting by. Watching them taught him the law of diminishing returns. They worked and worked and worked, and yet they never got ahead. And when Matt asked them why their whole life was a struggle, the only answer they had was, "That's the way it is. You work hard every day. You do right by people. You give your children what you can. You hope for the best." Following his parents' advice, Matt decided to study engineering when he got to college. He wasn't crazy about the subject, it was just the closest fit for an aspiring inventor. The most significant lesson he learned in his years of school was that a university couldn't teach him how to be an independent thinker, a tinkerer, or an inventor. And then, as if to add insult to injury, Matt couldn't even find an engineering job when he came out of college. Only after he dropped his engineering credential from his résumé did the St. Louis Telecommunications Company call back with an offer: as a cable installer.

The work came easy to Matt, and since he was good at it, he quickly moved up the ranks. In the ten years he worked in the industry he rose from home cable installer to chief engineer in charge of designing fiber-optic networks. The money wasn't bad, the job had its perks, and there was room for growth within the company. All in all, his future looked bright. But in the back of his mind Matt always knew working for someone else his entire life wasn't for him. Plus, he still had this burning desire to create something the world hadn't seen before, and then get rich from it. So, like any decent inventor, he started looking around for something that didn't exist, that people would be willing to pay for, something he could invent given his knowledge, skillset, and experience. Ideas came and went. Some were unworkable, others too expensive. A few already existed. Then there were those that were just plain old bad ideas. What Matt was really searching for was something he could throw the full weight of his energy into; something that would kick-start his life. But it couldn't just be any old thing. The idea had to make commercial and creative sense. Then, one snowy St. Louis day, he had an epiphany while watching kids ride their sleds down a local hill.

"I observed how popular snow sledding was," Matt says, "and I imagined, wow, what if [kids] could do this when there was no snow. The concept led to a sled-shaped device with wheels that could ride on grass. I'm working with an engineering mind now. I had not thought about marketing. All I knew was the concept made sense, that if people will go out there in extremely cold weather to sled down a hill, why wouldn't they want to do it in the summertime."

For two years Matt lived with that unanswered question. He looked at it from every angle. He played devil's advocate with himself. He scouted out sports supply stores, toy stores, chain stores. Then he got on the phone. Nothing. As far as he could tell, no one had thought of a summer sled before. He wasn't entirely aware of it at the time, but he was working through the self-doubt. "This was just so obvious," he recalls thinking. "White people sled. Wouldn't they think of this? This is just obvious. So I had to convince myself maybe it's not out there. And through that, I logged on, I got introduced to the Internet, I became a voracious research scientist, I learned how to use search engines and just started doing research on the patent process, what it takes, doing research on black inventors, trying to find someone I related to with my characteristics.

"I was completely outside the realm of the people I knew. They had no advice for me, so I started doing my research and realized black folks invented virtually everything and a lot of it is starting to come out. They definitely didn't benefit economically, and then half of them didn't get the credit for it. That was fuel for my fire."

Matt's first prototype was made out of cardboard and roller-skate wheels. The contraption was crude, but he just needed to check the concept. Once the sled was ready, Matt took it out on the hills he used to ride on as a kid for a test run. He brought along one camera for photos and another to record the prototype in action. Back at home he went into his basement laboratory and studied the footage. So far so good, he figured. Next came a wooden version of the summer sled, and again the videotaping and picture-taking and rounds of study. Following two months of testing, he built three more units and set up his first public demonstration.

"I went out and put flyers up, then I started a company called Mental Engineering. I was never going to let anybody know I invented it because I wanted honest opinions. People tend to lie. If they think it's you, they won't tell you the truth. I said, 'I work for the company, these guys developed this product, they want me to bring it to our market.'"

Once the demonstration was complete Matt knew he had hit on something big. People loved the Summer Sled. It appeared as though the hard work was set to yield dividends, and Matt was naturally ecstatic. "I was ready to quit my job," he says.

But then he overheard one spectator proclaim to another, "When this thing is made out of plastic, it's gonna be a huge success."

"I was like, 'Plastic! That's it!' That led me down a whole other path because I had to go get engineers who knew how to take what I did in wood and turn it into plastic. I started doing a lot of research, at that point, on CAD designers, CAD engineers. These people had to take what I physically did, measure it, turn it into a three-dimensional drawing so I could take it to a toolmaker and get quotes about what it would take."

In all Matt invested over $20,000 of his own money in the new prototype. "I was all systems go, doing patents and everything. I was convinced this was my way out." Moreover, he knew that once he recouped the research and development costs, his profit margin would increase dramatically. Unfortunately, he ran short on cash before he could get the prototype to market. He reluctantly went to the banks, all of whom turned him down. Next, he looked to the venture capitalists. They weren't willing to take the risk either. Matt then turned to his childhood friends, the ones he used to go sledding with. He organized a basketball game to get everybody together; meanwhile, he put together a videotape that had footage from the public demonstration as well as from a local news station that had run a piece on the Summer Sled. The cable truck came in handy then. After the game he gathered everyone around and played the video right on the street. When the tape stopped, he handed out a prospectus and said that he was looking to raise

$200,000. Interested investors could buy in with a minimum investment of $100.

"To make a long story short," Matt grimly recalls, "two people invested out of about seventy." What made the poor showing worse was that no one believed in him. Word made its way back to him that people were calling him a scam artist, while others simply doubted the product's viability. In an uncharacteristic moment of vulnerability an otherwise boisterous Matt opens up: "The negativity was intense," he says. "It was intense. It made me cry. But after I got them tears out of me, it fueled my desire. In about five months we raised $250,000."

"How did that happen?"

"I went to the street. I had video with channel five talking about the product and would ride down the block. I assumed everybody had one hundred dollars." Matt switched up his game plan and went into hustler mode. Picturing Matt scoping out a block, gathering a crowd of people and working them wasn't difficult. He has the kind of charisma that allows him to walk through many different worlds. It's a kind of dynamism that you encounter in successful people all of the time, and yet it is also authentic, genuine: real.

I can clearly see why people believed in him. In one sense he's your down-home cousin or uncle who drives a sporty pickup truck, wears his baseball cap backwards, and likes his jeans with a sharp crease down the middle. In another, he's a consummate professional. For instance, when he was raising capital, he wouldn't accept anyone's money on the spot. Instead, he developed an intent-to-invest contract that stated only after he'd found two thousand investors would he accept payments. Once he reached his goal, he sent out a letter requesting that potential stockholders send in their check. "We started raising money in June or July of ninety-nine and I quit my job in September ninety-nine. October first we had one hundred thousand dollars cash."

When Matt resigned he didn't hand in a letter of resignation and wait two weeks, as is the custom at most jobs. He didn't go through a formal farewell process, the long, drawn-out good-byes complete with empty promises to stay in touch. Uh-uh. A meeting in L.A. conflicted with his work schedule so instead of delaying it, he called the cable company, gave them an address, and advised them to come pick up the truck. Then Matt hung up the phone. In what amounts to a contemporary rendition of the frontiersman narrative—the classic story of American hope and optimism—Matt then went home, packed his bags, kissed his wife good-bye, and by four o'clock that afternoon he was on a plane heading to California.

Although the Summer Sled has had its share of success (it's available in Sam's Club, several home-shopping catalogs, and Wal-Mart has expressed a serious interest), it is what's happened in Matt's life since the day he quit his job to work on his invention full-time that is what makes his story more than just another parable of perseverance and conviction. Wading through the muddy waters of mind to market has fundamentally changed his outlook on life and transformed him from doubtful dreamer to devout believer. At times, Matt even sounds more like a braggadocious boxer than a businessman (though the two certainly aren't mutually exclusive). Take his response to a question I pose about the difference between the old and new Matt Walker as one example of what I'm talking about: "I'm past doubt and disbelief. I can do what I want. I can dream into existence anything I want. There's nothing nobody can do to stop me. All I have to do is sit down and think about it and develop a plan."

Likewise, Matt's drive to make millions quickly evolved into a mission to move millions once he uncovered an entire history of achievement by African-Americans that he'd never been taught about in school.

"I'll be honest, what put me on another path [was] *Message to the Black Man* by Elijah Muhammad. It was over then. I knew I was on the right path. I started to wonder how can I play my part for the black nation, for my people. My people are the ones who are the downtrodden, so how can I be one of the ones among them to rise above it and be an example of another way. My whole mission is to show there's another way. You don't have to be able to rap and play sports, you can use your mind. If you can use your mind, you can do anything. Saying that is one thing. Displaying it is a whole different thing, so I said, all right, I'm not going to be preachy, I'm just gonna get to work. Watch my actions, watch my work, and that alone should convince you."

Matt's phone started ringing off the hook once friends and family found out he was behind the Summer Sled. Everyone had an idea for an invention, it seemed. People talked to Matt about ideas they'd stored away, and ideas they'd doubted because everyone around them had been doubtful. And some of them were pretty good. Matt got to thinking again. What if he wrote a book detailing all the steps necessary to creating a marketable product? Besides one or two high-priced, high-risk invention submission companies, there was no resource on the market that helped people with their ideas. He looked at it from every angle and again it made creative and commercial sense.

"Remember," says Matt, "I documented everything. I was meticulous about documenting things and taking pictures and keeping records because in the patent industry due diligence is one of the ways you can prove you're the authentic inventor of a product. It all paid off. My phone rang so much from people who had ideas and I didn't have time to sit on the phone with everybody."

Matt's *Idea Development Workbook* is a comprehensive, no-nonsense guide to developing an idea. "My mission is to simply educate, motivate, inspire, and assist children and adults in developing their ideas into products." The book is only fifty-eight pages, and yet that's about all it needs to be. Matt doesn't waste time with fluff and filler or with telling his readers how he made it; rather, he shows aspiring inventors exactly what he did from prototype, to patent process, to business plan, to fund-raising strategies.

The only point in the book where Matt takes center stage and speaks from the first person is on the opening page. There, and in just slightly more than five paragraphs, he offers five pieces of advice: "Believe in yourself despite what anybody says," "Make sure this is really what you want to do," "Be creative," "Remember, you are special." The last bit of advice he offers is for people to stay away from invention submission corporations. Writes Matt, "They sell you on the idea that they're going to help you get your idea to the marketplace and they're getting people for their money. They prey on the vulnerability of an inventor. An inventor's idea is like a child. If somebody said I'm going to help you grow your child, you'd give 'em all you got."

As trite as it may sound, success like Matt's may be the final frontier for black America. On one level he's created a product that doesn't necessarily appeal to, nor is it marketed to, African-Americans. Summer Sled, in its own way, represents a reversal of the traditional modes of consumption. Typically, mainstream America produces and benefits financially from the products African-Americans consume; however, in Matt's case the tables have been turned. The people who tend to buy products like Summer Sled are middle-American catalog shoppers. Demographically, they're at least middle class, often conservative, and leisured. They slide their Summer Sled into their SUV or mini-van and drive to the nearest hill for a fun-filled afternoon, and that's just fine by Matt. He's the first to say that the last thing most black folks need to spend their money on is a sled. Like everyone else in this age of privatization, downsizing, and outsourcing, black America needs to create wealth, not necessarily wage-earning wealth either, but real, sustainable working capital in the form of real estate or intellectual property.

Which is why, aside from helping budding entrepreneurs develop their ideas, an even more crucial role someone like Matt stands to play is in preparing "urban" America for the next stage of capitalism. In recent years leading economists* have argued that what we are living through is a social and economic paradigm shift. Already, we have seen intellectual property law (the field of law protecting copyrights, trademarks, and patents) become the fastest growing law specialty in the United States. Ideas are literally becoming the engine of our economy and are arguably more valuable than physical property. The implications for this changing of the guard are enormous. An invention or innovation that fills a niche—online grocery shopping, for example—creates new jobs, which in turn creates wealth, which in turn builds and sustains communities. Moreover, ideas aren't subject to the law of diminishing returns, meaning, unlike fuel, which is destined to run out, they can be used over and over again. Finally, ideas are inherently democratic: anyone can have a valuable one. The question now is where and how people

---

*See Richard Florida, *The Rise of the Creative Class* (New York: Basic Books, 2002). A critically acclaimed national best-seller, Florida's book proposes that today's economy is "fundamentally a creative economy."

who've been traditionally (and arguably systematically) disconnected from the matrix of industrial and technological capital
will fit into the economy of ideas.

This exact dilemma prompted Matt to found the Entrepreneurial Development Corporation (EDC), a not-for-profit organization. The organization's goal is to one day fund the
research and development of ideas created by people who have
nowhere else to turn. Matt's vision is a broad and unique one.
Instead of simply teaching people the skills necessary to compete for a job, the EDC will guide people's ideas from mind to
market so that they are the ones creating jobs and wealth. In
turn, the company will sustain itself through partnerships with
the inventors. Unlike those who believe bringing a new stadium
or arena to a community is the most efficient means of redevel-
opment and growth, Matt believes the key to saving communities lies in tapping into the creativity of the individuals. The
difficult part, of course, is getting people to buy in.

THE GOOD FIGHT

These are the feel-good stories, the ones that can make even a die-hard cynic take a second look at the world and maybe even wonder if there's still hope after all. I could try connecting the four of them by more elaborate means, but at the end of the day the reason Kara, Michele, Gabriel, and Uchenna are in this chapter together is because they're all in the trenches with our younger generation making a difference. We all know someone like them. A friend from college. A brother or sister. Someone we admire for the simple fact that no matter what challenges they face, they don't give in to the urge to simply quit on humanity.

Although teaching plays a central role in all of these stories, they present compelling alternatives to the conventional classroom instruction that far too often pushes creative-minded people out of the profession. Kara Mitchell spent two years teaching and organizing in the rural countryside of the Dominican Republic as a Peace Corps volunteer. For the past several years Michele Luc has worked with a youth advocacy organization that unites teen activists in New York City with their peers from across the globe. During a year when Gabriel Benn left teaching to pursue his career as a rap artist full-time, he noticed there were no programs designed to bring artists like himself into the school system to work directly with kids. A year later he was back in school teaching and earning his master's so he could push his newly designed school arts programs. Finally, there's Uchenna Smith. After three years of teaching she was fed up with the public school bureaucracy. Uchenna was more than willing to go the extra mile to help her students succeed. But when her administrators discovered that she was staying after school to tutor students they reprimanded her. Rather than allow herself to grow old and bitter in an intractable system, she decided to start her own school. Now, at twenty-six, she's the one making the rules.

But there's also an underside to these kinds of stories that I try not to avoid. For those who go into the business of helping others, there's always more work to do. And while doing good work might guarantee we go to bed with a clear conscience each night, it alone doesn't promise us the fulfillment we seek in our overall lives. In fact, quite the opposite can happen. We can realize one day, as did Michele, that despite all the good work we've done in the world, something is still missing from the equation. For her part, Uchenna speaks to the issue of imbalance. Her life, she says with perfect aplomb, is out of whack. She works or is thinking about work all the time. One solution is to balance the altruistic impulse with something that is personally nourishing and equally important. For Gabriel that something is his rap moniker Asheru. Rap has taken him around the world and placed him on stages beside some of the biggest names in the music business. Another route is the one Kara took by joining the Peace Corps. She knew she was committing herself for a two-year period and not the rest of her life. There were other avenues she wanted to pursue, and that's okay. I'm of the belief that if everyone in the world did just a small part to improve our collective lot, then people like Uchenna and Michele wouldn't feel they have to do so much.

There's Always Another Way

Uchenna L. Smith: School Leader

> "Could I be more selfish, be thinking about myself, some
> dude, a family? Yes. But right now there's no guy that's more
> important to me than my school. This place is a dream; it's
> like magic."

If I hadn't spent the last three hours in Uchenna (the *U* is
silent) Smith's office talking to her, I'd be hard pressed to distinguish her from the kids in the picture she's flashing before
me. The one in her hand now was taken during her school's
year-end trip to Washington, D.C., and it features a crimson-
tinted Massachusetts senator Ted Kennedy surrounded by
dozens of smiling brown and black faces; the hundreds of others
in the shoe box it came from were taken over the course of
Buffalo, New York's KIPP-Sankofa's inaugural year. It was also
Uchenna's first year as a principal, or "school leader" as they are
called by the founders of KIPP (Knowledge Is Power Program).
Judging by her disinterested reaction, she's grown a little weary
of the "you look so young" remarks.

"People tell me that all of the time," she says. Uchenna's age
and appearance are and aren't that big a deal. In one respect,
most twenty-five-year-olds aren't interested in starting a school;
in another, Uchenna wasn't your everyday twenty-five-year-
old. I've known plenty of twenty-somethings with passion,
drive, and determination—big dreamers among this demographic
are a dime a dozen, as are people "with potential." Few, however,
are honestly ready to take on the responsibilities of running a

multimillion-dollar company, which is basically what a school is minus the profit motive; even fewer would go so far as to proclaim, "I feel like my whole life I was meant to do this," which Uchenna does.

Talk to Uchenna Smith's sisters, her mother, or her colleagues, and you'll walk away with the same impression: that this young woman is unusually focused for someone at any age, much less in their mid-twenties—a time when most are simply hoping to find themselves. Beneath the bright eyes, the glowing smile, and the bushy mound of hair; behind the mountainous mess of a desk; and below an eclectic book shelf where *Seven Days of Kwanzaa* cozies up with *The Art of War,* sits a remarkably stable and affable young woman who you wouldn't immediately guess was dealing with standardized test pressures, budgetary demands, teachers, staff, parents, contracts, deadlines, purchase orders—all of the things that make a school run—plus a brand-new class of fifth graders due to arrive at the door of her fitness-center-turned-single-story-schoolhouse in less than two weeks. Perhaps even more impressive than her cool manner is the way Uchenna tactfully fields eleventh-hour phone calls from frantic parents hoping to have their children admitted to KIPP-Sankofa. Briefly putting our conversation on hold, she listens carefully and patiently to each parent, before switching them over to her tireless assistant, Yeiza Arzuaga, who in turn makes an appointment for the parent to come in for a formal interview. While each of the thirty-eight KIPP schools around the country follows a similar protocol, Uchenna performs the seemingly rote task with such earnestness that it's hard to believe that up until three years ago she knew next to nothing about charter schools, and even less about being the principal of one.

"I'm a teacher. I'm really not into the whole principal thing too much. I really just love being with kids, teaching, talking to people, helping people out. The whole principal thing was just this power thing that people . . ."

"Trip off of?" I say, finishing her thought.

"Yeah. I really didn't want to be a principal. For the first three months or so of school I just kind of pretended like I wasn't the principal. There were decisions that needed to be made that were hard decisions that I kind of put off in the beginning, and a lot of them dealt with having students here that should have gone. I had to realize that if you have one really rotten apple in a barrel it can . . . When I was a public school teacher, those were always the kids I gravitated toward, those were always the kids I wanted to help more and more and more."

Early in the school year Uchenna found herself going to one student's house every night, with food, in order to make sure he did his homework until, eventually, the strain proved too much for her. She had to come to the difficult realization that she was an administrator now, and that while she still taught a class on character development, her chief responsibility was to the life of the school, not just to one child. After going back and forth on the matter for weeks a meeting with the child's mother was arranged where for the first time Uchenna had to play the role of the tough principal. Uchenna pulled out the "commitment to excellence" form that student, parent, and principal signed before the start of the school year. Among other things, what separates KIPP schools from other charter schools is their fully enforceable trilateral agreement that requires students to (1) be in school ten hours a day, (2) attend Saturday school, (3) attend three weeks of summer school, and (4) wear a school uniform that they must first earn. Along with these requirements, parents *must* make themselves available to their children and the school whenever requested. In turn, teachers give their students their cell phone numbers and make themselves available for students and parents at all times as well. In the meeting, Uchenna pointed out that the parent and the child were failing to hold up their ends of the bargain, and that no matter how much she liked the child as a person, she had to enforce the rules. The school would only be successful if everyone pulled their weight. Ultimately, the parent decided it was just too much work and removed her child from the school. But while the school suffered its first casualty, it also began to define its identity.

"When we started there were a lot of people complaining," Uchenna says. "Then you hold a piece of paper in front of them and you're like, 'This is what you committed to. I signed my commitment. I'm here. When your kid calls, I answer the phone. When they come to school, we've got exciting lessons for them. You've got to do your part, we're doing ours.' [That's when] we start having some real conversations."

Principal Smith started dumping students' book bags on her office table and literally showing both student and parent what organization looks like. If the student was having trouble studying, she'd teach them and the parent how to create study aids—math flashcards, for example. If a parent complained that they couldn't make it to a school meeting because they didn't have a ride, she or one of her staff members would go and pick them up. If a student couldn't get a ride to school, they'd do the same. Slowly, the parents started to understand that the young woman who had traveled door to door recruiting families to a school that didn't even exist meant business. Parents also came to understand that her door was always open, that they could call the school on a summer day like today and speak with Uchenna directly, or just stop by. Moreover, they found out that no excuse was a good excuse, and that failure of any kind wasn't acceptable.

Quite possibly you've heard of KIPP. In the last few years the program has been in the news nonstop because in a remarkably short time it has produced some of the highest standardized test scores in some of the lowest performing and most underfunded school districts in the United States. Numerous news sources including *60 Minutes* and the *Washington Post* have featured the program and its founders Mike Feinberg and Dave Levin. More than a decade ago both men enrolled in Teach for America directly out of college. Both had attended Ivy League universities, and both had shunned the lure of graduate school and a comfortable life to follow to give back to the nation's least advantaged communities. Feinberg and Levin were a pair of workaholic teachers who wanted to initiate change, but who found themselves in the often stifling position of teaching within a bloated, bureaucratic system. Instead of quitting at the first sign of defeat, however, they dug in and with the help of a pair of seasoned teachers designed the pilot for KIPP. After convincing the Houston Schools superintendent (and future education secretary) Ron Paige to let them pilot the program, they were able to expand into the South Bronx. Both schools were successful. More recently, the founders of GAP Clothing Company, Doris and Donald Fisher, gave KIPP $15 million, much of which has been used to build a school leadership initiative that identifies potential principals, and puts them through a rigorous yearlong course of study to prepare them to open their own school. According to the founders, good schools need good leaders. If a school has a good leader, then anything is possible.

The common thread running through all KIPP schools is the Five Pillars, a set of principles upon which each school is mandated to operate. One through five, the "pillars" are High Expectations, Choice and Commitment, More Time, Power to Lead, and Focus on Results. Working from the conceptual base provided by that philosophy, KIPP's approach combines a system of rewards and consequences to attract and maintain the interest and focus of students. The theory is there's no shortcut to success. Low-income students and their teachers simply must spend more time working harder because of their frequently fractured home lives, and their lack of preparation. The founders also believe school-based musical groups are a big part of the "joy factor" that students need in order be successful. Alternatively, students are given incentives for their hard work in the form of numerous trips, along with access to the all-important school store where students can acquire food and merchandise in exchange for the virtual cash they accumulate from good behavior and scholastic achievement. In contrast, students who break school rules are given demerits and must earn back the right to participate in the school's rewards program through both academic and behavioral improvement. In short, everything is earned in a KIPP school, and people believe that is what makes these schools work.

Uchenna doesn't have many fond memories of her three years as a Buffalo public school teacher. They were frustrating, disillusioning, and heartbreaking. Her first year at School 45 pitted her against an acting principal who she suspects felt threatened by someone who came in ready to rock the boat with new ideas. Everything, however, was supposed to change her second year. At the insistence of a fellow teacher she applied for and received a transfer to a brand-new technology-based school. Unfortunately, the school was so underenrolled that the principals from all of the area middle schools were asked to send a handful of students to help fill out rosters.

"But you know who they were gonna send. In the first weeks of school there was this kid in one of my classes who jumped on the desk and was just screaming. It was crazy. There were bloody fights, I mean *bloody* fights, that I had to break up in the hallway, people getting cut and slashed. I was just like, 'Oh my God. This is a beautiful school, brand-new building, a bunch of new energetic teachers who want to be here; who had to apply to be here; who want to be *at this school*.' It was a mess. I would go home crying. The woman who actually got me to go to the school ended up leaving. She claimed some mental disorder. The school was out of control. That year eighty percent of the faculty requested transfers out."

Uchenna, on the other hand, decided to stay and complete the second year of the two-year commitment she'd agreed to when she signed on. In contrast to much of the school, her classes were under control and even though her students often complained that she was too strict, she managed to create an atmosphere where learning could take place. Even still, the problems Uchenna and her fellow teachers faced during the school day only told half the story. The reason she would eventually leave the Buffalo public school system was because of what happened *after* school.

"When I worked at [School] Forty-five, the first school, I would stay after school to help my kids because math is difficult for some people and some people need extra help. When I went to school my teachers stayed after school and tutored us. As much help as we needed, they gave us. I thought it was my job, only I got written up by my principal for staying after school and tutoring kids. That really pissed me off. It was completely crazy to me."

The same thing happened the following year at the second school Uchenna taught in. Again, she started an after-school program—this time for gifted math students—and again the program was terminated by her principal. This time, though, Uchenna found a community center near the school and made arrangements with the center's director to bring her students there for tutoring. "Basically, the consistent message I got when I worked for Buffalo [public school system] was do not go above and beyond, do not do anything special for your kids. I wasn't asking for any money; someone was in the building; the parents were cool with it. It was just stupidity, that's all I can say. I got tired of dealing with bureaucratic stupidity."

Meanwhile, during that second year, a friend introduced Uchenna to a woman named Dr. Gail Foster, who had founded the Toussaint Institute Fund, a scholarship program for African-American boys who are at risk of being placed in special education, where they almost inevitably remain. Through Dr. Foster, Uchenna found out about the Black Alliance for Educational Options (BAEO), an organization that had been recently founded by Dr. Howard Fuller, and whose primary mission is to alert African-Americans to the wide range of educational choices available to them, including charter schools, home schooling, and school voucher programs. Although the organization has been accused of being anti–public education, BAEO's stated purpose is to give low-income African-Americans the same options for educating their children as their higher-income counterparts. What sparked Uchenna's interest in the organization was that "school choice," which is typically cast as a Republican initiative designed to suit elite interests, was being co-opted by blacks to suit the needs of their children.

That winter Uchenna traveled to Philadelphia for the BAEO's annual symposium, where she met Tracy McDaniel, a former Oklahoma Vice-Principal of the Year and a current fellow with KIPP, which Uchenna had never heard of. Tracy sold Uchenna on KIPP, and the need to have more African-American school leaders in a program that, while serving minorities primarily, had few minority leaders. Although she was intrigued, Uchenna had to consider the practical side. Becoming a Fisher Fellow would require her to give up nearly a year of her life without a guarantee that she'd have her own school at the conclusion of the program. As sour as Uchenna felt toward the school system, she was up for tenure, teaching was getting easier, she was involved in plays again, she was dancing for the first time since college, and writing and performing her poetry. Uchenna had also bought her first home, and she was in a serious relationship.

On the other side of the fence stood Uchenna's sense of responsibility. From the time she was five all the way through her high school years her mother had run a multimillion-dollar non-profit home ownership organization in Niagara Falls, New York. The organization bought dilapidated homes, renovated them, and then sold them back to poor people at a subsidized rate. Over time the program began to help families buy homes they had been renting, and in some cases it lent them the capital to renovate their own homes. "I saw my mother in a very professional setting," Uchenna says. "I saw her working with people who needed her help and how kind, how respectful it was, and how important it was for her to help those people."

Uchenna decided to go for it.

"My school ended June twenty-fifth. I had to be packed and out of my apartment, ready to go to [the University of California] Berkeley by July seventh. We were there for six weeks. Class was from eight to five, then we would have evening meetings. We had homework every night just like the kids would have homework every night. When we were in class they would quiz us. It was harder than any college course I've ever taken, more intense. The other thing was everybody just really wanted to do the work because you were about to be responsible for a whole school.

"After that, we came back to where we wanted to open up our school, started trying to make some inroads, and then we were shipped off to our first residency. It was a high-performing school where we could shadow the school leader, talk to the teachers, do observations, talk to the office manager. Just collect different documents and try to get a sense of what we had to build and create. My first school was YES College Prep, which was in Houston. Part of their requirements for graduation were to get two letters of acceptance to a college; they're really serious. The school is excellent. Chris Barbic is the leader there; he just taught me so much. I was in Houston for a month. We get a project that we had to work on, so my project while I was there was improving the school store. The next residency I went to was the Academy of Pacific Rim, which is in Hyde Park, Massachusetts, right outside of Boston, and I was there for a month. Again, I learned a lot."

"Was it ever overwhelming?" I ask Uchenna.

"Oh! Was it ever overwhelming?" Uchenna reaches across her desk for a pair of thick three-ring binders she says were part of a library of documents she had to be familiar with. "Every day was overwhelming. Every day you're in a place where you're surrounded by a bunch of people who are overachievers, who are workaholics. When you're part of KIPP you're proud to be part of KIPP, so you get there before any teachers get there, before the sun comes up. You stay there until the last teacher leaves. You're trying to learn what it is to be a principal. Then you go home, say by eight, nine, [and] you have to work on your charter for a couple of hours, work on your school design plan, read ten books that KIPP wants you to read, finish your e-mails, contact people back home."

Uchenna hit the ground running when she got back to Buffalo. If her school was going to open in the fall she had to find money, a staff, a building, an entire fifth grade class, and finish a four-hundred-page charter. Armed with cell phones and Yeiza's Toyota Corolla, they began making home visits, writing grants, visiting sites, and recruiting teachers. Outsiders wondered if she'd be able to pull it off in such a short time, but Uchenna never doubted herself. Not only had she put too much on the line, she'd already envisioned the school. "It was gonna happen. For me, this school was real years and years before it was even really here. To me, it was realer than reality. There was no doubt in my mind that it was going to happen because I knew I was going to do whatever it took, and that was just it."

As funds from a few smaller grants trickled in, Uchenna was able to run ads in the paper and on the local radio stations to attract parents. She was able to secure a lease on space for the school. Next, she bought the furniture, and the books. Suddenly, it looked as though the school would be ready to open its doors on time. But right when things started to appear as though they were under control, something happened that seemed designed to put Uchenna's resolve to the test. The contractor found a problem with the building's roof. Fixing the problem would require an extra three weeks of repairs, he said. Those three weeks were supposed to be the prep period for the new staff; without that time there was no way the school could open on time. "I had to scramble to find another building," Uchenna says. She appealed to a local minister who offered them the use of his church as a temporary base. "They had a school that they weren't using during the summer so we moved some stuff into there, set everything up for three weeks, moved everything out, then we moved everything over here."

The final preopening day hurdle Uchenna faced concerned the cafeteria furniture. The company they had originally ordered from called at the last minute and said they wouldn't be able to make delivery before October 15. That would mean her kids would have to spend the better part of two months without a proper place to eat breakfast or lunch. That just wasn't going to cut it, so Uchenna got on the Internet where she found an online wholesale furniture company. As karma or coincidence would have it, another buyer who had previously ordered the exact style and color Uchenna was looking for had canceled earlier that week. The only catch was the wholesaler only sold directly to distributors. Uchenna pled her case anyway. This was the first day of a new school, she told them. Everything needed to be in order. Would they please make an exception under the circumstances, she begged. When still they resisted, the shrewd, take-no-prisoners businesswoman in Uchenna emerged and she pulled out her trump card: the kids. Where would they eat? If they didn't have a good breakfast there was no way they could learn. Reluctantly, the company made an exception, only they said there was no way they could deliver by the first day of school.

But then something happened. Sifting through the shoe box once again, Uchenna finds the photograph she's looking for, looks at it wistfully, then hands it to me. In the photo Uchenna and Yeiza are striking their best schoolgirl poses before a row of lunch tables. "The first day of school I came in to open the building," she begins, "and there was the truck with the blue cafeteria tables."

As Uchenna guides me through a tour of Sankofa I try to imagine how she must feel when she wakes up each morning. I'm sure there were days this past year when even she wished she could stay in bed, days, as well, when she truly wondered whether the school would survive. But just by watching the way she saunters the empty halls clad in velvet sweats, T-shirt, and flip-flops, I'm willing to bet her worst days here far outweighed her best days anywhere else. Beginning the moment a student, parent, or teacher walks through the front door, they know there's something different about this school. From the banner welcoming the class of 2012, to the open office spaces where the staff and students mingle freely; from the vibrant, spit-shine hallways to classrooms named after the college each teacher attended; from the school store where the students can redeem the virtual cash they earn to the dance studio where they learn to play African drums like the djembe, everything in Sankofa has been thought through and designed to empower students while pushing them to new heights.

This is only the beginning, though. With a year under her belt and the basic systems in place, it's time now to begin the difficult work of building a successful school in the midst of the divisive school-choice debate. In fact, just weeks before my conversation with Uchenna, the Department of Education released a report indicating that students in charter schools were lagging behind their public school counterparts. Charter school critics, including some of the nation's largest teachers' unions, will likely use these findings as ammunition in their campaign against the trend. However, when I raise these points with Uchenna she quickly notes that (1) charter schools, including hers, typically attract the students with the greatest needs, and whose parents are looking for alternatives to conventional education, (2) charter schools only receive two thirds of the money set aside for each child, and (3) even despite these impediments KIPP schools have been enormously successful in achieving some of the highest standardized test scores throughout the country.

One reason charter schools, which are free and open to all, are viewed by many as a threat to public education is because teachers aren't protected by unions. Since each school operates by its own charter, school employees answer to the individual school, not the system. On the one hand that means teachers can be asked to work longer hours than those mandated by the typical public school contract, their pay need not be commensurate with their experience, and, perhaps most important, they can be summarily dismissed for noncompliance and/or the failure of their students to perform well on standardized tests. In effect, without unions to protect them, public school teachers become just as vulnerable and accountable as people working in the private sectors of the American economy, which many who support President Bush's No Child Left Behind legislation think is exactly what needs to happen. On the other hand, charter schools offer the freedom and flexibility that innovative teachers need in order to perform at their best. Also, teachers in KIPP schools are paid considerably more than public school teachers for the extra time they spend with their students. Third, charter schools tend to be smaller and more family-oriented, therefore teachers, students, administrators, and parents all feel as though they have a vested interest in the culture of the school.

Uchenna's response to the critics of charter schools is as simple as it is blunt: "Are unions helping children?

"I got written up for staying after school to tutor my kids because of union stipulations. If unions help kids learn better, cool. If they don't then something makes me go hmmmm. Unions are bargaining units for teachers. Teachers typically do not have a choice. They are forced to pay money into this political machine. Every year they get a blob taken out of their check, and some people say, 'Oh, it's good, it helps them with benefits, it helps them get more pay.' Should teachers be well paid? Yes. However, teachers are servants. Civil servants. That's what they are. There is no civil service that gets paid an inordinate amount of money. That's not really in the definition of the job. If someone wants to make a lot of money, they probably should not be a teacher. They should probably go into the private sector. And that's something they just need to grasp. If you're in it for the money and that's what it's about for you, then you're in the wrong place. That's how I feel."

If there's ever a point in which Uchenna shows the obstinacy of youth it's here, on this subject. Just as she doesn't take excuses from her students, she's intolerant of people who complain without making any changes, people looking for a free ride through the system until they're eligible for retirement, and people who don't have the interests of children at heart. The easy response to Uchenna's criticism of the system is to dismiss her as idealistic, single, and ignorant of what it's like to raise a family on a teacher's salary. But Uchenna knows as well as anybody else that she's not always going to be a young woman with the energy to move mountains. What makes her unique is that instead of watching her fire slowly die, she is putting it to good use.

"Could I be more selfish, be thinking about myself, a family? Yes. But right now there's no guy who's more important to me than my school. This place is a dream; it's like magic. I mean, could you imagine kids committing to come to school for ten hours a day? Two hours of homework? Not only do they have their teachers' phone numbers, they have my cell phone number so if they have a question at night they can call us, and they do.

"It's hard. It's a big commitment for everybody, but it works—that is the thing that drives me. When I see a kid come in who's struggling to read, I'm going to battle with the mom. She's cussin' me out, we're going at it, and then a couple of months later she comes to me and says, 'You know, Ms. Smith, I was gonna pull him from the school but we went out to dinner and I asked him to read this, this, and this, and he read it.' You get stories like that and you're like 'Yeah, I'm doing something and it's special.'"

Postscript: Just before Beat *went to press, I learned that Uchenna was getting married. After two years of spending all her time building her school, she was balancing the scales.*

Keeping Up with the Huxtables

Michele Luc: Global Youth Advocate

"Despite how many lives I have affected positively, I don't know if I consider myself successful."

Like most of her generation, Michele Luc grew up watching *The Cosby Show* on Thursday nights. In the eighties and early nineties, the hit series about an upper-middle-class African-American family living in a Brooklyn brownstone was an institution, perhaps even a template for black achievement. While *The Jeffersons'* gospel-infused "movin' on up" anthem signaled the African-American ascension, "Cos" and his clan informed us that we were now firmly ensconced within the American ideal. Nearly every aspect of the show—from the theme music to Cliff Huxtable's college sweatshirts, from Denise's various identity alterations to the range of multiethnic characters that popped in from time to time—illustrated the complete transcendence of socioeconomic barriers as well as the redefinition of blackness itself. In short, the show was as much a social commentary as it was comic genius. When Michele Luc, a middle-class girl from a small New Jersey town, first started watching *The Cosby Show,* she found in it a place to escape to; when it came time to decide on a college, the show provided her with a sense of direction.

"I knew I didn't want to go to school in New Jersey," says thirty-one-year-old Michele over breakfast one morning, our first meeting. Michele and I are seated by the window of a crowded diner on Flatbush Avenue in Brooklyn—her home now—on what might be the first beautifully sunny day of the year so far. "I loved *The Cosby Show* and Bill Cosby had attended Temple and Phylisha Rashad went to Howard. At the time, Theo had just started at N.Y.U. So I applied to Temple, Howard, and N.Y.U."

The irony is that as close as Michele was to New York, she didn't even know that the city had universities before Theo started at N.Y.U. "It's only a state over, but you only hear about the Ivy League schools," she adds.

To placate her mother, Michele also applied to Seton Hall University in South Orange, New Jersey.

Michele was accepted everywhere she applied. Straightaway she eliminated Seton Hall because she would've had to live at home. Temple and Howard were out as well. Both schools were too far away, her parents said. That left N.Y.U., which, despite its close proximity and prohibitive cost, Michele's parents reluctantly allowed her to attend.

"What were they so afraid of?" I ask.

Michele looks up from her menu and directs a peculiar look in my direction. Then she casually gathers her copious dreads and scoops them behind her ears. Michele has a rich complexion, and an expressive face. "You're talking about a Haitian family where usually the girls didn't leave until they got married."

However, when Michele's mother was twenty-seven and unmarried, she had left Haiti to take a nursing job in the United States. In the 1960s, West Indian women with nursing licenses were finding positions throughout the industrialized world. According to Michele, her mother arrived with only a crude handle on English, but within a year she had saved enough money to return to her island country for her beau. In her own quiet way, Michele says proudly, her mother had been a trailblazer.

• • •

After finishing at N.Y.U., Michele wasted no time reenrolling in school, this time in a graduate program farther uptown, at Columbia University. She was twenty-two and had her life mapped out. Michele saw herself starting off as a social worker and eventually branching into private practice so she could be independent. In the meantime, she would get married, buy a big house somewhere in Jersey, and raise four kids. She would have it all, just like her mother, just like Claire Huxtable. At Columbia, Michele took an internship with the Panel of Americans, an organization that provides workplaces with diversity training specialists.

"This was around the time of the whole Exxon thing with the CEO referring to his workers as 'his little black jelly beans' or something like that. When stuff like that happened, like for instance the Rodney King verdict, [the Panel] got people to go in and do a training on diversity, to talk about issues of race and gender." Her advisers at Columbia told her that this was a growing field for consultants, that if she was good at it she could make a pretty good living at it. "That's all I had to hear because I don't like working for people."

Michele found that the work suited her personality. It stimulated her and allowed her to discuss issues she felt strongly about. Unfortunately, the organization didn't hire her at the end of her internship, so she went back into social work, which proved to be horrible.

"I hated it. A lot of nepotism. A lot of backstabbing. A lot of ageism. In a lot of the nonprofits people get their jobs because of nepotism, which I don't have a problem with. What was problematic for older people was that I was the youngest person and the only person with a master's. It was a rough time."

Michele quickly decided that she wasn't willing to sit around and wait for things to improve. While interning at the Panel of

Americans, she'd met a woman who she thought had a pretty cool job at an organization called Global Kids. The woman had told her how the organization went into city schools and gave workshops on the death penalty in paralegal classes, AIDS in Africa in health classes, and third-world sweatshops in business classes. Perhaps more important, though, Global Kids also trained students to run global-issue workshops themselves. She'd never taught kids before, but she thought anything was better than staying in a miserable situation.

Michele dug up the woman's card. "I gave her a call and asked if there were any jobs available." Two months later she was teaching her first class on monsoons in India. She liked the work. She also liked the fact that she had to continue educating herself in order to stay on top of her job. "I was not a newspaper reader. If I did it was the *Daily News* and I did the crossword puzzle. I had to read a lot more from different sources like the BBC, Human Rights Watch, *The Guardian,* and make myself aware of all kinds of media, and that some of the stuff we get here isn't completely honest."

The purpose of an organization like Global Kids is to pick up where schools and parents leave off. It offers something outside of the exacting educational regimen of math, science, history, and English; it enables kids to grapple with real-world issues among themselves; and it encourages kids to believe that they can create the changes they want to see in the world. In Michele's opinion, the reason many kids join Global Kids is because they sense it is genuinely giving them something they aren't getting at school or at home.

"I think that for a lot of young people we deal with, we show them a reality that they didn't think was possible because they have a real polarized view of the world. They think that if you come from this area, you can't achieve certain things, you can't go to certain colleges, you can't do certain work. And even then there's the opposing viewpoint that if you go to college you have to be totally removed from the community, so if they go to school and have those benefits now, it means they have to abandon their community, they can only associate with these people and listen to this type of music. For them to see us as people who come to their 'hood to teach them things that are beyond their scope, but I'm still a black woman they can identify with, is just powerful. They can go to City College or Columbia and be equally blessed. If they go to a university and they're not surrounded by people who look like them that doesn't mean they have to relinquish a part of their identity. They can still be who they are and they don't have to make any apologies for it."

One of the crucial methods Global Kids employs to teach kids how to negotiate the global landscape is international travel. On three separate occasions Michele has led groups of kids to Croatia to participate in global peace and democracy-building conferences. (A fourth time she went alone to give a lecture on democracy building to fifty international educators.) For many of these kids, it's their first time out of New York City, let alone the country. Even Michele, for all of her education, had only been to Canada and the Caribbean prior to her first voyage. She still recalls the reactions of her friends, who looked at her as if she was crazy. Wasn't there a war going on there? they asked. In turn, Michele told them about the 1995 Peace Accord and the country's efforts to restore democracy. She also told them Croatia was one of the most progressive and economically recovered nations in the former Yugoslavia.

Michele didn't fault her friends and family for their ignorance. Before she started working at Global Kids she didn't know anything about the Eastern European bloc either. While many of her white and Asian coworkers had lived in places like Madagascar, Nepal, India, and Thailand, just going to a school in another state had been a big deal for Michele. The same could be said for nearly every other African-American working at Global Kids. At times, Michele's even had to defend applicants whom her coworkers were quick to eliminate because their curriculum vitae didn't list extensive international experience. As with most matters pertaining to race and class, Michele has her theories on why this is so often the case:

"I think that we've gotten so used to the struggle that we think struggle is our birthright and that certain things we aren't entitled to do, so the whole idea of travel to another place for black folks here in the States and in the Caribbean, and for working-class people, is not even a consideration. It's not a reality. When we go on vacation we go to the Bahamas or Jamaica; we do stuff that's familiar. We don't go to places that are foreign, strange, and where people don't look like us."

Life in the States, Michele and I joke, is hard enough for black folks, therefore we generally don't feel the need to embrace someone else's struggle.

What Michele discovered on her first trip to Croatia, though, was that like most any city in the United States, Croatia has its slums and its suburbs, its beauty and its ugliness. "I went to gorgeous places," she says. "The place where we stayed for the first week when we gave the conference for the European Union is beautiful. They have us in a resort town right on the Adriatic Sea. You really are on the water. Then when we went to other parts like Keenan, which is right on the border of Bosnia where they saw major fighting, I was like, 'wow,' yeah, you're like trucking through rubble."

For the most part Michele hasn't experienced racism during her trips to Croatia. People stare at her on the street. Skinheads roam about. She's had her share of airport run-ins. Nothing serious. Nothing she, as an adult, can't deal with, and even understand to a certain degree. There was, however, an unsettling experience in 2000. One of the youth delegates was a young man from the Bronx. This was both his first time out of the Bronx and his first time on a plane. As Michele describes him, he was a sociable kid, one who could joke around with anybody. "His 'in' was through his humor," she says.

"Everything had been cool for the first few days. Everyone knew us as the Americans who were coming to give a workshop. It was me and my coworker, who is white, and three students. We were supposed to meet with students who lived during the time of war who had to be underground and talk with them about what it was like. We get off the bus and we pass by a house where a bunch of guys were hanging out. They were staring. As we're walking I notice Anthony's demeanor changing. He's kind of squinting and looking back. They were laughing and pointing specifically at Anthony. At one point one kid runs up to him and says something to him then runs away laughing. It's one thing to be in a store and have security watch you. It's another thing to be one of only two black faces in a sea of white and people are pointing and laughing."

Michele took the boy's hand and walked with him. What troubled him most, he told her, was that he didn't know what they were saying about him, that they were just looking and pointing. And they didn't stop. Once Michele's group was inside the conference, the Croatian kids gathered around an open window and continued to taunt the boy. Eventually, he put his head down and didn't lift it until it was time to go.

Michele's story reminds me of an experience in Capetown, South Africa, when a street vendor I'd met asked, quite politely, whether I preferred being called a "nigger" since, after all we American blacks so frequently referred to ourselves as such in movies and music. I didn't get angry with the vendor, as I suppose the young man with Michele wasn't angry with his group of taunters. If anything, we were both hurt, because we'd been

reduced to something less than individuals. We were marginal-
ized, prejudged, thrown into a box that we didn't create. The
difference is that I could stand there on that street and educate
the vendor, while the boy in Michele's story could only wonder
what was being said about him.

"I really almost felt like a mother having to explain racism to
a child. I think the realization of race really started to hit him. It
was sad and it was hurtful."

The children who shout *Neger!* have no way of knowing the
echoes this sound raises in me. They are brimming with good
humor and the more daring swell with pride when I stop to
speak with them. Just the same, there are days when I cannot
pause and smile, when I have no heart to play with them; when,
indeed, I mutter sourly to myself, exactly as I muttered on the
streets of a city these children have never seen, when I was no
bigger than these children are now: *Your* mother *was a nigger.*

More than half a century has passed since James Baldwin
penned these words in an essay entitled "A Stranger in the Village," about his time in a Swiss village, and yet they seem equally
appropriate in today's context. One can only hope those Croatian boys had no way of knowing the painful history standing
behind their playful taunting.

"What's the most rewarding aspect of your job?" Several weeks
have passed and Michele and I are in her apartment. Bob Mar-
ley's voice simmers in the background while the scent of in-
cense chokes the air. Although Michele has been intermittently
distracted by the flow of instant messages popping up on her
laptop's screen, we've spent the last half-hour talking like old
friends. They're from a guy she's been seeing. Michele reads the
messages to me, asks my opinion. The tape runs.

Finally, Michele takes a seat on the opposite end of the couch and considers my question. "What's the most rewarding aspect of my job? It's gotta be seeing the development of a young person on all levels: academically, socially, emotionally, just the growth of a young person. I think it's really special to see young people who have their own thoughts and their own ideas and to expose them to all these different things they have no clue about, and to help give them a voice to articulate that with people outside of their immediate worldview. Giving them the chance to see that they have different options. I think that's what's really most rewarding. I mean the travel is definitely a perk, they get to see that the world is bigger than their block, bigger than their borough. It's so much harder to say, 'Well these people are like this' if you see those people in a different setting."

Nonetheless, working with kids outside of the traditional school context carries its own stresses. Unlike teachers who can choose to shield themselves from their students' lives and still perform their job satisfactorily, Michele's success or failure hinges almost entirely on her relationships with her kids. School is compulsory; Global Kids is voluntary. What this ultimately means is that her kids develop attachments to her that extend beyond the purview of their work together. Pregnancy, suicide attempts, date rape, homelessness. Michele has seen and heard it all.

"I've had kids come to my house on several occasions with no place to go. One of those kids actually stayed with me for a week because her mom literally threw her out the week before graduation. She showed up with a box and her bag. This girl was a senior, had a full scholarship to Vanderbilt University—tuition, everything! Was an A student."

That girl's mother kicked her out because she stayed out past her curfew. Other parents have called Michele at work to inform their child, through her, not to come home. She finds that kind of behavior particularly contemptible. Her job isn't to tell a fourteen- and fifteen-year-old that they can't go home. Much of the discord among her kids and their parents stems from what she calls the "Americanization" of second-generation immigrant children, which in most cases means little more than that they adopt values their first-generation parents don't approve of. One type of so-called Americanization that parents find particularly deplorable is homosexuality. One girl, who is also Haitian, and who Michele had been close with for years, "came out" to her in her senior year of high school. "I was able to tell her there's nothing wrong with being lesbian," Michele says.

Michele attended the young woman's college graduation a year ago. This past year the girl started law school. In a week, five more of "her kids" will be graduating from college. A few months ago she was able to hire a twenty-three-year-old who was a student of hers when he was fifteen. Seeing things come full circle in this way brings a smile to Michele's face, quickens the already fast pace of her speech. After seven years she still loves her job. But she's also wondering if it's time to move on.

Seven years at the same job by Michele's generation's standards, by the standards of the new economy, is a lifetime, a feat worthy of the gold watch. In Michele's case, it's also cause for anxiety. She hears the rumblings, sees the look on people's faces: Why is she still at the same job? Why hasn't she moved on? Is she stuck? "I'm so concerned about what people think. I shouldn't be. I question myself and wonder why am I still here."

Michele is extremely conscious of herself as a black woman. Her awareness of race and gender often colors her perception of people, and the things they say. If when she tells someone she attended N.Y.U. and Columbia an eyebrow gets raised or a mouth falls slightly askew, a part of her automatically registers racism. If a simple meeting that should take a half hour takes an hour because everything she suggests is being questioned and challenged, she wonders if it's because of her age, her sex, her race. At this point it's almost a knee-jerk response; perhaps it's even the price one pays for being conscious in what many consider a sexist, racist, and classist (among other "ists and isms") society. Ultimately, what happens when we don't know exactly how to read people, their intentions, or their words, is we begin to call ourselves into question. For Michele, the solution to her hyper-consciousness has been to throw everything back on herself. "Maybe I'm reading too far into this?" she'll ask, followed quickly by, "but what if I'm not?"

Michele is not alone. There's an infallible link between success and uncertainty such that even those blacks who achieve in this society feel weighted down by a sense of suspicion, even outright distrust of the system and the people within it. Having to deal with this kind of double consciousness can be paralyzing.

"I never really view myself how other people view me," Michele says. "I think I take for granted that I've done a lot of things that a lot of people I know have not done and I compare myself to other people. Despite how many lives I have affected positively, I'm still not completely okay with everything, so I don't know if I consider myself successful."

A moment later Michele will modify this last comment. She'll say she is successful in the sense that people can look at her life and say that she's achieved a great deal at a young age. She's just not successful in her own opinion of herself. Still, Michele understands that these conflicting perspectives are problematic, that they will only drive her to extremes, which is one of the reasons she sought out a therapist—an African-American woman—who helped her define the real issue: She had a superwoman complex.

"She really just made me see that and think about why and where does it come from. Where does my need to handle everything, take care of everyone, especially before myself, and be good at this and good at that . . . where does that come from? I think that definitely a lot of black women have that. It's this whole idea about being nurturers and caregivers—I mean I just picture running around like a chicken with the head cut off. And if I'm not able to attend to something, I feel really bad about it. If I forget to call someone and say Happy Birthday— and I remember everyone's birthday—then in some way, shape, or form I have failed. Then, I'm not superwoman and I have to deal with that. I do think that a lot of black women feel that way, oftentimes to a fault."

Michele is an incredibly intelligent and insightful woman who sees deeply into things, particularly herself; she is also someone who, despite her accomplishments, is still looking for answers and explanations to questions even *The Cosby Show* didn't deal with head on. Cliff and Claire Huxtable were African-American professionals whose children attended top schools, whose squabbles never rose beyond the range of a spirited debate, and who, most important, never confronted the crises of (black) consciousness. They were, as author Shelby Steele wrote in his book *The Content of Our Character*, "black bargainers." They made a conscious choice not to confront race, class, or gender as issues, but to ignore them in hopes of transcending them.

For someone evolving within this utopian sphere of tranquillity the road map to success undoubtedly appeared free and clear: get an education at the right institutions, get a job in the right field, raise a family in the right neighborhood. If you do those things, you've nothing to worry about. The reality, as Michele has since discovered, is much more complicated. Before one can transcend their reality, one must confront it; before one can confront, one must be conscious.

Once-in-a-Lifetime Opportunity

Kara Mitchell: Ex–Peace Corps Volunteer/Child Therapist

"Defer your loans. Pay your debts. Get up and get out."

I was expecting someone different. Someone with a rugged, outdoor look who wore a multipocketed backpack (complete with her own water bottle) and unwashed sneakers, jeans, and, since it was raining outside, a well-traveled parka. I pictured her with mushroom-shaped dreadlocks that fell to her shoulders or maybe a tiny Afro neatly framing a perky face.

And maybe Kara Mitchell was expecting someone else, too. Maybe she was expecting someone wearing a smart pair of glasses and with a slightly dull pencil stuck behind his ear; someone with a notepad in the front pocket of his lucky flannel shirt or the back pocket of his wrinkle-free Dockers.

We base our preconceptions on prior experiences, stereotypes, and our imaginations. The world is a much easier place to navigate when we have an idea of where people belong, who we should pay attention to, who we can discard. This is particularly so in urban centers, where we encounter far too many faces in a single day to grant them each a separate identity. To simply survive, we must assign categories, file away certain "types" in our mental Rolodex, and keep it moving.

In this case my interviewee and I sit right beside each other and, without even bothering to ask if perhaps we are who the other is looking for, wait for our prototype to walk through the door. We'd decided to meet in a Starbucks, the twenty-first cen-

tury's most generic meeting place. After five or so minutes I pull
out my tape recorder and place it on the table..

"Are you by any chance Dax?" the woman asks, suddenly
coming to life.

"You must be Kara."

But even after we've headed out the door for a bite to eat, I
wonder why I hadn't noticed Kara earlier, particularly when she
was the only black woman in the café that afternoon? A possible
answer relates back to the initial e-mail I'd sent out to the Peace
Corps home office two weeks earlier, in which I explained that
I was looking for past and present African-American volunteers
to profile in a book. I figured that since only 3 percent of Peace
Corps volunteers globally are African-American, the few who
had chosen that route must be an unusual bunch. Frankly,
whenever I think of the Peace Corps, I innately picture earnest
white kids in their early twenties who come from working- or
middle-class stock toiling away in bug-infested villages with no
running water. I see a slim John Candy and a young Tom Hanks
romping through a monsoon in *Volunteers*. I see granola bars and
Birkenstocks.

I don't see Kara Mitchell, at least not the incarnation sitting
before me at the Ethiopian restaurant we decide to eat lunch in.
There is an aura of sophistication about her that seems to defy
even the idea that she would spend two years living in a village
in rural Dominican Republic. It's the blond highlights in her
hair; it's the stylish, violet-tinted blouse; it's the discretion with
which she nibbles away at her food, even the uneasiness she feels
about talking into a recorder.

More than a little curious, I scratch my whole game plan and
cut straight to the point, asking her what possessed her to join
the Peace Corps in the first place.

Kara's answers are a combination of:

- **practicality**: "I chose the Peace Corps because I didn't have the money to just go ahead and travel freely, but I also wanted to stay for a long time so I could learn a different culture and another language."

- **opportunity**: "I had started graduate school and I was thinking when else would I be able to do something like that, because after I graduated I planned on getting a job and buying a house—all that stuff. I was still living at home at the time. I didn't have any real bills to pay so I just did it. Plus, I figured that it would give me a clearer idea of what I wanted to do when I came back."

- **impulsivity**: "When I was in college there weren't any study abroad programs for people who majored in psychology, and I was like, 'What can I do?' I remember thinking about the Peace Corps, but then I just sat on it and thought about it. Then I just did it. It was there and I just thought that was my time to take it."

"Were you at all scared?"

"I wasn't scared, I was excited."

"What about school loans?"

Oh, the loans. Most of us coming out of college these days owe tens of thousands of dollars. College debt is the new American way, the acknowledged price we pay to participate in an increasingly competitive and global job market. For many younger Americans the anxiety associated with college debt (particularly falling behind on monthly installments) is so draining, so mortifying, that they end up either putting their goals on the back burner or avoiding their obligations altogether. But for Kara, loans or not, she was going.

"I was like, *Loans?* That was the last thing on my mind. I had already had to defer them because I was in graduate school. I couldn't afford to pay them for four years. I know I'm paying a helluva lot of interest, but that experience that I had has been incredible. You can't even put a price tag on that. Those loans will be there." Here, Kara adds what might easily be interpreted as the bittersweet laughter of the inevitable: "You can always defer them. I had my bills so what I did with every paycheck was put a certain amount on my credit cards because I was that passionate about going. I was able to pay my bills down and I left. That's how simple it is. Defer your loans. Pay your debts. Get up and get out."

Certainly, if you're passionate enough about turning a dream into reality, you can make every sacrifice imaginable to make that happen. In a relatively free and open society such as ours, we have that luxury. But even a plan as foolproof as Kara's could've suddenly combusted without the unequivocal support of her parents. Her mother and father, a longtime social worker and police officer, respectively, were behind her all the way. From working-class stock themselves ("they shared shoes and wore hand-me-downs," she says), her parents made it their business to instill in Kara and her siblings a sense of moral obligation to those less fortunate.

"Both of them used to tell us we needed to help other people out, and that's something that I really agree with because I don't think my life has been completely . . ." She pauses to gather the right words here: "It hasn't been too difficult."

I like this about Kara, her honesty. She doesn't mince words, even when it comes to her own privileged background. Her parents' generation's struggle for equality is not the same as her struggle for clarity. That battle has been fought and while there is still work to be done, Kara is honest enough to see that her life has been, by most standards anywhere in the world, pretty good. What troubles me as an American, and only incidentally as an African-American, is our national obsession with identity politics. We are perpetually engaged in a game of one-upmanship when it comes to who's had it worse in America, yet the reality is that we all have it better, materially speaking, than just about everyone else in the world.

Kara was given three choices for where she wanted to be stationed for her two-year commitment. She could've chosen a location on just about any continent, but she picked Latin America. "I wanted to learn Spanish," she says. As her backups she chose Africa, then the Caribbean. "After that, based on my skills, they placed me in the Dominican Republic. I went as a community education provider."

But before Kara was sent to her work site, she was placed with a host family for three months in a community of roughly 140 people. There was only one working phone, and to get to town Kara had to take a forty-five-minute motorcycle ride. Fortunately, her host family made her feel right at home.

"There were so many similarities. It was just like being with family. They were like, 'If you're hungry, have whatever you want, let me know.' I could say to them, 'Oh, I'm hungry' and I'd have food right in front of me in like five seconds. You could go to anybody's door and they'd let you in and feed you. Not like if you were just some stranger off the street, but as if they knew you and you were a little hungry, they'd fix you something. They were very hospitable, really nice people."

In fact, the people were so nice that they would sometimes stop by to see Kara, unannounced. They'd ask if she knew Michael Jackson and Mike Tyson. They wanted to hear about life in "Nueva York," even though she explained that she was from Maryland. There was also a young girl in the house who was enamored with the guest from America. "She wanted to be in my room or just around me all of the time. It was like having a little sister." Other kids would throw rocks at her door to get her to come out. When Kara opened the door they would beg her for money, for they were under the impression that she was rich, and by their standards she was. What no one seemed to understand was that sometimes she just wanted to be alone. "That's a very American concept, so it was hard for the people to understand that. I had to think of ways to get around that."

In the beginning, there were also times when she wanted to speak English with someone who could understand what she was going through. But since the closest volunteer was forty-five minutes away, she chose to focus her energies on learning the language and the culture as quickly as she could. "I tried to be like them as much as possible. I stopped wearing short skirts. I wore jeans and slacks when I was there. I tried not to stick out too much."

Years later Kara sees that time as a purifying process. She had to cleanse certain elements of herself before she could go out and help others. "I learned a lot of things that I liked about myself and a lot of things I didn't like about myself," she says of those early days.

"For instance?"

"Like my lack of patience. I still have some problems with that sometimes, but I had to step away from that when I was there. The initial isolation prepared me for what was to come."

Kara's first test came two weeks into her stay. She was given a weekend assignment to go out and find another volunteer. Not only that, she had to find a way to get to the volunteer's village without any guidance. She couldn't log on to MapQuest and download the directions. There weren't any addresses, let alone zip codes, and her Spanish was terrible at the time. Kara was a ball of nerves the morning the father of her host family took her to the bus station. He got her a ticket and made sure she was safely on board. Then Kara was on her own. Once she got off the bus, she found a place to sit down and just looked around for a while. Overwhelmed, she asked herself if she'd made the right decision in coming to this foreign place. But then Kara pulled herself together. "I got out there and said to myself, 'Well, either you can sit over here and stare or go out there and find her.'" And that's exactly what Kara did.

Nothing, though, could've prepared Kara for Hurricane Georges. The cyclone hit shortly after she moved to her work site. The entire village sought refuge in the community's lone cement building where she watched her home crumble to the ground. For days, she was unable to contact her parents to let them know she was all right. Even when she did manage to make her way to the city, she discovered only ruins. The streets were filled with the bewildered and bedraggled. The electricity, which was unreliable anyway, was out. The phone lines were down. No one knew what was going on. Kara felt helpless, a little scared, and numbed by the sight of such pandemonium.

She looks back on it as yet another experience that she wouldn't trade for the world. By living through Hurricane Georges, sticking it out when her safety was certainly at issue, she gained a better sense of her resiliency and purpose.

"Once you go through something like that it just changes you, in a good way. It gives you a lot more confidence. Now I'll go anywhere in a country and not even care, not even think twice about it."

As a community education provider, Kara was assigned to work with deaf children at a community school. The job was disheartening at the outset because parents and teachers alike had all but written the kids off due to their disability. She came in with a fresh perspective and a sense of hope for them, though. After watching for a time, Kara began speaking with the teachers about differentiating their methods of instruction. Writing on a chalkboard and expecting the students to miraculously absorb the lessons obviously wasn't working, so she created her own set of materials and worked directly with the students. Kara also did AIDS outreach, environmental workshops, and character-building workshops.

As I listen to Kara's stories, I can't help but note how all of her projects had a similar proselytizing bent. Her character-building workshops taught children how to be responsible citizens. Her environmental workshops were mainly puppet shows that taught the importance of keeping the environment clean. The AIDS outreach project was basically Kara passing out condoms and pamphlets on safe sex. If there's ever been an argument against liberal institutions like the Peace Corps, it's that while they do good work, they also apply hypocritical standards of morality abroad that aren't even practiced at home.

I wait for Kara to finish, then I ask her, "Did you ever feel conflicted about your Americanness?"

There was one area in particular Kara felt uncomfortable with. "With our program they wanted us to teach an English class. I didn't feel like imposing my American values on them so I just didn't do it. I did not do it! I was like 'Why?' If they wanted to learn English they could come to me and ask me. I wasn't teaching a class, imposing myself on these people. I was trying to learn myself."

Many of the people Kara came in contact with in the communities she worked in, particularly those living in rural parts of the Dominican Republic, thought Americans only came in white. When she told them that she was from America they didn't believe her. They thought for sure she was one of them, until she opened her mouth and started speaking her broken Spanish. There was also the common (in communities of color at least) good hair/bad hair squabble, and a class system based on skin color. The lighter-skinned Dominicans lived in the cities and had far more resources. They were featured in soap operas, delivered the news, and held positions of political authority. Kara even found herself on the receiving end of this discrimination when she was turned away from a club one evening. The bouncers at the door said they didn't have any more space. But a few moments later a fair-skinned group came to the door and they were promptly admitted.

Kara was eventually allowed in after one of her friends came out to get her, but that experience stayed with her, left a bad taste in her mouth. "You leave the States to get away from that and people that look like you act like you're beneath them." Even now the mere mention of those experiences disturbs her otherwise calm demeanor. Her voice rises a pair of octaves and words she hasn't used to describe even the most uncomfortable living conditions abroad spring from her mouth. By taking action, though, whether it was putting up signs that read "All Hair Is Good" in Spanish, putting on environmental workshops, or teaching Dominicans to have tolerance for their darker Haitian island-mates, Kara showed the people she worked with, young and old, how to look beneath the surface of things in order to make better and more informed decisions about the world. Moreover, by choosing to live and work in a setting that was steeped in the kinds of race and class discrimination issues that are all too familiar to Americans, she helped dispel myths about blacks, about women, and about Americans.

When Kara returned to the United States she picked up right where she had left off. She finished her graduate studies immediately and is now a child therapist. She works mostly with minority families who come to her through Social Services. Kara also works part-time as a family development specialist. "Families come in and talk to me about any problems they might be having and I'll just refer them to resources because they're usually not aware of what's out there for them." Before she went away, she thought about getting a Ph.D. in psychology and opening a bilingual practice. Since returning, she's reconsidered that plan. Abroad, Kara realized that she didn't need a doctorate to help people. Of course, she still may go back to school somewhere down the line, but for now, what's most important is that she's doing work that matters. "I learned in the Dominican Republic that I wanted to devote my life to helping people. It means a lot to me to know that something I've done has benefited someone else. Doing humanitarian work makes my reason for being here that much better."

Our waiter has long since taken our food away. The rainy afternoon has cleared a bit and the anonymous city bustle is back in full swing. In a few minutes I'll be on a train heading for another interview with another ex–Peace Corps volunteer who's not nearly as adjusted to life back in the States as Kara is. While I wait for her to return from the restroom I review my notes. On my pad I had written the words "60% Rule." When Kara was still mulling the Peace Corps, still in school, and still unclear about the direction she wanted to go in, her mother, who had once applied to the Peace Corps, too, had said to her, "If you're sixty percent sure about something, do it, because you don't want to go through life having regrets."

When Kara returns from the ladies' room I mention this again.

"I go through life thinking about that," she says. "She's right. You don't want to look back thinking you should have done this or you should have done that. When I made my decision to go to the Peace Corps I was about sixty-five percent sure about it, so I decided to go ahead and do it."

"And?"

"And I'm really glad I made that decision."

Weeks after our conversation, I find myself thinking about Kara Mitchell and about how each of us had been looking for someone else in Starbucks that afternoon. The truth is that there is a certain strain of truth in most stereotypes; they wouldn't endure otherwise. I assumed Kara wasn't an ex–Peace Corps volunteer because she looked too fashionable, too in vogue, and because most Americans I know who work in the Third World are just the opposite. One of the things that Kara made very clear to me throughout our conversation, however, was that she is an "ex"–Peace Corps member. The Peace Corps is something she did at a particular moment in her life. There was never a point at which she seriously considered devoting her life to third-world humanitarian work. What she wanted was the "experience" of living in a different place at a time when she would've been in graduate school or working a low-wage job anyway. Younger Americans in general are often criticized for seeking their own ethnic enrichment in the poorest quarters of the world, and returning to the United States once they've seen enough, things get too rough, or they're ready to deal with the "real world." But when you consider the good work people like Kara have done abroad and the global awareness they bring back with them to the United States, it makes you wonder if even an ugly word like "stereotype" doesn't have its virtues, too.

Bridging the Gap

Gabriel "Asheru" Benn: Hip-Hop Artist/Educator

> "You're not going to read me coming. You can think I'm this, you can think I'm that; but once we sit down and build, whether we're talking about education or hip-hop, you'll see a brother is certified."

How cool would it be if your teacher was a rapper? If he came to class on Monday mornings and told you about the show in London over the weekend, or the fans in Finland who begged him to stay an extra week? How he turned them down because he had classes to teach, students depending on him? Well, the students in Gabriel Benn's class had a hard time believing their teacher was also a hip-hop artist.

At first, Gabriel casually dismissed his students' reaction to him, assuming that was a result of the mythology of fame and wealth surrounding the culture of hip-hop. According to the adolescent's hip-hop lexicon, rappers are big-willies, ballers, playas, dons, ghetto princes, and the like. They wear expensive chains and fresh-dipped gear. They drive tricked-out cars and (according to their videos at least) party all day and night. They certainly aren't holders of college degrees who drive eight-year-old midsize sedans with a car seat in the back. (And while on this day Gabriel happens to be sporting an orange hoody, baggy jeans, and Timberlands, you can be sure he won't be walking into class like that on Monday morning.) Like most kids influenced by the lure of pop-culture iconography, Mr. Benn's students had no clue how the music industry really works. That's part of the reason why Gabriel is in the school system. He wants to be the teacher who provokes his students to think critically and analytically about the world so that they can transform their material circumstances. He explained to his students that teaching isn't some side gig he does just to make ends meet, it's just as important to him as being an artist, it's what he feels he's "supposed to be doing." But even after this heartfelt appeal, Gabriel noticed that his students continued to look at him with an incredulous eye, as if to say, "There has to be some catch." After all, they're in "special ed," so obviously no one really cares about their education, certainly not someone they might look up to.

"They wondered why I even bothered with them," Gabriel says. "They were like, 'Why you messin' with us? There's retarded kids in here. You could be out there ridin' on twenties. You could be out there *really* rhyming and stuff.'" He lets go a hearty chuckle on this point: What does it mean to be "really rhyming and stuff"?

Does it mean rocking shows? He's done that.

Does it mean touring the country? He's done that.

Does it mean traveling overseas, performing with name artists, cutting an LP? He's done all of that.

Like any rapper worth his salt, Gabriel has had his share of what he likes to call "hip-hop moments," timeless reminders of why he fell in love with the music in the first place, why he became an artist, why he still chases his own dreams.

"I got a coupla stories about being out on the road," he says, folding his arms around his stomach. He's a big guy, stocky and tall, a lineman or an end, with dark brown skin and the gravelly beginnings of smoker's voice. "There was this one joint we did out in Oberhausen with ED O.G., J-Live, and Lone Catalysts. We got out there and it was packed. It was this little town in Germany and the crowd was just charged. There was a whole bunch of white Germans, but half of them spoke English. We was in there and the house was packed and we just rocked the joint for like two and a half hours. When we got off stage we was selling T-shirts." Gabe's excitement is just about to bubble over when he pauses long enough to take a breath. Then he shakes his head as if to say whatever words he can conjure for me won't be enough to put me there. He starts again anyway: "It was just so much shit going on in that one city. You walk around that area and you see cats rhyming in the cipher, rhyming in straight German. I didn't understand a word, but you hear people screaming. That's when you know this rap thing has transcended. I went back to my room and I was like, 'This shit is real. This is some real live shit!' "

There's a similar story about Denmark, and another about London. The trip to Amsterdam, Gabe says, was particularly memorable. "You're out there for two reasons. Because Amsterdam is Amsterdam." He stops long enough for me to catch his drift and we share a knowing laugh. "Then you're doing shows that are sold out on top of that." The Amsterdam show was with artists like Common, Jill Scott, and Bilal, to name a few. "That was just another ill-moment. I don't even sleep after nights like that. I'm just laid out, dozing but not really fully asleep."

> "Without getting all deep and philosophical,
> We creatin' a space where anything is possible."
> —GABRIEL "ASHERU" BENN, "Truly Unique"

Like most hip-hop artists, Gabe has a crew, a group of his boys to whom he would give the shirt off his back and vice versa. In one way or another, they are all loosely related to his rap group, Unspoken Heard. They travel to the shows as security and support. They stop by studio sessions and lend their voices for background vocals. If he needs a beat to rhyme over, and one of his friends has one, they'll give it to him. ("They're not trip-

pin' off the money," he says. "They just want to get it done.")
So naturally when Gabriel and I need somewhere to talk on a
damp Sunday afternoon, all he has to do is get on the horn and
five minutes later we're at a friend's front door.

But what distinguishes Gabe's crew is the source of their connection. Instead of growing up together on steely city streets,
they found each other on the campus of a southern university.
"We all went to the University of Virginia," says Gabe. What
drew them together was their reverence for classic b-boy hip-
hop by artists like Public Enemy, Big Daddy Kane, KRS-1, Eric
B & Rakim, Jungle Brothers, De La Soul, and Tribe Called
Quest.

"What is a b-boy anyway?" I ask.

"B-boys are people who know how to flip whatever they
have and make it better."

After graduation the crew went their separate ways. They
went off to become doctors, lawyers, writers—one even became
a psychologist. But one, Wes Jackson, started his own record label. "He approached me and another brother to be his first
artists on his label. That was how we started the Unspoken
Heard. Prior to that I was doing a lot of spoken word and
rhyming with a few other guys and live bands. I was doing that
maybe a year, two years. I was recording demos. I wasn't taking
it that seriously, but I was taking an interest in it. Once he started
the label we took it seriously. After we saw how people were responding to our music, the opportunities started opening up as
far as traveling, doing gigs. We've been doing it ever since."

Traveling with his closest friends, forming alliances with
other artists, eating and sleeping on someone else's dime on the
strength of what he's written with a pen and pad, that's what
Gabe calls the "love part," the "pay." "The hate part is when
you start arguing over stuff like money. Stuff you never argued
over before. It kind of messes with you." There's also the pres-

sure of the different careers and emerging families. Last year Gabriel had his first child during a period in which he could have been out on the road promoting his album.

"When my son was born I was like, 'I ain't goin' nowhere.' I needed to hold it down for a minute and get the family straight. That was a decision I made." The decision was a difficult one, and although he doesn't explicitly say as much, it caused a rift in the relationship with his longtime friends. Nevertheless, when you consider how important Gabe's friends have been in shaping his creative identity, his decision to be with his family illustrates the kind of person he is. In fact, that quality of character underlies everything from his lyrics to his approach to teaching.

"I want my kids to look to me as a person who cares about them. I always tell them I ain't their friend. I'm not. I'm Mr. Benn." Mr. Benn keeps in touch with his students' families and makes sure they're doing their work, even though he's not a stickler about homework. "I understand a lot of them go through a lot of stuff at home," he says, acknowledging a domestic reality many teachers and administrators often fail to take account of when dealing with inner-city students. Because his students often face the pressures of gangs, sex, drugs, and money, Mr. Benn also lets them know his door is always open. If they ever need to talk, he says, they can count on his honest opinion no matter what.

"They know I'm going to shoot the straight shit with them. I'm not going to hold my tongue. I have all boys. My school chose to give me all boys, so I have six of them in my room who I've been with all year. We go out and do field trips, all that stuff. I'm like the one constant for these kids. *I'm* their constant. They're going to always see me every day. I'm not going to just up and be like 'I just got signed to Def Jam, yo! I'm out! Holla!!'" A phlegmy laugh suddenly explodes from his lungs followed by a shaking of his head: "That ain't gonna be me."

The way Gabe punctuates his sense of obligation to his students causes me to think about my own middle schoolers, who, whenever I miss a day of school, don't hesitate to give me grief about it.

"Why you left us yesterday, Mr. Ross?"

"I didn't leave you. I wasn't feeling well."

"You was fine when you left two days ago."

"I'm not allowed to be sick."

"Whatever, Mr. Ross, you just wanted a day away from us."

Sometimes they're right on. Teaching isn't like going into an office every day. You can't sip that cup of coffee until nine-thirty. You can't check your e-mail until ten. There are no bathroom breaks in the middle of class. And long lunches are out of the question. Walking into a classroom is like stepping into free-fall, every day. You have no idea what happened to your kids the night before or on the way to school, or even in the hallway. All you know is that whatever it is, they're going to bring it with them into the room and you're going to have to deal with it.

Even Gabriel, despite his rapport with his students, acknowledges that teaching is a daily grind. Besides the home-life issues (overworked parents, single parents, parents who lack the skills themselves, poor nutrition, lack of space) teachers confront on a daily basis, kids are simply different from even today's twenty- and thirty-somethings. From the moment they're born they experience the world almost exclusively through a screen, be it television, computer, or film. What they get is a constant flow of stimulation and gratification. When something doesn't hold their interest, they have the power to click it, flick it, or tune it out, and find something else that does. In short, they are the on-demand generation.

All of these changes make it next to impossible for a teacher to hold a class's attention using the standard method of instruction. Standing in front of the class and lecturing for an hour simply won't cut it. They'll resist and act out. They'll disrupt class and make your life miserable, and it's all their way of demanding an education that speaks to their lives. In recent years, educrats east and west have dumped money into curriculum design in the hopes of finding a way to get kids to learn. Some plans are downright awful. Some have a few good ideas worth salvaging. Very few, however, have figured out how to harness the power of hip-hop and spoken word the way Gabriel thinks he has with Project NOMMO, his creative writing/exposure program.

"NOMMO is the power of the spoken word, taking a thought and putting it into action," he explains.

Back in 1999, while taking a year off from teaching to finish his album, Gabriel came up with the idea for a classroom curriculum. His thinking at the time was that by teaching kids to be more socially constructive and analytical, they could better navigate the system. "We use hip-hop. We use contemporary writers and poets. We use visual media like video, films, and dance. It's based off of this cat Howard Gardner's theory of multiple intelligences, where he says there are seven intelligences everyone operates on. Everyone has their own niche, their own thing that they do better than others. It's basically about identifying where a student's strengths lie and putting them through a program adapted to their strengths." What made Gabriel's program particularly unique was that it was targeted specifically to special education students. "The special education population is ninety percent black. Kids are getting thrown in special education just because they might be bad in class, just because they're hard to control."

From the outset people thought the idea was innovative. They just weren't willing to stake their careers on a project by a twenty-five-year-old without a track record or the proper string of letters behind his name. If that's the way the game had to be played, Gabe thought, then he'd go back to school to get the proper credentials. He believed in Project NOMMO that much. That was two and a half years ago. Now he's less than a year away from earning his degree in curriculum administration from George Washington University.

"Once I get out there with the program I've developed and I've got those letters behind my name, it's a different ball game than when I was saying it three years ago. I realized that's what I had to do to get that respect, so that's what I'm doing. And then when you walking in those circles and people are like, 'You have an album out? Wow! Can I hear it?' I'm talking forty-year-old white ladies. They'll come back to me and be like, 'I let my son hear it. I think he's heard of you guys. He likes it.'"

Gabriel, Gabe, Mr. Benn, Asheru—he gets a rush from surprising people with his arsenal of identities. He likes having separate worlds in which he can successfully operate, and he doesn't want to give any of them up. "Right now, my whole goal is to fuse hip-hop and education. I want to continue putting out albums, doing songs, collaborating with artists around the country. But then the end goal is also to shop this program so that we can have artists come into the schools and work with kids directly. I think it will give the artists more of a purpose and give the kids direction."

Gabe isn't alone in thinking artists, and others from various career backgrounds, may be at least one other solution to the problems facing public education. In the last few years school systems across the country have been instituting fellowship programs designed to attract creative individuals from other walks of life to the teaching profession. The hope is that these teachers, most of whom are in their twenties and early thirties, will resuscitate the classroom environment by bringing fresh ideas and energetic bodies. "You got all these kids running around singing whole Lil Kim songs, knowing all the words and they're like six years old. Some of them can't even spell the word 'cat.' People see that and they're like, 'C'mon, something's got to give. I think that's what's getting people to want to reach out and feel like they're being productive, feel like even though they're striving artists, they're doing stuff even when there's down time."

"Striving artist?" I repeat. "I've never heard that one before."

"I use the word 'striving' instead of 'struggling' because it might be hard, but brothers and sisters just have to strive through. It wasn't like I was ever desperate. I'm definitely grateful. Bottom line is, you got to strive."

> "I rock for skaters and thugs,
> Corporate account holders who say they
> Up in the club,
> Students who go to school
> Frustrated as hell,
> Parents who do their best
> To keep you up outa jail,
> Critics, cynics and mimics
> All the rest in between
> That hate to see a brother
> Mix intelligence with C.R.E.A.M.
>   That mean
> We either pro-black and conscious
> Or bankrolled up kicking
> Nothing but that nonsense
> But imagine a brother like Ash going out like that. . . ."
>
>   "Truly Unique"

While Gabriel waits for his curriculum to be accepted and Asheru strives as an artist, Mr. Benn teaches the seven principles of Kwanzaa to his middle schoolers. To introduce his students to the concept of Mia, meaning purpose, he played a song by the hip-hop group Blackalicious. After that, he had them write out a mission statement. "At the top of the page they wrote, 'Mia equals Purpose.' Below that they wrote out the statement, 'In my lifetime I will strive to be . . .' Below that they wrote stuff they wanted to be. They were writing stuff like doctor, football player, veterinarian, all kinds of stuff. Then they had to write what they would do to achieve their goals."

Much like when he talks about his "hip-hop moments," Gabriel's grizzly voice bristles with excitement as he relays stories about his students. Unlike many teachers, Gabe has been able to successfully bring hip-hop to the classroom; unlike many rappers, he's been able to bring his intellect to the page and stage. However, it's by bridging those passions to create an educational program that uses hip-hop that Gabriel may be making his most significant contribution to the success of the next generation.

Postscript: A little more than a year after we last spoke I called Gabe to see how he was progressing. I could hear kids in the background when he picked up the phone. The major record label still hadn't come knocking on his door, nor had the school system that wanted to buy Project NOMMO for a couple of million bucks. On the other hand, he'd finished his degree and the school where he'd been teaching for the last few years was now allowing him to pilot his project. "I got turntables in my classroom," he said, laughing. Among other things, he was teaching the kids how to use studio equipment and how to make their own beats. He'd also just returned from a three-week European tour where he sold a bunch of records and rocked a few houses. And in addition to that, he was in the studio recording his first solo LP. Gabe hadn't yet made it to where he wanted to be, but he was certainly still striving.

BLACK EXODUS

On Friday evenings a group of men meet at Tannie Stoval's apartment for wine and thoughtful discussions on literature, film, and politics. Democracy in Africa, corruption in the French government, and the generation rift between African-Americans are all particularly contentious topics. The conversations get heated, but never nasty, certainly not physical. Not with this group of expatriates. Tannie, the elder statesman, is the group's acknowledged leader. A scientist with a doctorate from the University of Minnesota, Stoval came to Paris in the early 1960s after accepting a position with the French government. Tony Clarke, a choreographer originally from New Jersey, is the other elder, having landed on French soil in 1969 with little more than the gleam in his nineteen-year-old eyes. They are the only two in the group who left the United States principally because of racism. Jake Lamar, Zachary Miller, and Darrell Moore, who spends half the year in Paris and the other half teaching in the philosophy department at DePaul University, are here because of love. Literally. Jake and Zachary are both married to French citizens and Darrell, though not married to his partner, shares an apartment with him.

These weekly conversations have been going on in one form or another for close to a decade. They began after the Million Man March as a small gathering of "brothers" living in the City of Light, and they quickly evolved into something of an event. Back then, each Sunday evening the African-American men living in Paris would gather at Tannie's for a feast. The one rule (besides the fact that you had to black, male, and American) was that you couldn't bring food. You could, however, bring a decent bottle of wine. At their height, the get-togethers attracted dozens and were so renowned that a Paris television station wanted to film a series about them.

Not only are Friday evenings at Tannie's a way for these men to feel connected to one another, they are a way for them to feel connected to black America. If you were to listen to them talk about the race between George Bush and John Kerry, you'd think they were going to have to live under the next administration for the next four years when in fact, besides Darrell, none of them has even been on U.S. soil since 9/11.

There are two factors at work here, both of which explain to some degree why their connection to black America endures despite the distance and the time. First, while most of them are French citizens, they are black naturalized citizens, which means their role in French politics is marginal at best. Second, they weren't looking to sever all ties with America when they moved abroad. They still have families and friends living in the United States. Moreover, they recognize the inescapability of their heritage. They've all read Baldwin and Wright and Himes, so they know being American is as much a state of mind as it is a state of being.

Invisible Presence

Monique Welles: Travel Guide/Veterinarian

"You're reflected in a different mirror here and it's so liberating and it bolsters one's confidence, one's sense of self-worth."

When I boarded the American Airlines plane bound for Europe, the only interview I had lined up was with Monique Welles. After I'd read an online article she'd written about her boutique travel firm, DiscoverParis, I'd sent her an e-mail just to introduce myself and the book. Not a day later she sent me a reply saying both that she was highly interested, and that she might be able to introduce me to other expats in Europe. I booked my flight just days later. The rest, I figured, would take care of itself.

Monique has been living in Paris for the past twelve years. She originally came over to work for a pharmaceutical company as a veterinary pathologist, now she does work on a consultancy basis. Depending on the company's line of business, Monique's job can range from evaluating animal tissue to understanding the causes of death, to evaluating the same tissue to understand the way an animal reacts to various chemicals before human beings are exposed to them. She'd studied French from her prekindergarten years in Houston all the way through college where she minored in the language. Her plan had always been to live abroad, if only for the experience, but gaining her French citizenship came as a surprise even to her.

The night I arrive in Paris I meet Monique, along with her husband, Tom, for dinner at a French restaurant in Paris's Latin

Quarter. Monique and Tom met more than a dozen years ago while they were both taking French courses in northern California. At the time, Monique wasn't looking to get involved with anyone—she preferred being alone. She'd grown up that way, and by adulthood she found her career and her quiet life of reading, writing, and contemplation stimulating enough. Besides, the thought of waking up next to the same person every day for the rest of her life didn't appeal to her. But then along came Tom.

They make for an interesting pair. Monique's the talker, Tom's the observer. She's a go-getter, he's laid-back. Tom is also noticeably older than Monique, who's in her early forties. He was married previously and has children who are adults themselves. He's also white. But Tom shares Monique's passion for French language and culture, and he was willing to take chances with his life. Their personalized travel company, DiscoverParis, was originally Tom's idea. Monique was the one who decided it should be aimed specifically at African-Americans. The basic concept, however, originated after the couple took a personalized tour of Italy.

"It was the first time I'd ever heard of such a thing. The company asked us, 'Okay you're going to Italy, so what do you want to do?' I said, 'I don't want to see any museums, I've had enough of those.' I said, 'I want to eat well and I want to see how the natives live so you plan a vacation for me like that. I don't want to be with a bunch of tourists. Take me on the back roads. Just take me where regular citizens are doing what they do every day and I just want to walk around and watch.' [The agent] planned what for me was the best vacation I've ever been on in my life. It was eleven days; we did three cities. We did Venice, Florence, and Rome. She gave us oodles of restaurant recommendations on the walks we did every day. She would give us tidbits of information, oddities that you'll see as you walk along. Your average tourist wouldn't even care, but that was the Italy I wanted to see and it was perfect."

Back in Paris, the couple got to thinking and researching. They found out there weren't any other businesses that catered specifically to people like them, people who wanted to explore on their own but who didn't necessarily want to be lost all day either. There certainly weren't any companies catering to African-Americans traveling to Paris. By then, Monique had been living in the city long enough to observe and somewhat understand her adopted countrywomen and men:

"French people want you to integrate. They don't care what color you are. They want you to embrace French things, Frenchness, France." As an example, Monique points to the intermixed Asian community down in the lower 13th arrondissement. Monique says Parisians frown upon that kind of self-segregation. Paradoxically, she says, Parisians let you be. "They're not worried about you. In some sense, they don't care about you. It's the antithesis of being a black person in America. You know, wherever you go, whatever you do, the first thing that someone is going to see is that you're a black person and everything else is going to be predicated on that. For French people you're almost invisible, so you can kind of create your own world."

So, if on the one hand, according to Monique at least, Parisians want you to fit in, while you're also supposed to create your own world, what you're left with is a very fine line to toe, and an enormous opportunity for hypocrisy. Nevertheless, it's still arguably a fairer bargain than the one African-Americans enter into at home. In Paris, you buy into a way of life that celebrates culture and leisure, conversation and contemplation, all on a daily basis, and as ends in themselves. In America, those same activities are largely the province of a privileged minority. As far as the vast majority of Americans are concerned, culture and leisure are weekend affairs, if that, while in the face of the daily grind conversation and contemplation are even rarer finds. When the rest of us do get a chance to break away from our routines for a week or two, we expect to have something material to show ourselves (and each other) upon our return.

Given these conditions it's little wonder that for Monique the most demanding part of marketing DiscoverParis has been convincing African-Americans who travel to Paris that there is something wonderful and unique about their relationship to the French capital, but that they may not be able to wrap it up and take it home with them. "It's a spirit," Monique says. "It's not in physical things. I tell people there are four or five physical representations of African-Americans and they're not likenesses, they are words. There's a plaque here, there's a sign there. You have to have somebody who can tell you what happened in such and such a neighborhood at what time. In that sense, it's difficult. People want to come to Paris and they want to see an African-American—they want to be able to just check things off. They want to be able to say, 'I saw this and I saw that,' and that's not the way it is. It's subtle. You have to be ready to exercise your intellect a little bit in order to appreciate it."

The Luxembourg Garden is a perfect example of what Monique means. There's an apiary there, a man-made orchard, and the French senate is housed in an old palace within its confines. Also the garden where Richard Wright used to sit and think, where Chester Himes used to pass from his hotel in Orleans to the cafés along Montparnasse each day. Unless you have your own prior knowledge of these facts or someone like Monique to guide you, you won't know any of this. You'll certainly feel something refreshing and relaxing, but just imagine if you could picture yourself a half century past coming from a completely hostile society to a place where you could simply

"be." That's when the experience takes on a profoundly different shape.

One of Monique's favorite places to visit is 51 rue Geoffroy-
Saint-Hilaire. The second-story flat was once the home of the
Nardal sisters, a pair of women who played a significant role in
the Negritude movement of the 1930s. Remembered as a kind
of Transatlantic twin to the Harlem Renaissance's assertion of
black creativity and thought, the movement was comprised of
young poets from the French West Indies like Aime Cesaire
along with future statesmen like Leopold Senghor, the first president of independent Senegal, while embracing the likes of
American writers Claude McKay, Langston Hughes, and Coun-
tee Cullen. The Nardal sisters, intellectuals and artists in their
own right, hosted a weekly salon at the apartment that brought
together the whole African diaspora, and featured music, discussion, and dance.

"If you know the history you walk through there and you
just feel there were great minds in here and they were revolu-
tionizing black thought," Monique says. "I always just like going over there and feeling something. You're reflected in a
different mirror here and it's so liberating and it bolsters one's
confidence, one's sense of self-worth. I don't [think] I've ever
been a person without self-worth, but I can just see so many
things appreciated so differently here. Regardless of what anybody says, you always appreciate being appreciated by others."

The trouble, says Monique, is that African-American visitors
to Paris tend to want to see a museum celebrating African-
Americans, a neighborhood in which blacks live and congregate,
or a monument of some sort commemorating their effect on
the life of the city, when the fact of the matter is you may go
days, weeks, without seeing other African-Americans. And
when you do see another black face, you can't always assume

they come from the same experience, or that they'll speak to you because of your familiar skin color. While it's true that most of the African-Americans here know *of* one another, they all don't live in one area, they don't worship at the same church, and there isn't a place they all meet up except at the annual Black History Month events sponsored by the American embassy. Even at the jazz and hip-hop clubs there's no telling who will show up on what night.

"One of the things I know about the African-American traveler in general," Monique explains, choosing her words carefully, "is that regardless of where he or she is going, the traveler wants to see other black people, and if they don't, they don't feel comfortable. Well, in Paris, you can see black people, but the black people you're going to see on the streets are going to be usually from the French Antilles, or they're going to be African, and they're not going to care that you're a black person. They're not going to smile at you and come up to you because you're black. This is what I hear over and over again and I'm like 'No, you come here, it's for you. This is not for you to be with other people, this is your experience.'

"What I would like for people to understand is that they really don't have to be afraid on their own. They don't have to travel with a group to be able to appreciate this city. I firmly believe that it is best appreciated on your own. We're a customized travel planning service. We will do whatever it is you want. Really. But we are encouraging you to get out there, walk the streets, look at the things up close, don't drive by in a car. People ask me why I like Paris. To begin with I say one of the reasons is because I can walk everywhere and I'm in touch with my environment. I'm not in a car with the windows rolled up and the radio going. I see, I smell, and when I see something, unless I'm rushing somewhere, I can stop, I can take a note, I can come back. This is what seeing this city and appreciating this city is about. Every day I discover something."

I found out what Monique meant about Paris being a place where one has one's own experience over the next two weeks. Early on, when I found myself excluded from the language and the culture, I felt frustrated, homesick, lonely, even angry. After a morning of writing, I'd spend long, uninterrupted afternoons observing life outside of the cafés, walking along the Seine, or reading at the foot of the Eiffel Tower. I routinely took my meals alone, and twice I went to the movies by myself. One night I sat in my hotel room with Chinese takeout wondering why I'd even come at all.

Over the course of those first few days, I became aware of how much of my identity had been formed in opposition to racism. I had grown so accustomed to seeing myself through the eyes of white America and defining myself against its stereotypes that when I found myself in a place where race wasn't such a polarizing issue, I had to ask myself who I was independent of my race. Ultimately, I wondered if I was really ready to relinquish my racial identity and all of the drama that came with it to become just another human being on the street as I was in Paris. I asked myself if being black meant far more to me than I ever imagined or acknowledged. And I questioned whether, perhaps, I wanted it both ways, meaning to stand out from the crowd because of my race, and to be regarded as the same as everyone else in spite of my race.

Had I not met Monique so early in my stay, Paris might've been a major letdown. I might've spent fourteen days walking and watching and wondering. But since I did meet her and she had told me what to expect of Parisians, rather than wait for the city to embrace me I gradually began to do what was in my power to become a part of its life. Despite my negligible knowledge of French, I took chances with the language. I learned how to take the trains, how to read the maps, and how to ask for directions. And the more I got out of my comfort zone, the more contact I had with people. After that, Paris became a real city rather than the idealized haven for artists and intellectuals and bohemians I had pictured. Those illusions eliminated, what I encountered was a place that has its share of imperfections, but that also values what I value, and what I wish Americans had in greater abundance: the time and space to enjoy life.

All that Glitters Ain't Gold

Jake Lamar: Novelist

> "I thought when I was twenty-five I wouldn't live anywhere [else]; New York was my town. I didn't know I'd find the unfamiliar that exciting."

At first glance, Jake Lamar's life seems charmed. He grew up in New York City in the sixties and seventies, an upper-middle-class kid. His father, a "Morehouse Man" as they like to refer to themselves, operated his own consulting firm while his mother raised Jake and his two siblings, Bert and Felicia. A standout student who showed literary promise from an early age, Jake attended the prominent Fieldston Academy in Riverdale, New York. His college choices came down to Harvard and Brown. He chose Harvard, where he won a position on the school's storied newspaper, *The Crimson*. Four years later—just ten days after graduation—he walked into his first day of work at *Time* magazine, where for the better part of six years he wrote for its "Nation" section. Then, on the cusp of his twenty-eighth birthday, he sold his first book to a major publishing house for an advance healthy enough to quit his fairly lucrative job. By thirty-two, Jake was living and writing in Paris. By forty-three, he was married, still living in Paris, and five books deep in his literary career.

But all of that's just surface, all just the glossy paint on a car with its fair share of faulty wiring under the hood.

Jake came of age in what you might call the John Shaft–Jackson Five era. The war in Vietnam was finally drawing to a close, Nixon had been exposed, and John Lennon's "Imagine" was the world's anthem. Meanwhile, the Establishment was actively seeking out youngsters of Jake's caliber: He came from a good family, he went to "good" schools, he had a rather pleasant, nonthreatening look about him, and he had talent. A new America wanted nothing more than to prove to the world (and itself) that it planned to make good on the promise of affirmative action. In *Bourgeois Blues*, Jake's first book, a memoir about the first twenty-seven years of his life, he recalls a pleasant secretary at *Time* stopping him in the hallway as he left his final interview. "We *want* you to do well here," the woman said, as though she had a moral stake in his success or failure. Jake always saw those kinds of condescending remarks for what they were and did his best not to feed into them.

Over the years Jake had watched his family disintegrate as their father's pursuit of wealth, power, and status consumed him. At bottom, Jacob Lamar Sr. was always looking to prove he was just as good as his white counterparts. By the time Jake Jr. walked through *Time*'s doors, however, he'd already decided that wasn't going to happen to him.

"He's from, 'Shingley, Georgia, population fifteen, including the cows and the chickens,'" says Jake, parodying one of his father's many grandiloquent homages to himself. The drawled impersonation typifies Jake's wit and his penetrating honesty. It also reveals his ambivalent feelings for his father. "To go from that to wheeling and dealing in Manhattan, and in his generation, too—this is someone who grew up in the thirties. He was born in thirty-two. He grew up in the Depression, World War II, the sixties. The civil rights movement was happening as he was starting his career. He worked in city government for a while, for Mayor Lindsay, in the sixties."

From government Jake Sr. climbed into private construction and later consulting. But what he wanted more than anything was to be a tycoon, and for his first son to be the lawyer who handled his affairs. Jake simultaneously admires and is repulsed by his father's dream of leaping out of the "garbage can" into the lap of luxury in a single generation. As his memoir describes in unflinching detail, Jake Lamar Sr. was a difficult man to get along with, to put it mildly. When business was good, he was Daddy Warbucks, flying the family to Hawaii for vacation. When business was bad, he was a maniacal villian who came home reeking of alcohol and in a violent mood. As a kind of placative recourse, Jake fashioned himself into the prototypical dutiful son. "I always wanted my father's approval from the time I was conscious," says Jake. "I went to Harvard because I knew it would make him proud. I had to go to Harvard. There was no question about it. I was that kind of person then. It would have been unacceptable in my own sense of myself if I had not gotten into Harvard."

The only problem was that Jake's father considered writing, the one thing Jake knew he was really good at, a trifling indulgence that he needed to avoid. While Jake was writing film and book reviews for the *Crimson,* his father bemoaned the fact that he would never make a living, never succeed in the world, and ultimately never fulfill the master plan he'd laid out for his boy. Throughout college Jake drifted between his father's rules and his heart until one day toward the end of his senior year his father called and informed him that he had gone bankrupt. Humiliated, Jake Sr. disappeared shortly thereafter. Five years would pass before Jake Jr. would speak to his father again. Of his reaction to that phone call Jake writes in *Bourgeois Blues:*

While my father's financial collapse was, in one sense, a nightmare come true, it was also sort of liberating. Money was the last tangible form of power my father held over me, the threat of financial cutoff the last lever he could pull to get me to do what

he wanted. Now that power was gone; and with it, any notion
I'd ever entertained about going to law school. I could finally
pursue a writing career without opposition.*

Paralleling his shaky relationship with his father was an ambivalence Jake felt for America. Like his father, America had opened
doors for him. But just as his father had, America was suddenly
burdening him with pressures he didn't ask for. In this case,
however, it was the pressure he felt to define himself along the
color line. As a teenager he'd only vaguely encountered racism
at the prep school he attended, but at Harvard, he had developed
a visceral sense of the way race plays out in America.

"I really didn't like it there," Jake casually remarks the afternoon we spent sitting in front of his favorite café in Paris, the
Cépage Montmartrois. His sleepy eyelids and the drifting voice
expose his fatigue even before he tells me he was up until four
A.M. writing. "It was the first thing that I wanted so badly that
turned out to be a kind of disappointment. I never really found
my niche there. I'd always had tons of black friends, but I wasn't
the sort of black guy who only wanted to have black friends.
Harvard was very much like that with the black community, at
least when I was there. The friends I did have were the other
sort of socially fluid people. But I felt much more pressure . . . I
think that's often people's university experience and either you
be a socially fluid person or you just stay with the black folks or
you just stay with the white folks. I found it hard for the first
time in my life. And then there was that other thing that I encountered much more afterward, but at first it was at Harvard:
white condescension. I'm talking about something very subtle,
this insidious kind of thing where they just didn't expect me to
make it and they would talk down to me. And then they would

*Jake Lamar, *Bourgeious Blues* (New York: Plume, 1991), pp. 104–105

realize I was as good as them and then they got hostile. You go from condescension to hostility."

Jake's experience at *Time* began as a continuation of the negative experiences he had at Harvard. But then, shortly after he was hired, he was reassigned from the Editorial section to the Nation section. That was when Jake started to notice the way his pieces were routinely edited to give them a conservative spin. He also noted that he was being given all the "black" assignments. Although he didn't mind writing about race, he did mind the way his stories were either shredded or shelved. In either case, his viewpoints were snuffed out by the magazine's editors who, on hiring him, had assured him *Time* was a "fair and balanced" outfit. After observing things awhile, Jake started wondering if his editors weren't simply using him, the lone black writer in the New York office, as a scapegoat for its racially biased articles.

Jake lasted nearly six years at *Time* before quitting just three months after he sold his first book. But even before the book was published he ran out of money and was forced to move to Ann Arbor, Michigan. Suddenly, he was back in a financial bind. His book came out, and though it received complimentary reviews, it didn't make the best-seller lists. Things got so bad that even the advance for his second book, *The Last Integrationist,* wasn't enough to dig him out of the hole. He needed a miracle.

"I'm sitting down at my kitchen table doing the math, figuring out the first half of the advance, how much it's gonna help me. I was so in debt because I had quit *Time* two and a half years earlier. I had lost all my credit cards. It was devastating. I was doing all my calculations and I was like, 'Damn, I'm still fucked.' I worked so hard on this proposal for this book, but I didn't get as much money as I wanted. I was feeling really hopeless and the telephone rang and this guy's like, 'Hello, is this Jake Lamar, this is Jack Murrah from the Lyndhurst Foundation in Chattanooga, Tennessee.'"

The man gave Jake the whole song and dance about the foundation, about how it gives out prizes to writers every year, how he'd been nominated by a former Harvard professor and how he'd been one of the year's winners. Jake, drowning in his worries and figuring the prize was for at most $5,000, thanked the foundation and was hanging up when the voice on the other end said, "'Oh, but I didn't tell you what the prize is worth.' I was like 'No.' He said, 'It's forty thousand dollars a year for three years.' I didn't believe it. I waited about ten minutes and was like, 'What just happened?' I called back and the secretary said, 'Lyndhurst Foundation,' and I said, 'I just got a call that I'm a prizewinner. I'm just calling to confirm.' And she's like, 'Yes, you really won,' and I hear all these people laugh in the background.

"That changed my life. I got a check in ninety-two, one in ninety-three, and one in ninety-four. [With] the first check I got out of debt. After a second year in Ann Arbor with the second check I came to Paris. The third check allowed me to stay in Paris."

Even now, twelve years later, a plumper and grayer Jake gets giddy when he thinks about that phone call. That he and I are sitting at our tiny table on a hill in Paris is a direct result of that phone call. Before that, he'd never been farther than Canada, let alone considered expatriating. Leaving America just didn't seem like a solution or an option.

"I was thinking in the American box. I was thinking, 'Oh, I can't live outside America. How could I? I come to Paris, it will be a lark, it will be an adventure, but it will have to end because I live in America.' I really did not envision back in 1994 the life I have today. I did not envision being married to a European. I did not envision speaking French. I didn't envision still being able to make a living as a writer. I thought I would have to do something else, teach maybe. That was another thing. I was always thinking I'll go back to the States and get a teaching job. I wasn't imaging getting a ten-year card. I got my *carte de residence* last week, that's a big thing. It's good until 2014. It's like a notch below citizenship."

A resident card is also extremely difficult to acquire. Since the French economy's downturn in the 1970s, foreigners have found it particulary hard to gain legal residence in Paris. Algerians and other immigrants from the African diaspora have been specifically blamed for the country's period of decline. Africans and Muslims in particular have been accused of taking jobs from citizens, overburdening the country's welfare and health-care systems, of committing violent acts, and of not assimilating into the larger culture. Meanwhile, Jake has had a completely different experience.

"Ten years ago it was inconceivable that I would do this; I didn't imagine teaching at a French university, which I have done now. It happens very slowly and very gradually. Just looking at things from a perspective of a different nation, it's just really something. It's opened my mind in a lot of ways."

As far as Jake was concerned, he'd read all of the great twentieth-century African-American literature before he'd even gotten to college. Baldwin, Ellison, and Wright—the holy trinity—had been his favorites. Through them, he was able to see himself as a writer. In order to really understand these particular writers' literary careers, however, one must factor Europe, and specifically Paris, into the equation. Arguably the most celebrated of them all, Richard Wright, lived in Paris the last thirteen years of his life, while James Baldwin migrated across the Atlantic at different junctures in his career. Jake knew these stories well, and was in large measure drawn to Paris because of them. However, it was only after he landed on French soil that he discovered the author that has affected his work more than any of the others: Chester Himes. After arriving in Paris in 1953, Himes wrote a string of popular mystery novels featuring black characters that the French simply adored and American publishers simply ignored. "It's baffling," Jake explains, "but the thing is he's a footnote in America. He's considered a major writer here. He's considered one of the great writers of the twentieth century here." In his book on the history of African-Americans in Paris, *Paris Noir*, Tyler Stoval notes that

> Like Wright, [Himes] came to France as a mature man and established writer, and similarly settled permanently in Europe as a repudiation of American racism. Like Baldwin, he never felt completely comfortable in Paris, remaining a loner and an outsider during his time there. Yet Himes was an original, both as a writer and as an African American expatriate. *To a much greater extent than Wright or Baldwin, he severed his ties with the American literary establishment, publishing many of his works in French translation and living off the royalties paid by French publishing houses, an amazing achievement for a foreign writer.* [Italics added]

The story with Himes was that he wrote a book called *The Long Crusade* that met with such resounding criticism in the United States that he couldn't find a publisher anywhere afterward. Himes's early work explored sexuality and violence between black men and white women in a way neither blacks nor whites were comfortable with. "Himes has the weird humor and this profane quality that just froze him out," Jake adds. The celebrated sociologist E. Franklin Frazier also met with a similar kind of commercial distaste after he completed his scathing social analysis *Black Bourgeoisie* while he was working for UNESCO in Paris. Though the book went on to become a university fixture, it wasn't until two years *after* its publication in France that it was published in the United States. For an African-American writer to leave the States in the forties, fifties, and sixties meant he or she was fed up with a system that relentlessly closed them in. Leaving meant he or she was willing to accept their status as political exiles; moreover, it meant he or she was ready to experience a new way of life.

"I do feel like I'm in a line. I don't think of myself as ever being in anybody's canon, but these guys inspired me and made me want to be a writer, Toni Morrison, too, Lorraine Hansberry, and then all of the white writers who've come before. But just because of who I am these black American writers especially have just meant more than other writers and I do feel . . ." Jake hesitates a moment, measures his words appropriately, "I don't feel like I'm writing in a tradition, but I'm definitely part of their progeny. But then again I do feel times are different and I'm writing things that are very different and there are so many black writers now whereas in the old days there were just a handful."

The key point of distinction between Jake's work and that of his predecessors may be *the way* he writes about race. The work of Baldwin and Wright and Himes is in many ways a haunting reminder of power relations among whites and blacks and how ultimately blacks are always powerless to define their reality in opposition to their white counterparts. Meanwhile, the four novels Jake has published since his arrival in Paris have simultaneously reconfigured and personalized that power dynamic.

"I find a lot of what I've written about in all my books is self-definition. I say self-definition more than identity because identity is something anyone can stamp on you. How you define yourself is something else. And so it's been the theme. The first four books I wrote were all set in America. That was sort of a constant theme of how you define yourself as a black person, how you define yourself vis-à-vis other black people, white people; how do you define you."

Jake's latest novel, *Rendezvous Eighteenth,* is set in Paris's 18th arrondissement. Easily Paris's most ethnically and culturally complex quarter, the 18th reminds one of New York City's grittier days, only different. The buildings are older and shorter, the streets are narrower, the cars are smaller, and the pace is slower. All of these factors make the intermingling of people from vastly dissimilar backgrounds that much more frequent and intense. Describing the neighborhood he now calls home in the novel's opening pages, Jake writes of the

> white French, black French and brown French—ostentatiously loitering, smoking cigarettes, trying to look bad, talkin' shit; a girl with dirty blond dreadlocks rollerblading in circles, walkman headphones plugged in her ears; a noble-looking, ebony-skinned man handing out leaflets, rotely, wearily demanding an end to the war in Sierra Leone; befuddled white American, German and Japanese tourists, maps in hand, cameras strapped around their necks, struggling to get their bearings in Montmartre, this curious puzzle of a neighborhood, full of hills and outdoor stair-cases with iron bannisters, hidden alcoves, ivy-lined nooks and crannies, narrow, labyrinthine, cobblestone streets.

The novel, though on its surface a thriller, internationalizes the themes of race and self-definition Jake has been writing about since the days of *Bourgeois Blues.* Ricky Jenks, his lead character, is, like Jake himself, an expat in love with a non-American; only in the fictionalized situation the woman is Muslim. "Her father was Moroccan, her mother's Cameroon, and she was born on Toulouse on the southwest of France," Jake says. "She's a Muslim, but a secular Muslim, [so] she drinks wine, she's had sex. But she tells Ricky that she will only ever marry a fellow Muslim. This freaks him out because he's like, 'We're both black. What's the problem?'

"There were things I just didn't know about how Muslims and Africans and North Africans thought, but I've learned since living here. Things just play out differently here and the book's really very much about that. In a way, you feel more American than you do in America. I've just found racism here isn't so much a question of black and white; it's about history and cultural baggage, and where in particular you're from. This is the experience I had being stopped on the street by police in my early days here. As soon as they saw that American passport, there was no problem. So the racist impulse was to stop me, but as soon as they found out I was an American and not Senegalese, there was no problem.

"I think Americans are obsessed with what they can see. Here, racism is also about what you don't see. 'Is that person a Jew?' That was World War II. Racism doesn't get much worse than World War II. People were turning in their neighbors because they thought they might be Jewish. So even if you couldn't see it, there was still that [suspicion] and that made them the enemy. I never thought about World War II in this way when I lived in the States. You thought about D-Day."

On our way to Jake's studio he and I revel in the beauty and the ease of his adopted city. It's the middle of the day on a sunny Friday afternoon and the cobblestone streets are only thinly peopled. Still, the quarter feels remarkably alive. Jake has had his ground-floor apartment since he moved to Paris a decade ago. In New York a similar-sized and located apartment would rent for $1,200 easily. Back in 1994, Jake paid $500 a month for it; even now, despite the falling dollar and the rising Euro, he pays the equivalent of $660 a month. Although he and his wife, Doreen, share an apartment nearby, Jake keeps this place as a safe haven for his work. In this way he can separate his writing life from his personal life. When he's here, he works. When he's not, he doesn't work. There's a couch, several bookshelves, a kitchen, a thirteen-inch television—he and his wife have been following the U.S. presidential race on it—and a modest writing table where his laptop and papers sit: everything a writer needs. What really sold him on the place, though, was the terrace and the courtyard it looks out upon.

Outside, Jake begins to really open up about his feelings for Paris. "I love this city," he says. "It's an easy city to live in. Health care is taken care of, education is taken care of. These factors I used to agonize about in the States." There is also the simple thrill of the "new." "Both my parents grew up in the South. For them to come to New York was incredibly exciting and they met the sort of people they didn't meet growing up down South, and were exposed to experiences and cultural things they didn't have in the South. I think for me Paris is kind of like that because New York is so familiar to me. This is so wild and interesting and everybody I meet is interesting to me because they're not familiar and when they are familiar, they're in a different context.

"But then, on a practical level, I love cities and Paris as a city just works. It's small, it's got a good metro system, you've got all these movie houses showing old movies, which I used to love in New York. I used to love when I was a teenager to go to the Bleecker Street Cinema and Carnegie Hall Cinema and the Thalia. I don't think these places are revival houses anymore. I think they're just first-run theaters, if they're still there. I used to love to go see a Fellini movie when I was seventeen. In Paris you can do that."

If there is one subject that riles the otherwise mellow Jake up more than others it's the publishing industry in America. When he discusses it you see his father's ire reveal itself in him; you also remember he's a kid from the Bronx. Writing and publishing, he reminds me, are two different animals. Writing is the easy part. You come up with the story, you write the story. Publishing, on the other hand, requires tangling with an industry that obsessively defines and assigns African-American writers. The industry decides who the audience is *and* the kinds of books it will be receptive to. If it's a book by an African-American author it has to be about "black" issues, involving "black" characters experiencing "black" life, and if it deviates from that thin line, perhaps in the way *Rendezvous Eighteenth* does, it isn't an authentic representation of blackness, and therefore risks being lost in the bookstore.

"I feel like I'm part of a generation of writers, Michael Chabon is my age, David Foster Wallace is my age, Trey Ellis is my age. It shouldn't be me against Trey Ellis because Trey is black and my age. I mean, we're all out there trying to get our stuff published and recognized. But the industry says, 'You're a black writer and therefore your competition is other black writers,' and it's terrible."

In the last few years Jake has watched his sales slip. As a result, his advances have shrunk as well. At this point he says he's happy to have a contract for his next book. After that, though, who knows. "It's a grim reality to face up to at forty-three, having published five books, but that's the ridiculous profession." Jake's saving grace might just be that, like his literary godfather Chester Himes, his books are now being translated into French.

A few months before our interview, Jake had reviewed TransAfrica founder and reparations crusader Randall Robinson's book *Quitting America: The Departure of a Black Man from*

His Native Land for the *Washington Post*. Written following Robinson's move to the island of St. Kitts in 2001, the book is meant to be both a political tirade against the Iraq war and a historical study of the Caribbean. "But, above all," Jake writes in the opening paragraph, "*Quitting America* is a love story; more specifically, a wrenching tale of unrequited love." According to Jake, Mr. Robinson's biggest gripe with America is that while he tried to love the country, it wouldn't love him back. Paradoxically, St. Kitts is portrayed as a utopian enclave untainted by the tourism industry that has simultaneously helped and harmed the rest of the Caribbean. In his review, Jake expresses a measure of doubt about the idyllic portrait of St. Kitts that Robinson paints for his readers. As an expat himself, Jake is cautious about portraying one country as better than another when they all have their benefits and their drawbacks. In the review's final paragraph, Jake asks:

> Why have the vast majority of black Americans with the resources and wherewithal to quit America opted to stay? There are millions of African-Americans who share Robinson's disgust with the Bush Administration and the Iraq war, who share his tortured knowledge of America's race-crazed history and his despair about the future, yet choose not to live in another country. Surely America must offer a great many black citizens—who have had the opportunity to leave—something that they have not found elsewhere.

Or maybe, as was the case with Jake himself, many African-Americans (like most Americans) find it hard to imagine making their home elsewhere. Despite the unhappiness and the longing for something different, the natural tendency is to stick with the familiar rather than try something new. In Jake's case, it took leaving for him to discover a home, love, a place where he can safely write, and people who appreciate his work. Even taking all this into account, Jake's decision to stay in Paris really came down to something as simple as the outcome of a quintessentially New York moment that even the best fiction writer couldn't brew up:

"I'd only been here a few weeks and the metro shuts down at one. And I had always been careful to get the last train. Then after two months I was out too late and I was standing on a street corner somewhere in the middle of town in my baseball cap and basketball shoes and I'm out there trying to hail a cab at two in the morning and it occurred to me, that at two o'clock in the afternoon in Manhattan no taxi driver would stop for me let alone two in the morning. So at two in the morning, a taxi pulled up and at just that moment this well-dressed white couple comes up on my shoulder. The taxi driver rolls down his window and says to me where are you going? He turns to the white couple and he's like where are you going? And immediately, I just went into a rage. It's not even like New York where they won't stop for me, this motherfucker stops and he asks where I'm going and then takes the white couple. The white couple tells him where they're going and he says 'Oh, I'm sorry, I'm sorry, it's my last run of the night and he's going in my direction so that's it.' So I hopped in the cab, and we drove off leaving this guy—I want to remember him in a tux, he wasn't, but they were well-dressed—and I was like, 'Wow, that was so nice.' It was just that my race wasn't a factor. I don't want strangers to love me. I just don't want my race to be a negative factor. And in this case, it wasn't. It wasn't in the equation. It was just 'Who's going in my direction?' But the funny thing is, if they had been going in his direction, it might have changed my whole attitude about France."

It Was Only Supposed to Be a Year

Zachary James Miller: Filmmaker/Psychologist/Activist

> "I'm a realist, and I know that life is hard and everything, but I am a believer in positive thinking. I've always felt that I could achieve what I wanted to achieve."

Including me, there are only ten people at tonight's Democrats Abroad meeting, and we're all jammed into two corner booths in the back of Paris's only American-styled diner, the Breakfast in America Diner. The owner, Craig Carlson, used to be a Hollywood screenwriter. He moved abroad to get out of that rat race. Soon after, Carlson realized that what the city was missing, and what he was missing, was a good old-fashioned diner, so he built one. The menu lists all the greasy-spoon basics like omelettes and pancakes, burgers and fries, assorted chicken finger-foods, plus a few frills you won't find on the menu in the States, beer and wine for instance.

The Democrats are having their monthly chapter meeting tonight. They've all had to weather the storm of anti-American sentiment since the start of the war in Iraq, they have all seen *Fahrenheit 9/11*, and all of them are pretty fired up to oust the Bush administration this November. Across from me sits a young Muslim woman who recently graduated from college and is in Paris teaching English to businessmen. Next to her sits a rancorous octogenarian who hasn't voted in an American election since he left the United States in 1952. He has trouble hearing the conversation so to keep himself involved he randomly denounces the Bush administration. "Those fascist bastards call everyone who doesn't agree with them unpatriotic," he says in one of his outbursts. The computer programmer next to him, the one who looks like the prototypic middle-aged Deadhead, didn't take any interest in politics until Howard Dean came along. Now he's campaigning for Kerry. On my right side sits a dapper businessman, who until moving to Paris seventeen years ago says he never thought twice about things like America's foreign oil policy. Now he's always lecturing his family back home about their SUVs. He's been sparring with a WASPy woman who claims her father and George H. W. Bush were in the oil business together. She happily dishes her dirt on an adolescent George W. Bush. However, at six-four and roughly 250 pounds, the person who really sticks out in this motley group of expats is Zachary Miller, the group's only African-American and the vice chair of Paris's chapter of Democrats Abroad.

Zachary lets the chatter run its course before he politely introduces the meeting's agenda, which includes a possible fundraising event for John Kerry. Zachary's idea is to organize a concert, but he says he's open to other suggestions. After leaving the floor open for suggestions, he moves on to a discussion about venues. That's when others get involved. Pretty soon, they've got one list going for possible locations, another for bands they want to contact, and a third for expat celebrities they want to invite. That done, Zachary again steps in, this time to see who's willing to take on which job. Finally, he makes sure he has everyone's e-mail address. Apart from London, Paris has the biggest delegation of American citizens outside the United States. If the race is as close as it is expected to be, then this might very well be an election where the chapter's votes make a difference.

"Some of my earliest memories are of politics," Zachary says once the others have left the diner. With his clean, round face and thick head of dark hair, Zachary could quite easily pass for someone in his twenties from a distance; even up close, he looks to be in his mid-thirties. More than his appearance, though, his high-pitched cackle and spontaneous, theatrical mannerisms give him the aura of a much younger man.

"This is the sixties. I'm sitting at the foot of my father watching television as Kennedy is killed and King is killed and the other Kennedy is killed. I'm an only child, so I'm included in the parents' discussion. I'm listening, learning, sitting and watching all of this stuff going on and I started getting interested. I was a little boy when Kennedy was killed. When Robert Kennedy was killed also. We were all rooting for him to win the California primary. He was going to be the nominee. I went to sleep praying that he would be alive and would win, and then he died."

Zachary traces the origins of his involvement in political activism back to a place called Humanity House in his hometown of Akron, Ohio. Humanity House was a progressive umbrella organization funded by the American Friends Service that supported the activities of groups as wide-ranging as the United Farm Workers, the Vietnam Veterans Against the War, and the American Vegetarians. Zachary was all of thirteen when he joined Humanity House and became its youngest member. Pretty soon he was standing on picket lines and giving up meat.

"Looking back on it, Akron was a really good place to grow up. It was a medium-sized town in northeast Ohio. Everyone worked in the rubber plant, the tire factory. My father was a tire builder, my uncles were tire builders, my cousins, too. For the longest time it was a good union job for black Americans who had left the South to come to the North. My other uncles in Detroit worked in the auto industry. My mother did day work, but she didn't have to do it every day. She was just supplementing. We had the middle-American, median-income kind of thing. I was sheltered from a lot of racism that I didn't know was happening. It was a black neighborhood, but the only places that the dentists and doctors who were black could live were the black neighborhoods. So we had upper-class blacks living with middle-class blacks living with poorer blacks, all in one neighborhood. It was just a pretty gentle, positive way to grow up. That gave me the idea of doing whatever I wanted to do. I wanted to try acting so [my parents] let me try acting. I wanted to do karate, so I went to karate school."

Zachary's experience was startlingly different from that of his cousins in Tuskegee, Alabama. He still recalls the change in his parents' demeanor the first time they took him down South. He wasn't aware of it at the time, but they worried that Zachary would make a mistake when he was out with one of his cousins and wind up hurt or worse. A year earlier his cousin Sammy Young Jr. had been murdered for using a white restroom. Young was the first college student killed in the civil rights movement. What Zachary remembers most vividly about that trip was the way his father ignored him whenever he asked why they didn't stop and rest along the way. "I'd say, 'Daddy, can we stop? There's one, there's one.' As a child they never told me that we couldn't stop at any of the motels and I wanted to stop at the ones with the pools."

Zachary had planned to attend Yale after high school, but when his father developed pancreatic cancer at the end of his junior year, and then again during his senior year, plans changed. With his father gone, he knew that his mother would need him, so he decided to stay close to home and he enrolled at the University of Akron. Although he didn't want to be there, he made the best of the situation and started a campus organization called the Committee for Social Change. "We attracted a number of ragtag radicals and we were selling 'Kick the Bum Out' stickers against Nixon and having demonstrations on campus. When Jane Fonda was going around speaking at colleges we had her." From there Zachary got into local politics, where, as one of a very few young African-Americans working in the Democratic party, he got to know and work with his senators and congressman.

In the midst of his political endeavors, Zachary also began pursuing a career in psychology. After graduating from Akron he entered a specialized psychology/holistic health program at Antioch College's San Francisco campus. Zachary later had a talk-radio show in Pasadena where he gave health advice. He enjoyed California, but when his mother became ill he returned home. This time, however, he wasn't alone. He'd met a young graduate student from France who had come to the United States to volunteer in a social services program he was running in the summers. Together, they opened Akron's first wellness center.

"Running the residential treatment center was a joy. Usually I was working with kids or people who were really disabled, so they had a five-year-old's mentality, but you just felt like you were accomplishing something, you felt you were changing someone's life, one by one. Reagan had almost destroyed the whole psychological health-care system in America, and all these people were on the streets and homeless, so we felt we were affecting lives."

The center stayed open until Zachary's mother passed away five years later. At the time, Zachary's wife, Violet, needed only a year to complete her master's in education. But it could only be done in France. Zachary didn't know the language and didn't care much for the French, but without any familial ties holding him in Akron any longer, he figured a year away would do them both some good. They needed some healing time, after which they could come back and resume their life in Akron.

"The first year was almost surreal in that [Violet] was working, doing the teacher training, and I was in the apartment quite a bit. I was trying to write and I was very much inside my head a lot. My mother had passed away six months before we moved. I'd just left a career and really my best job in psychology, running the residential treatment center. We both had a lifestyle we liked there. It was a new adventure to come to Paris, but it was a struggle for the first year. But, I [also] don't know if I would have gotten into the things I got into here and had to basically reinvent myself. I treated myself like a client. And I asked myself the same questions I'd ask someone sitting in front of me. One of the things I said was, 'What would make you most excited to be doing right now? What would you most want to accomplish? What would you most want to do?'

"I've always felt entrepreneurial. I was the kid with the lemonade stand in front of the house. Then it dawned on me that if I started a production company I could do documentaries."

Zachary began traveling to London to study filmmaking at the London Fimmakers Co-op Workshop. There he met Elliot Grove, one of London's premier independent film gurus. The two became fast friends, and soon thereafter Grove asked Zachary to run his indie-film seminars in Paris. Suddenly, Zachary started to emerge from his shell and find his way. That's when he met the late beat poet Ted Joans.

"The first black American I met here was Ted. One Sunday I went to Shakespeare and Company and I'm in the back looking at books [when] I see this brother looking at me out of the corner of his eye. This is how people do it in Paris. You say, 'He's American,' [and] you give each other the nod. He starts talking to me and at one point he says he's Ted Joans and I said, 'I know you,' and he said, 'You should.' "

Ted invited Zachary to dinner that evening at the home of Jim Haynes, also an American expat. According to Zachary, for the past two and a half decades Haynes has been hosting a potluck dinner every Sunday. Through that dinner and many to follow Zachary met other Americans living in Paris. Later, Ted introduced Zachary to the jazz musicians who in turn would spark the idea for his first documentary: a jazz series set in Paris.

With a little persistence, Zachary presold a documentary on saxophonist Steve Lacy and pianist Mal Waldron to ARTE television, France's art channel. The program was successful and it later aired in Germany as well. Although Zachary's quick to add that no project has moved either as quickly or smoothly since then, that initial success gave him enough in the way of confidence and contacts to live principally from the income his production company generates through workshops, private investment, and licensing and distribution.

Through that fortuitous first meeting with Ted Joans, Zachary also got plugged back into the political community. After meeting other Americans, he learned about Democrats Abroad, which has been around since Lyndon Johnson defeated Barry Goldwater in 1964.* And on a night when he was merely hoping to catch a glimpse of the Democratic hopefuls running for the party's 1992 nomination, Zachary was unexpectedly inserted into international politics.

"They were having these events at the American Church and Violet and I just went because they were showing the debates, also that night was going to be the French caucus. I had no intention of running [for Paris delegate position]—we were just going because we didn't have cable and I hadn't seen any of the candidates on television. At the end of the evening they said, 'Okay, we're going to have the caucus and anyone who would like to run for office you have to fill out these forms.' I'm looking at my wife and she's looking at me, you know. I was for Jerry

*Many of the estimated 6 million Democrats living abroad are members of the military and diplomatic communities, or they are involved in business enterprises that require them to live outside the United States. Since it is formally recognized as a "state" committee by the Democratic party, Democrats Abroad allows those Americans in particular to participate in the political process at home.

Brown against Clinton and whoever else was running, so I went and I signed up. Those who sign up go into the caucus room with all the people who are for the candidate and make a speech about yourself, why they should elect you, [and] why you're for that specific candidate. A lot of people had prepared because they knew they were going to do this. I knew I was going to do this like five minutes before I did it. But they elected me! I went up and made this off-the-cuff speech and I was elected to go to the global caucus, which that year was in Brussels. That's how I got introduced to Democrats Abroad."

What I find most invigorating about Zachary is his attitude toward politics. Even though he hasn't lived in the United States for over a decade and a half, he still passionately believes in and is actively committed to the American political process. After the 2000 election he felt, like millions of people, that George W. Bush had stolen the White House by violating the civil rights of more than twenty-two thousand mostly African-American voters in Florida. But instead of just talking about it, he and his fellow minority caucus members organized a peace protest. Then they followed up with panel discussions and various other outreach projects to galvanize the democratic electorate abroad. When Howard Dean came out of the gates fired up and angry at both parties in early 2003, Zachary was the first person in Paris to throw his support Dean's way.

"I felt like everybody was being so timid and cautious and weak and Dean had a strength. Dean came out fighting and that excited a lot of people. That was the main thing about Dean. Then I looked at the issues and I agreed with him on most of them."

Zachary then wrote to Governor Dean and started a local Dean meet-up where others in support of his candidacy could strategize on ways to get the word out. Soon after, Dean's campaign chair got back in touch with Zachary and officially assigned him the position of France's chair. He studied Dean's platform, debated the other Democratic candidates' chairs, spoke on Dean's behalf to the French press, and in the process managed to build Dean's second-largest support base outside of the United States—London being the largest—before the campaign collapsed in early 2004.

"I'm a realist and I know that life is hard and everything, but I am a believer in positive thinking. I've always felt that I could achieve what I wanted to achieve. I don't have a negative attitude. I try to accomplish what I want to accomplish and I do affirmations and I do meditations and I have a background of working on myself."

Ultimately, Zachary's belief in civic responsibility and his belief in himself go hand in hand. His ability to leave one country and start anew in another, to leave a stable, secure profession and take on the indeterminate world of independent filmmaking (in a foreign language no less), and his ability to negotiate a political voice for himself abroad are all testaments to the power of the human mind to reinvent its notion of reality, and the human heart to resist the temptations of cynicism.

The Triple Conscious MC

Mike C. Ladd: Poet/MC/Producer/Professor

> "I often meet a lot of other people out there like me. That's the whole thing about doing shows. In every city I meet one other brother who's like me. There's like this secret army of alternative black people."

My buddy Jeremy was the one who insisted I interview Mike. Whenever the book came up in conversation he'd say the same thing: "You need to meet Mike, he'd be perfect." After months of pressure from Jeremy, I finally made the call, and Mike and I made plans to catch up. The only problem was that he was so busy preparing to move across the Atlantic to be with his fiancée in Paris that things just never worked out. I figured I'd given it a shot and I forgot all about Mike until a couple of months later when I found myself inside the Bronx apartment Jeremy had once shared with him, surrounded by thousands of thumb-sized army figurines. Jeremy had called from out of town a week earlier with an urgent plea for me to gather his belongings from the apartment before the landlord threw them onto the street, and there I was on a simulated World War II battlefield, itty-bitty plastic rifles and bayonets pointing at me from all directions: the floor, the windowsill, the shelves, some even lined the dusty sill above the living room doorway. That night, after I got home, I called Jeremy and told him what I'd seen in his otherwise abandoned apartment. He laughed and said, simply, "It's insane, isn't it?" He then told me about Mike's fetish for war toys.

When Mike came back to Brooklyn to finish recording his latest album three months later, he invited Jeremy and me to the studio. Although I still hadn't heard any of his music, I figured any grown man odd enough to wage wars with plastic, pint-sized infantry men was worth meeting.

Mike was recording a song entitled "Housewives at Play" when we arrived. He was inspired to write it by a racy comic book of the same name about suburban infidelity. Although he had originally performed the song as a parody, a lyrical prank—one that wasn't expected to generate much more than a few audience chuckles—it turned out that people really liked it. The next thing he knew a record company in Europe was offering him a deal to record it as a single for overseas distribution. Now he was putting it on his upcoming album, *Nostalgialator*. Stories like this one typify Mike's creative career.

The one conversation Mike and I squeezed in between takes was about Colson Whitehead's novels. In addition to being a hip-hop artist with a penchant for simulated military combat, Mike also taught literature and poetry at Long Island University for several years, and is an avid reader. In fact, poetry, not rap, is his first love, what he told me he hopes to one day seriously pursue.

Whitehead's two novels, *The Intuitionist* and *John Henry Days*, are both post–civil rights allegories that use satire rather than melodrama and realism (think: Baldwin and Wright) to comment on race. Whitehead's novels blur the lines between fantasy and reality, between past and present, between black and white. Mike's music takes the race rhetoric even a step further into what he calls the "After-Future," where even the blur between fact and fiction are wiped out. Take, as an example, Ralph Ellison's *Invisible Man,* where the nameless narrator rises from nowhere and nothing to become a charismatic leader and spokesman for The Brotherhood, a kind of quasi-communist organization. In the span of a day, Ellison's hero bounces from near starvation to leading a tenants' rally in front of an apartment building, to being wooed into the upper echelons of The Brotherhood. In Mike's After-Future, Barack Obama's ascendence from state legislator to senatorial shoo-in in the four months following his speech at the Democratic National Convention would signify the moment in which Ellison's fiction meets our reality's fact.

"Post-futurism is the point where even the blur has disappeared, and science fiction and reality are completely unified and symbiotic," Mike says over breakfast a week later. He looks as if he's just rolled out of bed, but it's hard to tell with him. His fluffy amber-stained mane exists in a state of perpetual disarray, his jeans sag haggardly, and his walk is more lope than b-boy swagger. Were I judging Mike by his disheveled appearance this morning, I would never guess that he was raised in suburban Cambridge, Massachusetts, by the celebrated former Harvard professor Florence Ladd.

"[My mother] comes from that older generation that really had to find those things that were very specific career paths, and she went into academia. Her mom was a teacher, my grandfather was a carpenter. She had a Ph.D. by the time she was twenty-six. She got her Ph.D. in environmental psychology so she started teaching in schools in the Boston area. Then she met my father and had me. My father passed away when I was one. He was a white archaeologist, he died of a heart attack, so I grew up strictly with my mother as my main influence and she had these conventional ideas about life."

Those ideas included a heavy dose of education both in school and out. "Keep your eyes on the page," Mike recalls his mother saying throughout his childhood. In fact, her values are still so ingrained in him that after picking out a World War II army tank at a toy store one afternoon, he declares, "I'm an adult! I can buy what I like!" as though defending his expensive obsession with war toys against an invisible figure of authority.

Part of the reason Mike has always been fascinated by history, war in particular, is because his father fought in the Second World War. "He'd be eighty-three now," he says, "so I create a fantasy of what that was. And what he was." Mike's need to justify his alternative lifestyle, however, demands a closer look at his mom's effect on his life. Aside from teaching in both the environmental and psychology departments at Harvard, Dr. Ladd also worked as a dean at Wellesley and ran the Bunting Institute— an advanced women's studies research center—at Radcliffe College. "I've always really revered my mother coming from a working-class neighborhood in D.C. to being a prominent intellectual force in Cambridge," he says. Dr. Ladd was also adamantly opposed to war, and when it came to U.S. policies abroad, she didn't hesitate to offer her views to her son. At thirteen, she began sending Mike to Quaker meetings so that by his eighteenth birthday he could sign up as a conscientious objector and avoid a possible draft. "Thanks to my mother, I had a real early understanding of America as an empire and all the crimes that this country commits to sustain its position in the world. This is the eighties, so Central America was really central. I was aware of America's investments in South Africa during apartheid. Because my mother paid a lot of attention to international issues I became very involved in a lot of those issues." As Mike recalls it, his mandate was simple: watch what was happening around the world, understand it, and become a leader in the next wave of change.

Cambridge, as Mike describes it, was "a slice of non-America in the middle of racist Boston." The city was intellectual, cultural, beautiful, fairly open and active. Of course, it had its problems, it just did a better job of suppressing them. Racism or sexism or homophobia—any of the views associated with stodgy mid-century values—were considered bad form in Cambridge. The only trouble was that Mike was the lone African-American kid in his neighborhood. Then, once he hit high school, he went off to boarding school, which was even more alienating because there he encountered African-Americans with whom he felt no connection or kinship. Despite everything his mother had done to ensure that he understood what it meant to be black—she had immersed him in African-American culture and history—the world she had raised him in didn't reinforce that sense of pride. That's where Boston figured in.

Some of Mike's family, and most of his friends, lived in Boston, so when he visited them he saw firsthand the disparities that his mother had always talked about. His cousin Dean's apartment was where he watched *Sanford and Son* and listened to Funkadelic, where hungry street beats collided with the smooth melodies of Kool and the Gang. Boston was where he went to duck his mother for a few hours and to be the free-wheeling street kid he couldn't be at home. But traveling between the two worlds did more than just give him a place to mingle with "the people" whenever he needed to get away from suburbia. That contact planted the seeds of dissonance in him. He saw very clearly that the people living in the 'hood were mostly of color, that the people living in his Cambridge neighborhood were mostly white, and that there he was, a mixture of both, caught in the middle, fitting neatly into neither. During this period of angst, Mike decided to convert to Islam. "At that point I was very cynical about America. I was very anti–United States," he says.

In the midst of this period of disillusion, a boarding school buddy asked Mike if he was interested in moving to India for a year. "I'll go," he replied. Mike, perhaps naïvely, was captivated by the "otherness" that the Southern Hemisphere symbolized. India was not only the unknown, it was an unknown populated by brown people outside of the United States. There, he figured, he could create himself anew. He did all the research, saved money, and later pled his case with his mother. Living in the Himalayas for the year would cost less than his boarding school, he explained. *And* he would be experiencing a new culture. *And* it would look really good on that college application. Mom agreed.

But in an essay Mike would later write about the experience he explained that it was the shock of arriving in the foothills of the Himalayas only to be called a "nigger" on his first day of school that would show him that he could not escape his background.★ "I was beat by Hollywood," he writes. The year wore on and as it did he found himself in the oddly ironic predicament of feeling like a full-fledged representative of the Stars and Stripes. Whether he was walking through a village peopled by "untouchables" with a Walkman on listening to Funkadelic, witnessing the graphic violence between Muslim and Hindu students, lying on top of mountain peaks overlooking the snow-capped Himalayas, heading to Tibet with three thousand U.S. dollars in his pocket, or rapping over tablas at the talent show with a kid named Jivaid, Mike continuously discovered how American he really was. Of this cultural experiment Mike writes:

I was on both sides of the coin, as a black American, I had felt America's teeth sink into me. As a black American in a "third world" country, I was sinking my teeth into the disenfranchised Indians around me. I was beginning to develop triple conscious-

★*Rip It Up: The Black Experience in Rock 'n' Roll*, edited by Kandia Crazy Horse (New York: Palgrave Macmillan, 2004). pp. 73–74.

ness. Simply by being American, despite the African and the hyphen, I was associated with American imperialism. No matter how many people I tried to convince of my African roots, my build alone said well fed, well paid.*

At tiny Hampshire College, Mike studied literature and made plans to pursue a responsible, civic-minded career. In a thesis he wrote on nineteenth-century African-American expatriation, he concluded that exile ultimately wouldn't help the black race, and that it was a form of escape from the struggles happening within the country. Mike was thinking of going to law school, getting into government and politics, perhaps running for office, and becoming an African-American leader. Even after he moved to New York to live out his revolutionary/bohemian/artist dream, he figured he'd find his way back to formal education and its promise of ascendency into the corridors of power where he could effect real change. In large measure, that's what he'd been raised to do. Even now, thirteen years later, and though he's proud of his accomplishments and convictions, a voice inside of him still wonders where he'd be had he walked that path.

But that's not the road he chose.

After a stint in construction (where he discovered that everyone he worked with had also moved to New York to become an artist), Mike began writing and performing at open mikes around the city. Coming from where he'd come from, seeing what he'd seen, and finding a multitude of voices to bring it all together, put him on the map. In 1996 he won the Nuyorican Poetry Slam Competition, the coffee shop precursor to the *Def Poets' Jam* Russell Simmons has since brought to Broadway and HBO. Next came a self-produced album *Easy Listening 4 Armageddon,* which gave the world a glimpse of his unique fusion

*Ibid., p. 74.

of live instrumentation, new-age technology, and rhythmic and melodic variation, all beneath his sometimes raspy, sometimes rowdy, sometimes bluesy, sometimes breathless cadences. In the United States the album was practically ignored outside of the small spoken word set, but abroad journalists and DJs hailed it as an indication of where hip-hop could go. Like the albums that immediately followed, *Live From Paris* and *Welcome to the After-future*, Mike's music had a fresh, fearless, imaginative, and improvisational construction that led journalists to label it as "genius rap" because it simply didn't fit into any of the other hip-hop categories. His sound wasn't gangsta, it wasn't underground, it wasn't West Coast or southern, it wasn't radio-friendly formatted, and it didn't pay homage to gaudy materialism or gritty asceticism. Mike derived his eclectic sound from a mixture of live instruments, turntable samples, tape loops, and programmed beats. There were also elements of punk, jazz, funk, soul, classic rock, and drum 'n' bass all interwoven.

On the albums Mike pushes as many envelopes lyrically as he does musically. While "The Tragic Mulatto Is Neither," "I'm Building a Bodacious Bodega for the Race War," and "Let's Discuss Disgusting," a response to the book *The Bell Curve,* all formally address race through his sardonic wit, they each also emphasize an unfiltered free association wordplay that allows Mike the space to collect and distribute the many experiences that have influenced his life in one steady stream of consciousness.

In 2000 and 2003, Mike produced a pair of concept albums parodying the commercial/undergound rift in hip-hop through a centuries-old war between the Infesticons ("a spartan people interested in ideas and the content of their minds") and the Majesticons (a group "fascinated with their own exterior").★ Again, both albums were critically acclaimed as breakthrough works, and both,

---

★*Infesticons:* Gun Hill Road, 2000, Big Dada Records.

again, were largely ignored by the mainstream. In early 2004, Mike and composer Vijay Iyer produced *In What Language,* an international spoken-word project based on the experiences of people of color in airports across the globe. "I wanted to do something about airports and about prejudice [so] I traveled to different airports for about a year interviewing working folks in transit." Those interviews in turn inspired a series of poems written in the voices of airport workers, foreign businessmen, and cabdrivers, which were then set to compositions written and produced by Iyer. Although Mike and Iyer developed the idea pre-9/11, once the catastrophic event occurred Mike says the project "practically started writing itself." NPR did a segment on it and the *New York Times* gave it a favorable review. Even Mike's mother, his hardest nut to crack, gave him a nod of approval for the project.

If anything, Mike's musical predecessors aren't so much the likes of Eric B. and Rakim or even P-Funk, both of whom have figured heavily in his development, but the free-form, improvisational jazz of players like Ornette Coleman, Don Cherry, and Freddy Hubbard, and even, to an extent, John Coltrane. Just as these musicians experimented with, and expanded, the popular black music of their day only to encounter deaf and even appalled ears, Mike's conceptual sound tends to produce an extreme emotional reaction as well. People either love what he's doing or they can't stand it. The people who are bothered by Mike's music see it the way Miles Davis saw fellow trumpeter Don Cherry's free jazz style. "It just looked to me like he was playing a lot of notes and looking real serious, and people went for that because people will go for anything they don't understand if it's got enough hype," Miles writes in his autobiography.* Meantime, the people who love Mike's stuff think it's visionary, years ahead of its time.

*Miles Davis, *Miles: The Autobiography* (New York: Touchstone, 1989), p. 251.

"My career has been based on being able to do whatever I want. I'm constantly either surprising or disappointing my audience. If I'm going to do this, I'm only going to make so much money, [so] I'm going to do whatever I want to do. I get off especially on sort of blowing away the expectations of the audience. That's my own personal thing. I'm interested in showing all the dynamics of being a black person. I know I make black music, and I make black music for black people even if it's only five of them in the audience.

"[My music] is a tool to express all the different sides of what a black person can do or what a person of color can do. Being a black person for me also includes the white side. Part of my understanding of being black is that it is intermixed over several centuries. I'm producing a perspective of the world that is influenced by certain things that have informed me, which are a very wide variety of things. Simply by making that statement I then show all of these different things that have informed me. For the outside world to see a black person who's been informed by those things enhances their notion of what a black person can be."

"And what are those things?"

"Absolutely everything. From going to high school in India, to understanding Kool and the Gang, to getting taken to Senegal by my mother when I was twelve, to exposure to Langston Hughes at eleven, to discovering Funkadelic at thirteen, to my discovery of punk rock at twelve, to listening to Run DMC, to the first time I ever visited New York, to understanding that my father was a white archaeologist, to understanding what it meant that my great-great-great-grandmother was one of five black people on Portsmouth Island on the outer banks of North Carolina. Only by understanding our personal history and our personal complexity can we then help better understand our collective history and progression."

Mike's approach is a rarity in hip-hop today. The multibillion-dollar, multinational rap industry has very little space for creative deviation from the standard sixteen-bar, catchy hook, R&B slickified, guest appearance–laden, lyrically anemic, rhythmically repetitive, melodically monotone rap-tune format. Turning on the television or radio these days invites the same ten mind-numbing jingles into one's brain; choosing an album at the record store is as much a gamble as playing a scratch-and-win lottery game; and the live show complete with a stage full of inaudible voices, a DJ spinning records, or a programmed beat droning along, just isn't cutting it anymore. That the handful of notable exceptions to the new hip-hop rules, The Roots, De La Soul, and OutKast are consistently trotted out as the eclectic vanguard, lone wolves in the wilderness of pop-hop, means there's that much less space for the Mike Ladds of the world.

As with his free-jazz forefathers, Mike has found his most receptive audiences in Europe. In an especially insightful segment of the liner notes accompanying Mike's *Live From Paris* album, one critic remarks that "Mike, like many other American musicians before him, has been appreciated and understood in Europe before being recognized in his own country. I think this is somewhat due to his music not fitting neatly into any category."★ That Mike's music is original, fresh, clever, and deep is perhaps also an indication as to why he remains an obscure figure in a culture that seems to thrive on repetition, nostalgia, superficiality, and simplicity.

"If I thought about it too long, I'd be dead," Mike says after I ask him how he feels about being effectively blocked out of the radio rotation. "I would have killed myself a while ago. You gotta get over that one. People are tired and busy, and your role as an entertainer is marginal. On one level it's vital and I do be-

★Lars Weiss, Liner Notes, *Home Style Cooking*.

lieve there is power to say something and that you should never underestimate the influence you can have. At the same time, you don't affect policy. These are things you don't do, despite what you think as a spoken-word artist at the Nuyorican on a Sunday.

"I believe that my work influences other artists who have an aspiration to do something different. As an artist, I can only create what is in me. I'm a pretty alternative guy to begin with. I grew up atypical. My interests are atypical. But not enough to make me completely alone. I often meet a lot of other cats out there like me. That's the whole thing about doing shows. In every city I meet one other brother who's like me. There's like this secret army of alternative black people."

Six months after our winter brunch in Brooklyn, Mike and I are cutting through a line of tourists waiting to take their tour of Notre Dame, while he breaks down the causes of World War I, colonialism, and the rises and falls of Napoleons I, II, and III. Our original plan had been to spend the afternoon inside Cluny, a medieval museum near the Sorbonne, but since the museum isn't open on Tuesdays we decide to let the day unfold as it will. As we move along I note how, already, Mike seems comfortable in the city, at home. He moves through the streets like a seasoned Parisian and his French is coming along nicely.

On the other hand, Mike still doesn't know how he feels about being so far from the only struggle he's ever known. Although coming to Paris wasn't a political move ("I moved primarily because I could and because it's cheaper than New York") or an artistic move ("If I was moving some place abroad as a black writer I'd move to Bombay or Lagos or Johannesburg"), he still remembers the guy who after college saw living abroad as a form of escape, and he wonders if he's sacrificing his political and artistic integrity by being in Paris.

Mike also remembers the guy who, because of his politics, might've burned bridges he'd like to cross now. In three months he'll be getting married in a small village outside of Paris. After that he and his wife will be looking to start a family. Aside from recording and touring, his life seems to be settling down at thirty-four. He even wonders if it's time to retire from rap altogether. One of the four albums he's working on, *Negrophilia*, will be strictly jazz. The others will experiment with a range of musical styles that go way beyond hip-hop. Rap requires an artist to keep his ears on the street in order to stay fresh and relevant, and the only time Mike really gets to be around "the people" these days is when he takes one of his sporadic train rides out to the suburbs where Cameroons and French West Indians reside.

One avenue Mike has been exploring more is his writing. He's been taking his notebook to the café in the mornings and seriously trying to put his thoughts down. He says he's been working on a few essays for books and magazines. But since he's a perfectionist when it comes to his poetry, it takes forever for him to let a poem go. Mike's manuscript has been finished since 1997, but only a few people have seen it. There's just something about poetry for the page, maybe the romance of it, that appeals to him, that he wants to be a part of.

As he tells me this I think back to our earlier conversations about his mother, the old-school academic, and the sense of reverence he's always had for her. Saying that his life up to now has just been a series of rebellions against his inevitable ascendency into a nice bourgeois life complete with a tenured teaching position and a shelf full of books would be overly simplistic. But it wouldn't be too far afield to say that, in the end, Mike is still his mother's son and that, therefore, much of her lives in him. His aspirations to write poetic tomes may well relate back to a childhood in which child's play was checked and constant reading was required. Maybe he'd eventually give up his fascination with war toys.

I didn't hear from Mike over the next few months. The funny thing was that even after the time we spent together, not to mention the distance I'd traveled, I still wasn't sure if I'd include his story in the book. But then I got a call from Jeremy, who said that Mike had sent him something he wanted him to pass along to me. I eagerly awaited the arrival of the e-mail. When an essay entitled "How to Play War" finally popped up on my screen, I was neither surprised nor disappointed, only relieved to know that Mike C. Ladd is just as eccentric as ever.

WANDERLUST

Some people live life as though it is a race against time, steadily accumulating accomplishments, accolades, even acolytes. But others choose to look at life as if they are the heroes of their own quest for truth. For them, life is a journey filled with forks in the road, calls to adventure, and obstacles in the path to enlightenment. Quite often, these kinds of people are guided by the belief that the day must be seized. And what better way is there for us all to feel as though we are seizing the days of our lives than by changing the scenery. Change can force us out of our routines of thought and action and into a physical, mental, and spiritual place where we can ultimately define who we are independent of the identities our society forces on us all.

More than any other section in this book, "Wanderlust" interrogates the nature of the individual's search for meaning and joy and fulfillment against the collective and historical consciousness of struggle that has defined "the black experience" for several centuries. For so long the fortunate few (or "Talented Tenth") who have acquired an education or a modicum of economic wherewithal in this society have felt obliged to use what they have been given to help uplift others. That could mean leading a school, fighting for civil rights in the courtroom, or opening a hospital in the 'hood. However, balancing this sense of social responsibility with one's individual aspirations to live freely and independently often leaves people feeling torn, perhaps even guilty. Each of the following stories raises thought-provoking questions about to whom we owe our highest allegiance: ourselves or the group.

Desperately Seeking Clarity

Sariya Wilkens: Undecided

> "I feel like the work you do, that's your life's work. It's where you spend the majority of your time and you can't take that lightly."

Sariya Wilkens didn't understand why I was so interested in her story. She didn't get it a year ago when I first tracked her down in her friend's Harlem apartment, and she doesn't get it now that I am making a Sunday-morning sojourn from Brooklyn to Philadelphia, just for lunch. In an e-mail she'd sent me earlier in the week she expressed her concerns:

> i must admit i do have a few reservations about this. i guess i'm somewhat perplexed and i don't want to waste your time. i mean what you're wanting to find out is what i'm doing right? well, i'm not really DOING anything. i'm simply feeling. feeling my way through life and seeing every moment as my destination. i'm not working to some grand goal. i am simply relishing in the act of being. so, if you wish to come to philly to discuss...i dunno...Being...well, what can i say. i am by no means an authority on such a thing, simply a student. but if that's your wish i'm more than happy to comply....

For months I'd been trying to track Sariya down. She didn't have a phone number and she usually didn't reply to the e-mails I sent her from time to time. Now that I'd finally caught up with her, a mere two hours away, I had to make the most of the opportunity. Sariya's misgivings never crossed my mind. I was that sure that her story belonged in this book. But when I was on the New Jersey Turnpike and I had nothing but time to think, I asked myself what exactly was it about Sariya's story that kept me hounding her? Generally, the people I interviewed wanted to tell their story. Most, if not all, thought they had something valuable to share with a wider audience. Rare was the case of the person who just didn't get what I saw in them. Sure, she appreciated the premise of the book, that it was about African-Americans walking nontraditional paths; she just didn't see where she fit.

In a sense, I could see where Sariya was coming from. Her story was pretty blah. When we first met she was an overeducated, underemployed twenty-something living on a mattress in her friend's apartment. Big deal, right? She'd spent the requisite year "slumming" in Europe before heading to law school, where she took a vague interest in human rights law. But then, so do a lot of people. She took the bar because, well, that's what people do when they finish law school. Then, like any sane person who owed tens of thousands of dollars, she looked for a job. In fact, I had gone through pretty much the same experience myself. What kept me interested, however, was what happened after law school. Almost a full year had passed since she had graduated from Temple Law when we met way uptown, and still she hadn't found a job.

"I'm fighting desperation," Sariya said, her weary eyes and heavy voice echoing the sentiments of many unemployed Americans circa spring 2003. "I am trying not to panic and not to worry about where I'm supposed to be. I need a job. I need money. I need to be doing stuff. The world has expectations of me, especially since I've been in school so long."

Sariya's ideas about what she needed to be doing stemmed from her father, a lifelong Detroit schoolteacher, who passed away several years ago. "He had a great deal of integrity. Everything always came down to just doing good for him. Everything was always a moral issue for him. He worked in the school system for however many years and hated it, but he just felt like he had a responsibility. I think that played a large role in who I am."

Her father's commitment to educating African-American kids in downtrodden Detroit complicated Sariya's search for work. While she spoke the rhetoric of finding a job just to pay the bills, the more we talked the more she and I realized a "job" wouldn't be enough to satisfy or motivate her. Money wasn't the issue. Prestige didn't matter much to her either. There had to be more. Sariya needed to feel like her work mattered.

"I would take a job that I'm working crazy hours and getting paid nothing if I felt like I was helping somebody, as opposed to taking a job where I'm making all kinds of money that is pointless. I feel like the work you do, that's your life's work. It's where you spend the majority of your time and you can't take that lightly."

Cool. The next question I had for Sariya was what was she looking for. She'd entered law school with the notion of doing something "public interesty." She'd even spent a summer in Israel, as she says, "seeing the state of the Palestinians and seeing the way they were talked to and treated." But she still didn't know how she wanted to go about effecting change in the world.

"Most people in my life are like 'What are you doing? What are you waiting on?' They don't understand. They think I'm waiting for something to fall out of the sky and I'm sure that's what it looks like. But quite often what I hear from people is that I can do this and I can do that or they've heard about good jobs here or good jobs there and I can't really express to them that I don't care about those jobs. I want to do what I want to do. I want to do what makes me happy. I can't really explain to somebody if they say there's this great law clerk position that I don't want it and I'm sitting here jobless and homeless. Even if I come in on a stupid entry-level position for a really good organization that's really making some changes, that's fine."

Finally, I asked Sariya, point-blank, what her dream job would look like.

"I don't want to create a dream job. I don't like to leap into anything. If I think of a particular job as a dream job I'll become stuck on it and I don't want to lock in on anything and block everything else out. There are too many things out there that I don't know. I feel I'm necessarily working with flawed information. I don't know all the facts. There's a lot out there."

At that point it became apparent to me that what Sariya was really struggling with had more to do with the issues of this generation of African-Americans than with her specific need to find a job. Unlike our grandparents (or in some cases our parents, for that matter), for whom a job was a job and work was work, and you did it in order to provide and that was that, we've been given a different set of experiences, some shaped by integration, others by the sheer force of economic transformation in this country over the last thirty years, that have caused us to expect more from life.

"You can pretty much find a job doing anything," Sariya added. "You can find a job traveling, just simply to travel and write reviews. The way people deal with each other has broadened so everyone has evolved. We're [blacks] just coming along in that. It's like we're caught in the middle. We're still coming out of that old school of thought, but we're not completely out of it. At the same time, we've seen where we want to be whereas before they couldn't even see out this far."

Suddenly, Sariya and I had hit our stride and now I understood that what she and I were dealing with really spoke to a shift in our collective consciousness from a sense of America the land of opportunity to America the nation of entitlement. Whereas our parents' generation had looked at college as a chance to make a better life, we felt entitled to go not only to college, but graduate school and then to do the work we wanted to do. In Sariya's case, she discovered along the way that the professional career she had so ardently pursued wasn't all it was cracked up to be. Sure, her law degree qualified her to some extent to legally perform a certain trade, but beyond that she didn't know any more about the world or her place in it by virtue of her education. If anything, Sariya was less clear about her place in the world. She had this education, but she didn't know what to do with it. She'd had these experiences traveling the world, but she didn't know how to make use of them. She couldn't start her "adult" life because she didn't have a job. Sariya couldn't even go back to Detroit. "There's a lot of desperation there. It's like a dark shadow hangs over the city. Whenever I go back my mood just drops."

With no place else to turn, Sariya looked to her mother for advice.

Ten years ago Sariya would've scoffed at the idea of seeking her mother's counsel. In her words, her mother was "completely out there." In an era of perms and relaxers, and to the chagrin of her two daughters who wanted a cookie-cutter mom, Sariya's mother staunchly retained her Afro as a political statement. When Sariya was in middle school, her mother quit her social services job to study astrology and tai chi. Now, she was making her living as an astrologer, tai chi instructor, and spiritual reader. "Growing up I used to always talk about her. I'd say to her, 'Why don't you just act like a regular mother, do what they do and be normal.' My sister and I used to call her crazy when we were younger."

That was way before Sariya traded in her own perm for the natural hairstyle she now wore. That was also before she came to realize that perhaps her mother had been ahead of her time.

Mom advised her daughter to pay attention to what was going on on the inside. She told Sariya that anything happening or not happening externally was only a reflection of what was happening or not happening internally. But the most important gift her mother may have given her was time to figure things out, even time to struggle if need be. And with that time Sariya gained some important insights.

"I didn't realize how serious I was about my dreams. I felt like the only thing that was really important to me was finding a job doing something helping people, but there are other things besides that." Like the need to be creative. In recent months, Sariya told me she had been playing her guitar again. She'd had it since law school, but she'd never had the time to practice. Then there was her writing. For the last year Sariya had been able to write when and how she pleased rather than for a grade, under time constraints, and with certain required criteria in mind. She really enjoyed what was coming out, how it felt.

"I've been broke, but I feel like I've been pretty happy," she said. "I feel like I've grown a lot. Like I've solidified a lot of things for myself."

Shortly after that first conversation, Sariya was hired as an assistant manager at a café in Washington, D.C. The pace suited her. The hours weren't too bad. She seemed content for the time being. But then she told me she was moving to an ashram in southern Virginia. She'd visited Yogaville on a whim one weekend, and she liked it so much that she decided to make it her home.

That would be the last I heard from Sariya for almost a year.

• • •

Sariya's sister just graduated from dental school. In a couple of days she'll be heading off to begin her residency in Flagstaff, Arizona, on a reservation. The only reason Sariya agreed to leave Yogaville, where she'd been living the past eight months, is to help her sister move across the country. Otherwise, she'd still be there. A few days ago they bought a tent, sleeping bags, and cooking utensils. The plan is to camp out all the way across country. No hotels. No fatty highway food. No wasted money. This is how Sariya lives now. Spartanly.

One of the first things I notice about Sariya is that since the last time we spoke her hair has started to lock.

"Has it?" she asks. "I hadn't noticed." She keeps walking.

We're in West Philadelphia, the same neighborhood Sariya lived in when she was in law school. The University of Pennsylvania is here so a lot of the people hanging around campus on this early June afternoon are students with apartments and houses off campus. Although it is parked in the middle of a major city, West Philadelphia has a college-town atmosphere. There are quiet, tree-lined streets, old homes, coffee shops, a shopping center, bookstores, clothing boutiques, shoe stores, and exotic cuisine.

"What's it like being back here?"

Sariya doesn't reply right away. Instead, she digests my question. If there's one thing I detect about her that's different it's the calm, even pace at which she moves. She walks more slowly, takes her time answering questions: She's in no hurry.

"I was a completely different person. There are very few things that haven't changed. My personality. The way I operate in the world. It's been a very painful process, being stripped of that, and led to recognizing that none of that, even this personality, the things I present to other people, none of it is me. And I'm releasing that as much as I can."

"So describe Yogaville to me. What's it like? How does it exist?"

Another pause. "It was out in nowhere Virginia. Luxenburg. Not much else was around. It's in the Blue Ridge Mountains. The total space was about eight hundred acres. It's a huge place. There's a central quad area with buildings all around, a main dining hall, dorms, a dedication hall, a little library, a teaching academy where they teach yoga teachers and a main temple area that's dedicated to honoring all faiths.

"In the immediate quad area people live right there. There's also a monastery because it was started by a Hindu Swami. Including the monks there's probably forty people. In the extended community, the houses all around, there's probably one hundred people. You have a lot of people who come when it gets warm so that boosts the number. In the summer you have one hundred and fifty people."

The land for Yogaville was initially purchased by the singer Caroline Keene back in the early eighties. She was a disciple of the Swami. The property is sustained through meditation retreats, yoga retreats, and reiki retreats. There's also the yoga school. For people like Sariya who agree to work a full day the lodging and food are free. For those who prefer to have at least half of the day to themselves, since many of the residents are artists and musicians, the cost is roughly two hundred dollars a month.

"What kind of work did you do?"

"You just work. Whatever it is you want to do. I did landscaping work. I did farming work. I did kitchen work. It's a very unique environment that you really can't explain. You really have to experience it."

A typical day, Sariya said, went something like this:

Wake up

Morning meditation

Yoga

Breakfast

Service (i.e., work)

Afternoon meditation

Lunch

Service or free time, depending on the schedule

Evening meditation

Dinner

Once dinner is over a person can spend their evening however they choose. Some people take in movies. Others play music. There are even those who choose to spend their time socializing. Sariya chose to spend a lot of her time "observing silence," meaning she went days, weeks, without saying a single word.

"I came to some clarity in silence. You can observe yourself, observe the way you interact in the world in a different capacity. Once you make the decision not to open your mouth, you're forced to draw within. It's what you do when you meditate, but it makes your whole day a meditation. I always had a tendency to overeat, to absolutely stuff myself, and I had been struggling with it for a while. I started to eat all of my meals in silence and after a few days of this I noticed this voice that said, 'You better eat all you can because you don't know when you're going to eat again.' It took a while for me to get to that point. It wasn't words. It was a strong feeling."

Sariya has had many other revelations in the year since our last conversation, one of them being that more important than finding the "right" job at the "right" organization that does the "right" work so that she'll feel she's doing the "right" things in the eyes of society, she needed to take responsibility for her life. For Sariya that meant not getting a job right away just because that's what everyone says she's supposed to do; it also meant doing what she wanted to do and not feeling guilty about it.

"All of my conscious attention was going toward my personal evolution and I needed support. I needed to be in a place with other people of similar focus."

"And you met those people there?"

"Yeah, definitely. I think that was one of the reasons I said, 'Okay, I'm living here.' Encountering people who were genuinely devoted to their growth, their awareness, that's what I saw and I was like, 'This is it. I need to be here.' "

The whole experience sounded so idyllic: being in an environment where one can walk around in silence, not have to speak to anyone for as long as one likes, working, sleeping, meditating, not being bogged down by the trivialities that tend to mar one's days in the outside world. As I listened to Sariya describe Yogaville, I found myself longing for a similar kind of life. But something in me, the eternal skeptic perhaps, cut short those daydreams. As much as the thought of living on a commune sounded like a good idea, I know I need the balance of hustle and bustle. I also know nothing is perfect, not even paradise. Life in the city, the constant collision of wills and bodies, is our modern reality. Cities are where most of us have to be in order to survive. Ultimately, it's a heckuva lot easier to be tranquil and optimistic and healthy on a farm in southern Virginia than it is in Philly or Detroit or D.C.

Sariya nods as I voice my skepticism. "This is the understanding I needed for my development. I established a pretty sound foundation, but like with anything else you gotta come out in the world and deal with things. In order to be solidified it has to be threatened."

That threat came as soon as Sariya stepped off the bus in Philadelphia. The American bus station tends to attract the lowest of the low. People with hard-luck stories. People who can hardly scrape together a pair of nickels. Bums. Drunks. And this was the first thing Sariya saw when she returned to society. Al-

hough nothing particularly shocking took place, it was nonetheless a difficult moment for her. She felt herself slip back into her
old ways of thinking. The desperation kicked back in again. She
couldn't let herself end up like this, she thought. She had to find
a job; she had to make some money.

"It all came up, but it was okay because I could see it in light
of my new understanding, and walk away."

"And your mom? What does she think of all of this?"

"My mom is tickled to death. She loves it. When she was in
her twenties all she wanted to do was live on an ashram, so she's
living vicariously through me."

The next stop for Sariya is Flagstaff. She plans to spend some
time in and around the Grand Canyon helping her sister get settled in. Then who knows. The big city grind just isn't for her,
not right now. There's an ashram in California she's interested
in visiting, perhaps she'll even return to Yogaville, but nothing's
etched in stone. In fact, since that first conversation we had back
in Harlem more than a year ago, very little has changed about
Sariya's life. What has changed is Sariya.

Change Is Constant

Azikwe Chandler: Shepherd

"There's liberation in saying I can't do it all."

Azikwe Chandler was raised to the beat of a different drum. His parents were part of a collective, many of whom were ex–Black Panthers, who started their own community school in Brooklyn. While other parents around the country allowed their children be bused to integrated schools, African-Americans who had been heavily engaged in the Black Power movement elected to educate their own. Rather than send them to schools where they knew they would only learn about their ancestors one month out of the year, schools that were underfunded, under-staffed, and overpopulated, parents like Azikwe's wanted to in-still pride in their children so that when they did encounter a hostile society they could defend themselves with knowledge *of* themselves. This was a unique moment in America. Despite all that had happened in the sixties, from riots to assassinations, black folks still believed they could change the system and not just their place within it.

"We never celebrated Christmas growing up. We grew up celebrating Kwanzaa. The Nguzo Saba wasn't just at Kwanzaa, [though] the Seven Principles were throughout life for us. My parents really tried to live that. They gave us African names. We went to a school called Uhura Shasa. All of our classmates had names like Monsoor and Kenjufu and Assata and Taji—the whole nine. Every day we'd pledge to the red, black, and green. In the auditorium and on the walls we had big murals of Marcus Garvey, W. E. B. DuBois, Benjamin Banneker, [and] George Washington Carver. The teachers' names were Baba Yusef and Mama Amanesha, all of that kind of stuff."

Even when Azikwe's mother briefly separated from his father ("Pops had acted up," he says) and took him and his brother to live in Charleston, South Carolina, his father found a creative way to continue their education. "He'd send us books of *Anansi the Spider*. He'd be reading these books to us on the tape. My brother and I would sit down with the books and my father's voice would be like, 'Turn the page.' It was like he was there the whole time, so when I talk about being raised with the Nguzo Saba, that's what we had."

But despite his father's best efforts, moving to South Carolina was, to put it mildly, a culture shock. Suddenly, Azikwe was in Pepper Hill Elementary learning about Benjamin Franklin and George Washington. Suddenly, his classmates had names like Bobby and Johnny and Petey. He vividly recalls his first day of school: "This little kid was looking at the globe, I guess it was homeroom or something like that, and this little boy said, 'Look, it's the *Nigger* River!' "

Azikwe punched the boy in his face and he was sent home with a note. Although his little brother was sent home with pink slips nearly every day, after his first fight, Azikwe played it cool, kept a low profile, and came home, instead, with migraines. "I guess I was internalizing it rather than acting out," he says.

At all-black Burke High School, Azikwe excelled. He took AP courses and received the highest score on the SAT in the school, prompting the principal to declare "Zik Chandler Day" in his honor. Everyone patted him on the back, told him how proud of him they were, and asked him about his plans. All he knew was that he wanted to go to a school like Hampton, Howard, Morehouse, or Tuskegee. Then the vice principal spoke to him about Notre Dame; Zik blew him off. "I was like,

'Yeah, whatever.' I wanted to go to a black school." Still, the vice principal persisted. After making little headway with Zik, he spoke to his English teacher, who then spoke to his father. "When Pops said I should apply I couldn't tell him no. That wasn't an option."

Azikwe ended up at Notre Dame, where he studied architecture.

On the afternoon of our first meeting, lean, angular, and lengthy Azikwe, which means "healthy and vigorous of body and mind," sits crouched over a tiny outdoor table, his long legs ambling out onto the sidewalk. He just came from a morning of soccer, he says, and, seeing as it was his first time out in a little while, he thinks he might've overdone it. Behind us, just inside the sliding-glass doors of the café we're seated in front of, sits a crowd of young women celebrating a bridal shower. They've suddenly become boisterous, and while I'm listening and nodding, I'm worried that my recorder isn't capturing everything. Zik, on the other hand, doesn't seem to notice the women, much less mind their loud chatter; nor does he mind the people repeatedly interrupting our conversation to ask for directions. He takes it all in stride, smiles, takes a sip from his bottle of water, and with his deep disk jockey baritone picks right back up where he left off:

"I read two books back in ninety-seven, back to back. *The Celestine Prophecy* and *The Alchemist*. There were a bunch of themes that ran throughout the books, but there were two that really spoke to me. In *The Celestine Prophecy* it said there was no such thing as coincidence, everything happens for a reason. If you take that into mind, bigger things in particular, then you realize that certain things are put in your path to make you stronger and help you attain what it is you want to attain. You're supposed to learn from all of your situations, that's what it comes down to.

"The other theme, in *The Alchemist*, was that if you make up your mind that you really want to do something and you follow that commitment, you put your all into it to make that thing come to fruition, then the universe conspires to make it happen and you have all of these signs and omens that show you the way and tell you that this is what you're supposed to be doing."

Zik was the product of a shot in the dark e-mail I'd sent to some friends when I began writing *Beat of a Different Drum*. I was just looking for people to interview when he sent an enthusiastic reply that read: "Returned Peace Corps Volunteer (Brother) on an alternative path" in the subject box. The message opened: "Based on the e-mail below, I believe I'm one of the folks you'll want to talk to." A year by year time line, starting with his birth and ending with his present position as a projects director for AmeriCorps' National Civilian Community Corps (NCCC) program, followed. Since graduating from Notre Dame with a degree in architecture in 1994, Zik had never lived in a single place longer than two years. Among other jobs, he'd tended bar in London, led groups of high schoolers on tours through Italy, and taught in Nicaragua. Noticeably absent from this improvised curriculum vitae, however, was any mention of architecture beyond his Notre Dame years.

So what had happened?

Italy.

As a kid Zik had travel experiences. One was the journey he and his family took between South Carolina and Brooklyn and the other was reading his father's *National Geographic* magazines. "In Charleston, things are slow and everybody's nice and you can speak to everyone on the street. In New York, it's colder and some people say the people are colder. My mind was open from that travel. In the *National Geographics* they'd always talk about different places and foods and I always thought, 'Man, wouldn't it be cool to be able to see some of these places.' But how was I going to be able to do that? I'm this broke kid, my parents had never been outside of the country, so I always had the idea, but I didn't know how it was going to happen."

"*. . . when you want something, all the universe conspires in helping you to achieve it.*"—from *The Alchemist*

Every student who studies architecture at Notre Dame is required to spend their junior year in Italy studying classical architecture. Zik was no exception. "I loved it. That whetted my palate for international travel, being that far from home. It was rough, too. I had managed to save about two thousand dollars that summer, but then I was in Italy trying to keep up with my white friends who really didn't have to live off their own money. Every five minutes they were talking about a cappuccino break. I'd run out with them every time they would run out and then a month passed and I didn't have any money."

Even after Zik spent all his money, even during the four- to five-day stretches when he ate bread and jelly for every meal, even after he maxed out every credit card he could get his hands on, he had the time of his life. And when he felt like he'd reached the end of his rope, inexplicable things happened to keep him going.

"I know I had some spirits looking out for me," Zik says, recalling the time when a young woman he'd met on a bus in Rome invited him to one of the city's open-air markets. He thought she was shopping for herself until she handed him the bags and said they were for him. "It blew my mind. I had just met this woman, didn't know her. There was no reason for her to do that. I was moved. I knew she didn't have any money either. She was a student herself. She said she had a feeling that if the situation was reversed I'd do the same for her. I was just like,

'Wow.' Karma is a mug. I definitely think it was God and karma. I know I had some spirits looking out for me."

Meanwhile, Zik's mind was starting to wander away from architecture. More than the classically built churches he was supposed to be studying, Azikwe was fascinated by what was going on around him, the people in particular. He questioned whether he wanted to become an architect, if his heart was really into building. By the time senior year rolled around Zik had already decided he wasn't going to pursue architecture any further after graduation.

"There's a lot that you learn from the university, and what they teach you in class is only a minor part of that. For me, it was a question of where was I going to have the greatest impact on my people in terms of making this world a better place. I knew that architecture was something I could do. But in terms of what I could do to best assist my people really has to do with education. I knew that was what I had to do."

Zik also knew he could see the world without a lot of money. He didn't need a lot to survive on once he was there. Plus, the spirits would watch over him. Initially, he thought about the Peace Corps, but he figured before he could go overseas to help other people, he needed to address the problems here in the States, in the 'hood, on the "block" so he joined AmeriCorps for two years. "I got to see parts of the States I'd never seen before. In Denver I learned to ski and got hooked on that. I never thought I'd be on skis, but you learn all of these different things and your horizons get broadened." From there it was on to the Peace Corps and, among other places, Nicaragua, where he taught high school. Zik warmly recalls his two years in Central America. "Sometimes people would offer me dinner, sometimes we'd drink a little rum. It was just socializing. We'd play dominoes, whatever. It was beautiful." Those were good years, his twenties, where without a television to crowd his evenings he reignited his creative flame. "I read a whole bunch of books. I also wrote a lot of letters. My relationships, even though I was far away, were a lot more intimate."

Since 2001, Azikwe has been a project director for the National Community Service Corps, where he oversees a number of community service projects performed by groups of eighteen- to twenty-four-year-olds who have devoted a year of their lives to full-time community service. He heads up groups in Virginia, West Virginia, Ohio, Pennsylvania, and D.C. Zik's job involves negotiating partnerships with larger entities like the National Park Service or Habitat for Humanity and delivering the man- power. But while he certainly believes in the mission of the pro- gram, particularly bringing together kids from vastly dissimilar backgrounds to work for an uplifting cause, something has al- ways been missing.

"I want to see this resource in the 'hood. We need houses built in the 'hood, we need rec centers built, we need to clean up these lots that are strewn about with glass and turn them into community gardens."

The trouble is finding organizations that will sponsor the types of community projects he's interested in doing. In a field driven by aggressive grant writing and continuous networking, many smaller community-based organizations often can't com- pete. Ultimately, what ends up happening is that NCSC gets of- fered the same kinds of projects that, while laudable in their own right, rarely touch or concern the people and places closest to Azikwe's heart.

"My job is tough, but I'm learning a lot and I feel like I'm bringing those resources in. I've got another year or two. I've got to be successful at this. When I'm done I have to be able to say we helped x, y, and z communities in the inner city in D.C. or in Columbus, Ohio."

I pay particular attention to the way Zik stresses the phrases "I've got to" and "I have to." There's an earnestness in his voice. He wants to be a part of social change. He wants to lead something, to serve some significant purpose for black people, only he feels stifled by a combination of forces that are beyond his control. He can't rub his hands together and make the money to rebuild a community just appear. Someone else has to decide it's worthwhile to invest in a vacant lot, or an after-school program, or in building homes for the poor. Also, his thick-skinned idealism is beginning to wear thin.

"I think the hardest part is now. Up until now it really wasn't that difficult. Now I'm thirty-one. I've never been caught up in society, but now it's like society is saying I should have a house and be married and trying to raise kids. That's the hard part, trying to think of myself as a responsible man now as opposed to gallivanting across the world, as my folks have said a few times. I don't have any regrets, none at all, so it's only hard for me when I think, 'Well, why don't I have this or that? Why didn't I get caught up in that materialism?' That's what our society is about, so it puts it in your face all the time. When you see that type of thing nonstop and it's just pounding on you to own this car, live in this house, have this much money, to invest, fly here, and cruise on this ship. When you hear that constant 'Buy. Buy. Buy,' and you ain't got no money, you start to wonder, shoot, 'Why don't I?'

"Then you get to wondering if that means you're less of a person than the next man. I think that's what can become difficult. Of course, I remind myself that I've got ten times as much as somebody my age in Central America or, shit, Asia or any place else in the world outside of an industrialized country."

Azikwe was born and raised in America, though, and like the rest of us he has to deal with the influence of an unyielding consumer society. Nevertheless, I wonder if he holds himself to an unfair standard; if he isn't applying 1960s dogma to a twenty-first-century paradigm; if he isn't denying himself the possibility of financial freedom out of a fear that money will somehow corrupt the values he's stood by his entire life, or an even deeper fear that he might enjoy having money. After all, like his father has said to him on numerous occasions, he can still be a positive influence on young people by being a successful architect. Moreover, he could finance his own community works projects. With money, all of the hard work gets a little easier. But in order to get that money, Zik would have to follow the very conventions he's spent the last decade circumventing.

Seven months after our first conversation, Azikwe sent me an e-mail. He'd finally hit the wall and said he was leaving his job. A week later we meet up again. He's been on the road for ten days, logging a total of two thousand miles, he says. For the last couple of months he's been pulling fifty-plus-hour weeks. He looks exhausted but relieved. "There's liberation in saying I can't do it all," he says.

For the record, Zik adds, he still believes in the program; he just didn't think he's the right person for the job anymore. His boss was set to offer him a contract extension, but at that moment he decided to be honest with himself. The fire with which he'd come into it just wasn't there anymore and he couldn't fake it in order to meet society's demands that he play the responsible thirty-something role. "Administrivia" wasn't his forte, and for the last two years his life has been dominated by it.

"A lot of the systems weren't in place before I got there, so a lot of the work for the last two years has been building that up, building standard operating procedures, protocols, setting up policies. Necessary things, but they kept me away from what I really wanted to do, which was get back into the community and actually develop these projects. It's been a whole lot of stress. I feel like my department was understaffed the whole two years."

Azikwe and I talk for another couple of hours, mainly about his plans for the future, which are up in the air. He's experiencing a heavy bout of wanderlust, but he still wants to get his master's or doctorate in education so he can open his school one day. Already, he's been looking into a community service project in Belize, this one an experiential learning program where he would lead a group of college-age kids around the country for a few months. If that doesn't work out he's thinking about packing up his car, loading up his snowboard, and taking off for the winter to a resort where he's sure he can find some work. He wants to do some writing, maybe even some designing. Either way, he has a window of time and he plans to use it wisely.

None of that's to say Zik doesn't still have his doubts. Like the frustration that once manifested in the form of migraines when he was just a boy in South Carolina, he says his anxieties are appearing in his dreams in the form of an intruder. The intruder comes to his door and tries to fight his way in. Zik battles him at the threshold. In the end, neither of them is able to defeat the other. The battles just go on and on.

In December, Zik sends out a mass e-mail to his friends and family explaining his plans for the near and distant future. He has accepted a position as a group leader of an experiential learning program that will tour Peru, Bolivia, and Ecuador. From time to time over the next several months I receive journal entries from Zik. In one he tells of spending four days climbing Machu Picchu with fifty pounds of gear on his back. In another he writes of trudging through the Amazon rainforests in Bolivia. Others follow, but the common thread tying each of them together (despite his constant vexation with the kids he's leading) is his joy. Once again he's writing poetry; in fact, the logs themselves are often intense and vivid, the writings of an invigorated person. An excerpt from a poem entitled "Counting Blessings" I found to be particularly poignant:

> This could be a poem about despair. Of living here and
> there but being nowhere. I could speak of longings and
> desires, and smoldering fires. Of being broke, feeling
> sick, and not having sh_t. I could speak of places
> I've never seen, or not meeting the woman of my
> dreams . . . I could speak of racism and misogyny, and
> police brutality . . .
>
> But I'd rather speak of travels, good food, and having
> the right attitude. I'd rather speak of following
> dreams and other good things, like the joys life
> brings. How about sunrises and sunsets, and having no
> regrets?

After reading this I am inspired to reread *The Alchemist*. A sentence that I had overlooked the first time around, probably because it was so simple, pops out at me. The young shepherd, Santiago, is being described, but I think of Azikwe Chandler, a shepherd in his own right, and that maybe he is exactly where he is supposed to be. The sentence read: "His purpose in life was to travel. . . ."

A Nomad Knuckles Down

Heidi Brooks: Nonprofit Consultant

"Where can I be most effective? That's always what guides me. Where can I make the most difference."

Heidi Brooks's story embodies the ethos of a generation: its restlessness, its ambition, its blend of social consciousness and self-involvement, its linguistic fluencies and cultural fluidity. From one job to the next, one location to another, they leap; always in search of the new and the more fulfilling. And why not?

When Heidi and I first meet, in the back of a Manhattan Starbucks, she is finishing up work on her second graduate-level degree, this one an M.B.A. from Harvard. (Heidi already has a master's in international affairs from Johns Hopkins School of Advanced International Studies.) She's already landed what she calls her "dream job" and she's looking forward to staying put in her Boston condo after years of living either overseas or in temporary housing situations. Having a permanent residence, with her own furniture, a normal kind of life, will be as new to Heidi as traveling abroad is for the first-timer.

Since she was a teenager Heidi has lived in a single city for more than a year only once. The only time she's had the same job for more than a year was when she was an auditor for a humanitarian organization in third-world countries. Even then, though, Heidi lived in twelve countries over twenty-four months. Whenever she and her team showed up at an aid site, that meant another program was phasing out, shutting down. Her job was to make sure the books were balanced. More likely than not, she would never have been an auditor in the United States, but abroad, even something as mundane as inspecting an organization's accounts was an interesting experience.

"When I first went overseas I was going to Hungary for the summer to study. People were like, 'Why do you want to go to Hungary? Why there?' I was just, like, 'I need to go *somewhere*.' I was pretty open. A friend of mine [had] found this fellowship. I got it and spent two months in Hungary and Budapest traveling around. It was amazing. [It was] 1990. There was all this transition that they were undergoing. The fall of communism was about to happen. I was in Czechoslovakia months after the Velvet Revolution. The Berlin Wall had just come down. I was in Yugoslavia a few years before the war started. I was nineteen!"

Following that summer Heidi found it difficult to go back to college life at the University of South Carolina. Abroad, particularly in Eastern Europe at that time, each day had been as an adventure. Back at school, though, her days followed a standard routine of classes and social events. Heidi just wasn't interested in being at the school, so two weeks into her sophomore year she left again, this time for a semester at the University of Massachusetts.

"I didn't know anyone at U. Mass. I just got there and wandered around and met people. After that I came back [to South Carolina] for a semester, then I spent the following summer at Amherst, then I went to D.C. for a semester and worked on the Hill, then I came back to USC, then I went to Ann Arbor for a summer program, then I went to Argentina for five months."

"Why Argentina?" I ask.

"The Dominican Republic was my first choice, but [the school] canceled the program. I knew I wanted to live somewhere Spanish-speaking because I studied Spanish growing up. I grew up in Arizona. I'd been to border towns in Mexico. I knew someone who had gone to Argentina so I was like 'Okay,' not realizing that those were two polar ends of the Latin spectrum. It was a learning experience. It's a beautiful place. But I didn't get to enjoy myself. It kind of killed my interest in Latin America. I think if I'd gone to the D.R. I'd still be there."

Heidi is down to earth. She has a sense of humor and can tell a good story. She also strikes me as someone who doesn't stress easily, someone who can fit into any situation without much effort. That her self-assurance sometimes verges on overconfidence is excusable. Being fluent in three foreign languages (Spanish, French, and Vietnamese) while more than 90 percent of the American population doesn't even own a passport puts one in a very exclusive group. In fact, I think part of the reason Heidi has chosen her path is because it's different from the one most people walk. In an age when so many people are striving to fit in with the crowd, "difference" is social currency. Being different from the norm gets you in places; it also gives you access to people and experiences (and conversations) that can change the way you view the world, as well as your place in it. Perhaps that explains why, as an African-American woman, Heidi chose to study government and international affairs, and why, when the opportunity to attend a premier graduate program like the School of Advanced International Studies (SAIS) came, she took it.

"Coming out of USC I didn't feel like I got to be with the best people in the world. So going to a world-class graduate school gave me much more confidence about that. That exposed me to so many things. I feel like I'm in a world now that I would have been in earlier had I gone to Harvard [College] or another school, but I'm there now."

"What is that world?" I ask.

"I don't know, the Talented Tenth. You can divide the world into the people who know, the people who don't know but suspect, and the people who don't know at all. I'm definitely in the second group. There is so much out there, whether it's secret societies, or the way boards work. These are networks that I have access to now, that I might have had access to earlier had I gone to a private high school. I can't say I know how all these things happen, but I definitely suspect."

While acquiring access to knowledge, and to an extent power, has always been Heidi's driving force, the burden of finding the right occupation, one that matches her ambition, has hit its share of dead ends. Heidi initially took the internship on Capitol Hill because she thought she wanted to practice law or get into national politics. Later, she made an earnest effort to get into medical school, but she could never get the scores on the MCAT. More recently at Harvard, Heidi thought she wanted to be an investment banker.

"There is nothing on this earth I am less suited for than investment banking, but I went to a summer program. I was really repressing parts of myself to make myself fit this mold. I finally realized, this is not what I want to do, this is not for me. Even if I managed to get a job doing it, I would have been so unhappy. It would have been really hard. I definitely don't pick the path of least resistance, but there was a logical story for why I wanted the things I wanted."

If that is the case, then that story most likely began the summer Heidi spent at Ann Arbor.

"The program I went to in Michigan was called the Woodrow Wilson Fellowship for International Public Policy. They pay for people of color—Asian, Latino, black—to go into policy schools so they will get into the public sector. They have so few people of color who are going into international affairs. It's really, really a big problem because people [of color] think, 'Oh, I want to do something for my community.' I'd already been overseas and I was just like, 'People over here do not need my help. There are real problems overseas.' What's poverty here? Poverty here is nothing. It doesn't even compare to the poverty

I've seen overseas. I felt like there were so many more needs overseas and that was really where my calling was."

Heidi's first job overseas was on Africa's Ivory Coast, where she managed an aid organization's HIV/AIDS outreach program. "I developed a reproductive health program for refugees from the Liberian War who were in Côte d'Ivoire," she adds. The country's HIV/AIDS crisis was and is one of the worst in the world. Heidi's job was to figure out ways to educate Africans on the risks of the disease. One way was through what's called social marketing. Instead of simply giving them away, health workers sold condoms to villagers. "If you just gave away condoms people won't value them, won't use them, but if they understand the risk of AIDS and STDs, they'll actually buy them." A year later Heidi was still in Africa, this time interning with the State Department in Zaire (now the Democratic Republic of Congo). She was a liaison between local NGOs (nongovernmental organizations) and human rights groups and observed the transitional parliament and opposition party as the country prepared for its first free elections in more than thirty years. That the work was unending and frequently left her feeling defeated didn't dampen her hope for the future of Africa or the value of international aid work.

During her two-year stint as an internal auditor, however, Heidi started questioning the impact she was really having abroad. As a rule, by the time the auditing team arrived at a site the aid team had already returned to the United States or moved on to another location. But the locals came anyway. They didn't understand that their time was up, that the charity had moved on to a new cause in a new place. Without fail, Heidi had to tell them there was no more grain or medicine and turn them away. In most cases the natives went right back to whatever they had been doing in order to survive before the humanitarians came with promises of a brighter, more plentiful future. Before long, she says, it was as if the organization had never even been there.

"I didn't think development, the way they were doing it, was working. You have an impact on a small number of beneficiaries over a very limited period of time. I felt we were too vulnerable to what donors wanted. I have friends who are very happy being program directors, helping their two thousand people in a particular community, with the money they can get together through writing grants. They're there for three years and they're happy with that. That frustrates me. What can I do in three years? I can help these people for this amount of time? In some ways [we] make their lives worse because now they're dependent. I felt like I was seeing more and more of the bad impact of development."

After her second year of auditing Heidi decided that relief work wasn't for her either. Like law and medicine, it didn't fit her personality. She was more a big impact person than she was a humanitarian. Whereas the latter can survive on small victories and find joy in helping others as much as they can for as long as they can, the former needs the big picture complete with definite end goals always in view; otherwise they have a hard time staying focused or interested, or there.

Heidi's next post was as a project officer with the International Finance Corporation's Mekong Project Development Facility in Hanoi, Vietnam. "I was very interested in economic development, especially in Asia," she says of the move. "There seemed to be some very big differences between Africa and Asia in terms of development. Africa is still where it was, in fact sliding backwards, and Asia is moving ahead, even with the Asian crisis."

The IFC works with small businesses in underdeveloped regions to improve the quality of their services. The idea is that by developing entrepreneurs, you strengthen the overall economy of a country, which in turn fuels job growth, thereby empowering thousands of previously disenfranchised people. Heidi loved

Asia: the people, the language, the culture. Being an expatriate there also had its perks. She lived comfortably, better than she would have in the United States, and though the work was demanding, she had time and money. But even with an established, well-funded organization, Heidi felt she wasn't having the impact. There were wasted resources and inflated salaries and in the end very few people ended up benefiting from the program. She stayed on board for a year, then left to become an independent consultant. Finally, in her second year, she started asking herself if the expatriate life was what she wanted. She could've stayed in Vietnam. The money was good. She didn't have to work all that much. Her life there was fairly simple, and yet she felt disconnected.

"I missed black America. It's important to me and people don't necessarily understand that outside the U.S."

Abroad, whether it was West Africa or rural Vietnam, Heidi was identified as American first and foremost. Her race didn't matter nearly as much to the outside world. In Africa, she'd been called La Blanche, meaning the "white woman." In Vietnam, the fact that she wasn't Vietnamese meant no matter how long she remained there, she would never become a full-fledged community member. It didn't matter that she spoke the language or that she had the expertise.

There was also the challenge of being single overseas. She'd just turned thirty and she wanted to be in a relationship. While her Western male counterparts found companionship abroad with relative ease, it was a different ball game for a single woman. There were cultural obstacles, issues of custom and complications of gender that at twenty-four she hadn't taken into account. However hard it is to find a mate stateside, it was that much harder in a completely different culture. Added to an already complex plot, Heidi, in her ideal world, pictured herself with a black man and she realized that the chances of finding him on the streets of Hanoi were not just slim, they were nil. Six straight years abroad, fifty-six countries stamped in the pages of her passport, a box full of journals and photos: she'd had a good run; it was time to go home.

Earlier I mentioned that Heidi found her "dream job." What I didn't mention is the job itself. Halfway through business school, Heidi heard about the Bridgespan Group, a consultancy that works exclusively with nonprofit organizations and donor foundations. After a professor at Harvard used Bridgespan for a case study, Heidi had done her own research on the organization. She was impressed. What set Bridgespan apart from similar firms was that it had the expertise and technical support of its parent company, Bain & Company, a leading for-profit consulting firm.

"Where can I be most effective? That's always what kind of guides me. Where can I make the most difference? Nonprofit activities are being geared more and more toward the private sector, partnering with the private sector, trying to manage organizations in a way that's consistent with some accountabilities demanded by the private sector. There's an increasing awareness that we need to get at more root causes, even if there's less money to go around. It's a really amazing, changing time in the nonprofit world now."

After 9/11 and the tech-bust there was significantly less charitable money to go around. As companies faced sliding profit margins, corporate foundations and individual donors alike cleaved to their wallets and purses. Traditionally, nonprofits haven't been held to the same standards of their for-profit counterparts because, for example, you can't judge the success or failure of a community outreach center over a fiscal quarter. That takes years. Notwithstanding that, as the nonprofit sector congests and donors become more discerning, organizations are having to show results. That is where nonprofit consultancies come in. They help organizations that have operated without systems or ascertainable end goals develop those structures so they can compete in the new business environment.

Although Heidi has at last found what she wanted to do, she knows it would never have happened without the other stops along the way. "I think being overseas just gives you so much more perspective on the U.S. For better or for worse. Some people come back and are like, 'Oh, thank God I'm American. I'm not burning my passport any time soon.' I feel like the U.S. is a great place, it's home, it's my favorite place in the world. But there are so many things that are wrong, so many things that could be better, so many things other countries do better."

So Heidi is staying put in Boston. There'll certainly be more overseas travel in her future. But for the time being her stake is with America. Here is where she believes she can have the impact she spent her twenties looking around the world for. In a way it's fitting that she ended up longing for the very home she couldn't wait to get away from.

There's a lot worth taking away from Heidi's story. It speaks to an uncompromising generation and it shows a kind of profound logic that people in their twenties and thirties aren't often given credit for by their elders. We are often told by those who say they have our best interests at heart that we should stay put awhile, lay down some roots, become responsible, dependable members of society. Employers, we're told, like to see that you've stayed at the same job for more than a year or two. They say it looks good when you don't jump around too much. And yet, a quick glance at Heidi's résumé suggests that the exact opposite might be true as well.

What impresses me most about Heidi is how she's measured her moves as though her life were a game of chess. One of her gifts, it would seem, is her ability to see the big picture. Think about it: Every new experience, new job, new school, in some way piggybacked off what she'd done just prior. Moreover, nearly every one of her overseas excursions was paid for by someone else: a foundation, a university, an organization, even the U.S. government. What she always had was a plan, and while it wasn't perfectly scripted, the outline was in place. Meet the people who can open doors. Make the follow-up phone calls to show them you're serious. Shake the hands to leave an impression. Set up the lunches. Do your research. Go after what you want. Who cares if it doesn't make sense to people on the outside. One day it will.

Perhaps what sets Heidi's and my generation apart from earlier ones isn't so much our arrested development, our eternal restlessness, our demand for inclusion or our unwillingness to compromise, so much as it is our ability to exercise our mobility. Maybe if our parents, the "Boomers" or "Me Generation," had the same knowledge of and access to the world, they would have chosen to live their lives differently. When you consider access and opportunity as the two drastically distinct forces shaping modern American existence, jumping around makes sense. It isn't at all irrational. In fact, I'd even say anything less in a world of uncertainty such as ours defies logic. The global economy is in a stage of transition. Once stable, reliable jobs are being shipped all across the planet. No one is guaranteed, let alone wants, the same job for a lifetime. There's too much world to be seen, too many lives to be lived.

Postscript. Less than a year into her new job, Heidi's firm launched an initiative to recruit and retain senior-level leadership. Nonprofits, she explained, were dealing with the same employee turnover issues that every other industry was confronting. People burned out, moved, changed careers, leapt from one charity to the next. Heidi was appointed associate director of strategic alliances. Once again, after only a year, Heidi had a new job.

Throw the Masterplan Overboard

Bill Collins: Principal/Sailor/Chef

> "Passion for something plays an intrinsic role in my ability to not only grasp but work with it and go with it. And when the passion wanes, then I don't fight it."

At the age of thirty-four, Bill Collins boarded a wooden forty-foot sailboat and he said good-bye, for good. Everything he owned in the world was in or on the old boat. The other sailors down at the marina said it couldn't handle the rough waters ahead. He wouldn't last long, he was told. The boat was too old, he was too inexperienced, and nature was too unpredictable. Besides, how would he make money? How would he afford the repairs? They gave Bill a few months tops. Then he'd be back. There was just no way a guy who four years earlier had never handled a boat in his life could survive alone on the open seas.

Bill wasn't supposed to be going off alone. The woman in his life at the time was supposed to be beside him. But at the last minute she realized that the idea of living on the water, of moving on and on without knowing when it would all stop, was too much. She promised Bill she'd wait for him. But for Bill this wasn't a romance novel or dramatic screenplay; nor was he embarking on a year in Japan or a summer in Europe. He was surrendering to the uncertainty of life.

"My plan was very clear from the get-go," Bill says, "there was no pretentiousness about it; there was nothing covert about what it was. [I said] 'I'm checking out. You ain't gonna stand up there on no dock and wave no handkerchief at me and expect me to come back.'"

This isn't to say that it was that easy to leave. Bill had a promising career, a son he adored, friends, and family. Certainly, he wondered if he was putting his life in jeopardy, if the other sailors knew something he didn't, if the couple hundred dollars he had in his pocket would be enough to survive on until he found a steady source of income. But when it came down to it, this was the single dream he'd allowed himself to want completely and entirely. He'd given the last four years of his life to learning how to be a sailor; he couldn't give it up now.

One of Bill's earliest memories is standing on the platform of a train station, beneath a boiling Texas sun, waving good-bye to his father for the summer. For the first few years the train carried Bill's dad to New York City; later it took him to Ithaca, New York. Of course, back then, he didn't know this. "All I knew was the train was going somewhere," he says, recalling his childhood in Austin. "And as a kid, the train took on the whole symbolism of freedom. It was cool because my exposure to that at the time was 'Wow!' . . ."

When Bill was finally old enough, his father explained that the reason he went away each summer was because he was working toward his doctorate in education. After starting his studies at Columbia, he had transferred to Cornell. He traveled north for school for a number of reasons, the most significant being the racial bigotry that kept Texas's foremost institutions closed to blacks. Bill's father began his graduate studies in the mid-1940s; not until 1950 did the Supreme Court rule that the University of Texas Law School was in violation of the Constitution's equal protection mandate when it refused to enroll Herman Marion Sweatt after he had been admitted to the school.★ In his opinion reversing a state court decision, Chief Justice Vinson stated that because the black law school the university had opened to accommodate black students was not comparable to its all-white counterpart, the separate but equal doctrine established in *Plessy v. Ferguson* had been violated, though only as it regarded graduate institutions that received state funding, not elementary and secondary schools; that part would come four years later with *Brown v. Board of Education*.

In all, Bill's father would make the trip eleven summers in a row. The twelfth and final year the entire family moved to Ithaca so that Mr. Collins could finish his dissertation. For Bill, the move was very well likely the experience that set the stage for the life he has since lived.

"I went from an all-black situation as a kid. It wasn't like I was in a cave; I came from an educated family. But in my neighborhood there were no white people. I didn't go to school with white kids, the mailman was black, the policeman, the bus driver. Everyone I came in contact with for the most part was black. I never really got downtown. My mother didn't have no money to be spendin' downtown. When we went somewhere we got in the car and went down in the country. My only exposure to white folks in terms of authority was white police on the highway. You know there was always the fear of the sheriff stopping you. I wasn't driving but that was a prevalent thing, always an ongoing conversation in our family. Whenever we got where we were going, there were stories that went back and forth, but I had no contact with white folks."

From the moment he arrived in Ithaca, Bill's world expanded. His teachers challenged him with ideas and books that made him think critically about the world, while his new class-

★*Sweatt v. Painter,* 339 U.S. 629 (1950)

mates accepted him as an equal among them. "I literally thrived," he says. "It was totally provocative to me because it was a challenge. I'd never seen shit like this in my life. We jumped right off into it. It was an absolutely excellent situation. It was just what the doctor ordered."

Bill returned to Austin a year later a different person, that one year up North having placed him so far ahead of his classmates that he cruised through high school. Admittedly, he could have pushed himself harder, challenged himself in areas where he had more difficulty, but by then he saw school merely as a means to an end, and not the end-all be-all his family members made it out to be. Despite Bill's deep admiration for his father's accomplishments and lifelong dedication to education, he looked at school as but one kind of education.

"I believe in education for education's sake as opposed to education for a degree," Bill says. "[But] I understand that you gotta have that degree if you want to make some changes, maybe not in your life but in somebody else's life. This is something that's been going on for ages and ages, and it's not to say it's right or wrong, that's just the way it is, so you gotta make the most of it."

For Bill, that meant heading off to all-black Southern University in Louisiana shortly after his seventeenth birthday. The eldest son of the man everyone called "Prof" had to go to college. But by then Bill was more intrigued by the idea of leaving home than he was thrilled with the thought of more school. He started out full-time, but then he got a job at the post office and switched to part-time.

Bill abruptly cuts off his retelling and he looks at me as though there is something he needs me to grasp thoroughly before he goes any further. "I *like* to work," he says enthusiastically. "That's my connection with the real world. Nothing wrong with being a student, but I'm a student all the time. I find that I'm able to grow more, expand broader, when I have a way to support my independence. Work never bothered me. I made the most of it and it wasn't a matter of how much I was making as long as I had a job because I could then manipulate the money."

After dragging his feet for close to six years, during which he'd gotten married and had a child, Bill decided it was time to finish school and move on with his life. Although he'd be graduating with a degree in education, and despite holding down a stable job at the post office, he wanted to leave the South. "I wanted to expand. I wanted to travel. My travels at a very early age were limited but they were travel. They were down to the family farm, down to family things. But it was exposure and that was the point. I was constantly being exposed to something. My mind was growing. There were constantly things I had to challenge myself about. The experiences I had at an early age weren't always good, but they were always enlightening."

Bill had been reading about the opportunities for African-Americans, particularly those with college degrees, in places like Los Angeles, and he figured that that was where he wanted to be. Explaining all of this to his parents, however, would be its own ordeal. He would have to stand up to his father, to his family rather, and tell them he was leaving in order to discover a world he'd only known about in books and magazines and movies.

Bill leans in closer, presses his elbows to his knees, and sets the stage for me. He was sitting at the very table he'd grown up eating at. His new bride and their son were beside him and his parents were seated across from him. Then he tells me about his grandparents to really paint the picture for me. They were farmers—poor black-bottom black folks, he calls them. The family farm set on five hundred acres of land was all they had. Bill's father had been born on the farm in 1908. He'd been the oldest of twelve children, six boys and six girls. They'd walked twelve miles to school each day, *after* they'd completed their morning chores on the farm. Some had shoes, some didn't. Recalling all of the details, Bill suddenly swells with emotion: "We talking about dirt roads, little one-room schoolhouse with the potbelly stove in the back, off in the woods next to a cemetery. We ain't talking about no beautiful environment. It was almost surreal." On the strength of the livestock and crops the farm yielded, as well as his grandparents' wisdom and thrift, though, they had seen nine of Bill's uncles and aunts through college at a time when the average African-American didn't even get out of high school. All of this and more was hanging over Bill's head when he looked his father in the eye and said he was quitting the post office to find his calling.

Breaking into his wide, toothy grin, Bill dabs his cigar in the ashtray on the coffee table between us, leans back comfortably on his couch, crosses his legs, and says, "I might as well have dropped a nuclear device on the table because that provoked some shit . . . 'What do you mean you're quitting? Do you realize how much money you're making at the post office?'

"I was making more than my old man was making and he had a doctorate degree."

In L.A., Bill weighed his options. There was a "scene" (as he likes to often say) for just about everybody, depending on what your inclinations were. Fresh out of college, and still fairly green in the ways of the city, he dabbled, taking work as it came. Since he came from a family of educators, his task was to carve out a path for himself, by himself. His father had already blazed a trail by getting his doctorate, and in a way that relieved the pressure Bill's contemporaries felt as firsts in their families to graduate from college; instead, the pressure he felt was rooted in his personal drive to be an individual at all costs.

Ultimately, he decided law school was his best option at the time. A law degree was practical, and it would allow him to keep his options as open as possible. It was also free.

"The University of California system had UCLA, USC—a couple of others had scholarships for young black graduates. At that point taking the LSAT wasn't even required. If you wanted to take it, take it. I took it only because when I got to L.A. there was no way in the world I was going to be able to go to school. There were too many things happening. I took the LSAT, I don't even know what I got, but it was enough points that the scholarship I'd been promised at UCLA could be exchanged for a scholarship at USF (University of San Francisco). Another brother wanted to come to L.A. so we traded.

"There were two programs that were available. One was the full-time day-student scene; the other was a night program that was a five-year program tied to an M.B.A. I decided I needed to work. I ain't have nothin' else to do in the evenings so I thought it would be really cool to go to school from six to eight every night or six to nine. It was about business then. There was a different mentality in the night school than in the day school."

Bill liked certain aspects of law school. The classes challenged his mind, and then he was surrounded by interesting people from all sorts of backgrounds. There was also no place better for someone looking to expand their horizons than the Bay Area in the late sixties. Oakland had laid the groundwork for the Black Power movement, San Francisco had a thriving arts and culture scene, and the counterculture movement was practically bursting at the seams in Berkeley. Bill loved the Bay Area's diversity, in part because it was so far removed from his experience in Texas.

A pair of his classmates at the law school approached Bill with a proposal they were working on for an all-black alternative school in Berkeley called Black House. Although he had left the

South precisely because he wanted to escape its rigid color line, *and* because he didn't want to end up teaching like his father, he agreed to become the school's creative writing instructor.

"They were tackling some interesting problems, I thought so at least," he explains. "The whole issue of urban education, the changing urban environment was going on. Everybody wants to confuse what the free speech movement did, [but] what it did was make people question things. Berkeley just had a higher degree of sensitivity to that. That was something that at that particular juncture in the history of education in the United States I thought was kind of interesting."

Bill stayed on for two years, but by his third year the militant rhetoric had taken hold of the school and he knew it was time to move on. "The Panthers were all over our school. As an adult you're a little more worldly than a kid. When you're a kid, you're trying to shape your views. You don't create a scene where there is a confrontation always going on in terms of you buyin' into my line, my dogma. "I understand my history as a black man in this country. The ideals of what America is based on, I relate to that. This is the only country in the world that gives presence to life, liberty, and the pursuit of happiness. No other country in the world has that as a guide for its citizens— the pursuit of happiness. I take that literally. How does that figure with my African roots? We know we got here not by choice, but we ended up here and whether we came from the Caribbean or we came directly, we as a people have been very involved in the making of this country. We done paid some dues. I ain't about to say I'm going back to Africa, I'm sorry. I will visit, but I have no desire to return."

Bill's intention was to leave teaching altogether and finish up his law studies. He was two and a half years into school by this point, exactly halfway home. But when the school superintendent heard that Bill had left Black House, he offered him the principal position at an experimental school that was specially designed for kids the system had failed. Reluctantly, Bill took the job. But while the idea of the school excited him, something still didn't sit right with him.

Another eighteen months would pass before Bill worked up the courage to admit to himself that what he really wanted in life was to travel the world and experience other cultures. As Bill remembers it, he was on a retreat with a group of educators when it dawned on him that the people he was surrounded by were all committed and believed in what they were doing. They were living their passion; he was the one faking it. He finally did tell his group members what was truly in his heart, and they all applauded his honesty, but even now Bill struggles to articulate the conflicted emotions with which he was dealing at that moment. Mainly, though, he was confronting the guilt of leaving a noble profession in order to do something that was purely about him. Ultimately, Bill had to give himself the permission to pursue his happiness.

The more practical question of exactly how Bill was going to go about seeing the world was the one he had to answer next. Flying he couldn't afford; he'd never been much for walking; and cars and trains could only travel where there was land. That only left sailing. "That was the most logical way for me to travel," adds Bill. He dedicated the next four years of his life to learning how to sail. He joined a sailing club so he could get a feel for the water. When he felt confident enough to go out on his own, he bought a used twenty-four-footer. He used that as his training boat. He went out in fair-weather conditions at first; later he took it out in less favorable conditions. To cut his living costs he housed the boat at the marina in exchange for a laborer's job. The money hardly covered his essentials, but he had a place to keep his boat, and he was also surrounded by sailors all day.

"That almost mirrors what your father did in terms of him working through that dissertation process," I say.

Bill merely nods; he'd already drawn a similar conclusion long ago. "It was nothing instantaneous. It was very premeditated, very much planned out in terms of 'This is the goal; this is what you gotta do.' That's what it comes down to in terms of knowing what you want and going after it. It was a big move because it was like moving out of a real comfortable scene, moving onto a boat. It wasn't the best living conditions by any stretch of the imagination; working conditions were no better. I'm sure I shortened my life years by the fumes and the toxins I was exposed to cleaning the bottoms of boats off and sandblasting 'em and scraping the bottoms with lead and mercury and all the shit that's associated with paints. I wasn't paying attention then. The gas mask ain't shit, you need to have a respirator.

"At any rate, the tradeoff was it wasn't something I did all my life. The greatest thing was I had the rapt attention of some very capable tradesmen and was enthusiastic enough to pay attention and learn and listen and adapt and mimic and do the things I had to do to develop a better notion of what this thing I'm putting together was and trusting my life to in terms of putting it out there in harm's way. When you talk about going to sea you don't know where you're going. All I knew was I was heading south and I was going to find some trade. I didn't know how to sail; I taught myself on that. I did everything formally and informally to acquire the skills that would give me the confidence to move to bigger and more challenging situations. I went to school at night out at a college at Alameda to learn maritime navigational skills. Again, timing. I knew it was there, I took advantage of it."

"Did you have to get used to that feeling of being off of land?"

"I guess that's why I got off into racing. They call it single-handed racing. There was double purpose for it. One was to be in charge of your own self, to take care of yourself without having to have assistance; to be able to have a small boat and take it wherever you want to take it given the conditions. That was a level of, for me, the challenge. My understanding was there's a price you have to pay for this: confronting your fears, coming to grips with emotions. What do you do to deal with an imminent sense of change, an imminent sense of danger? Pay attention. When you see all signs are telling you, 'Hey man, you need to lay out, take it easy, go in and get you another brew, wait till it blows over.' You come to grips with that. That in and of itself is a good growth experience. You have a chance in a real, meaningful kind of way to understand yourself better. That was the notion of being out of sight of land, of learning to sail."

The next step was buying the forty-footer. The boat had been built in 1948, and it was prone to leaks, but it was big enough for two to live on, and it could entertain three or four times that amount for a day if he ever wanted to charter it out. Bill restored and treated the wood and replaced all of its missing equipment. Then he tested it out:

"There were a lot of experiences I put myself into that forced the issue if you will; to me that's great. If I force an issue on myself and not on somebody else, more power to me because it takes a lot of the handiwork out of waiting for something to happen. So you force the issue and see how you react to it. You see what it's going to take to get you to a particular level where you have the confidence in yourself, [and] confidence in the boat. I could literally have stayed there another two years working on the boat. You could do it forever so after a while you've got to draw the line, so that's what I did, I drew the line."

Twenty-one summers ago a yacht sailed into St. Thomas's Charlotte Amalie Harbor. On board were three crew members, the boat's skipper, and his girlfriend of two years. They were delivering the boat for a wealthy businessman who wanted it brought from Panama to St. Thomas. The following day the boat's owner was supposed to meet them on the tiny island, pay them, too. Two of the crew members were from Panama, and one was from Canada. The skipper's girlfriend was from Australia. She and a friend had left home at eighteen promising each other they'd live adventurous lives, and that they'd never return to their native land. She'd met the skipper in Costa Rica and they'd been together since. The skipper was Bill.

Six years had passed since he'd left San Francisco. And the boat everyone thought wouldn't last but a few months had lasted all six years. In the interim, he'd figured out how he could use his management skills to captain ships. It had taken some time, but now he had figured out he could continue to live on the high seas while making a decent living. From St. Thomas the plan was to fly down to Jamaica to pick up another boat, which had to go to Gibraltar. From England he was supposed to take another boat back to Panama. In all he was looking at more than twenty thousand miles of travel at a cost of a dollar and a half per mile. "I was gonna make me some money," Bill says, grinning, "we was gonna really do it."

What made the job all the more appealing was that he'd finally get to cross the Atlantic. Bill had spent the last six years in and around South and Central America, but never had he crossed to the other side of the great ocean.

But first he had to get out of St. Thomas.

Bill had sailed in from the east, bypassing Puerto Rico in order to catch the sun rising over the island. Looking up at it from sea level he thought it was the most brilliant sight he'd ever laid his eyes on. "It was green, absolutely green, gorgeously green. It was like a storybook scene. I had always imagined what St. Thomas was like, what it was about."

After they went through customs, Bill, his girlfriend, Linda, and the crew waited to hear from the owner. When a day passed without word, they continued to wait patiently. There were worse places to have to pass the time. Besides, their expenses, eating and such, were covered in the contract. But then things suddenly turned sour.

"They didn't have faxes and e-mails and all that, they had telexes, so I got a telex a couple of days later saying he wasn't going to be able to make it and that I needed to wait for him. It really changed the tenor of everything. I became very despondent. I was pissed. I was furious. We'd made a deal, I did my part, now the guy's telling me he can't make it? He doesn't have the money?"

Instead, the owner made Bill an offer. Since it might be a while before he could get to St. Thomas, Bill could charter the boat in the interim. The only catch was he wanted Bill to give him a portion of the proceeds. Bill didn't take kindly to the offer. He didn't see why he should have to work for something that was already owed to him. Bill chose a different route. There was no way, first of all, that he was going to leave the boat. But since he couldn't expect his crew members to stick around as well—nor could he afford them to—he bought them plane tickets back to Panama, paid the bill at the marina where the boat was being held, and went to see a lawyer. By the end of the day he'd blown all of his cash, but he had acquired a seaman's lien, ensuring that he'd be first in line to receive any proceeds from the sale of the boat. At that point it was just Bill and Linda.

To make matters worse, hurricane season was coming on. Leaving the boat could have been disastrous. Then again, he couldn't seriously look for work because any day he could've received a telex saying the money was on the way. Bill ended up working at the marina, while Linda found a job bartending at a local restaurant.

"It was probably one of the most introspective times in terms of what was going on, whether or not this was really meant to be, why did I do this, why did I do that—that kind of thing."

Bill thought about the opportunities he'd left behind for this adventure he'd set out on, and he wondered if it was time to settle back down. The boat had lasted. He'd met someone he could see himself spending the rest of his life with. He'd had a chance to explore cultures he never would have had he stayed in Berkeley. Maybe this was a sign. All things being equal, he'd had a good run.

"When I looked at the six years of travel and how I lived and the exposures of different people, of different notions, of different things that came into play, it was fantastic. What it basically did for me was it afforded me time to create a mutual offering, if you will. One of the greatest things about traveling is not only sharing but learning. If you meet somebody they can always make a better extension to you than you can to them because you're in their place, their time. If you have your own space that you're traveling in, you can share, too. You can invite me to your place, I can invite you to my place. This is where I live, this is where you live. We've got a mutual kind of scene going on in terms of sharing. I can be easily unobtrusive in my own controlled environment. I can bring about some interplays I could never bring about being in a hotel. It's an expression of who I am, this is my set."

During his period of reflection Bill wondered what he could do to make money should he opt to stay in St. Thomas for a while. What he knew was that he didn't want to work for anyone. He'd lived too long on his own terms. The only other viable alternative was starting a business. The question was what kind of business; moreover, what kind of business did an island like St. Thomas need. Then there was the obvious issue of what service could he provide given his limited resources. That left few options, among them barbecue. He'd grown up surrounded by it in Austin; he had even worked at one of his uncle's restaurants.

Bill started cooking up ribs and chicken and selling them each evening at the waterfront. People loved it. His barbecue became so popular that by the time he arrived at the docks each evening, people were lined up, waiting. Then, through connections Linda had been making at the bar where she worked, he was offered a catering job for a six-hundred-person party. He'd never done anything that large before, but he put together a team of people anyway, and the party was a success. Soon Bill bought a truck and started selling his food out of the back of it. By the middle of 1984 business was booming to the point that he was able to buy a piece of land that stood on the highest point on the island. In 1987, he was among a group of sixteen chefs from across the country honored for their innovative recipes at the third annual American Chefs' Tribute to culinary legend James Beard. In the following years he opened Bill's Texas Pit Barbecue locations throughout St. Thomas as well as in St. John and St. Croix. Bill's barbecue even took him across the Atlantic to places like Moscow, where he was part of an American delegation for the first Eastern European barbecue. And in 2000 he traveled to Cuba with Congresswoman Maxine Waters as part of the first official trade delegation to Cuba in forty years. In the end, Bill had traveled thousands of miles from his Texas roots only to discover his calling was Texas's signature cuisine.

From where Bill and I are standing on his deck you can almost see the harbor where the yacht pulled in twenty-one years ago. Pointing out toward where Puerto Rico sits behind the fog blanketing the Caribbean Sea, he maps that fateful morning for me in vivid detail. Then he takes another pull from the cigar he's been puffing on all morning. A still very lean and vigorous sixty-one, Bill has the pleasant air of a content and wise man. When you're around him you feel you're with someone who's comfortable with the choices he's made in life, and who no longer has anything to prove to anyone but himself.

Perhaps that's why in the last few years he's downshifted business. He no longer has operations in St. John and St. Croix, the trucks he has scattered throughout St. Thomas are only open after four each day, and they only take cash. One of the trucks doesn't even have a phone number. To our American sense of endless expansionism Bill's step back probably seems foolish. He has a thriving enterprise with broad potential and yet he's decided to relegate it to a tiny island. Bill's reasons are simple enough, though. He enjoys hitting the golf course as frequently as he can; he and Linda are also still avid travelers; and besides, it was never about the money or the recognition in the first place. Even as Texas Pit restaurants using his signature recipe have opened in Atlanta and New Orleans, albeit with his consent of course, he's not too concerned with whose name is on the front door, and whether everybody knows he's the man behind the sauce.

And what, I ask him as we lean against the deck overlooking the harbor, ever came of sailing? "Do you still go out?"

"Passion for something plays an intrinsic role in my ability to not only grasp but work with it and go with it. And when the passion wanes, then I don't fight it. When it came time for me to get off the boat, for me [it was] one of the biggest downers in the world because it's like going back to something and knowing that you never will again have that relationship with it. It's not just a recreational thing. I can't go day-sailing. I can, but you know what I'm saying . . ."

After spending the previous six years living on a boat, Bill estimates that in the last twenty years he's been sailing maybe four

times. I can tell that just talking about that time in his life is difficult for him. It brings back too many memories that with the
passing of each day seem farther and farther removed. Nevertheless, there is a silver lining. Bill's and Linda's present home is
made entirely of wood, five different kinds to be exact. Light
pours in from all angles, and even in the stifling tropical heat, air
circulates freely. When you're inside you feel like you're in tune
with everything that's happening around you, including the
constant crowing of the roosters outside. The couple chose to
build a wooden home after two concrete homes they lived in
blew away in a pair of hurricanes that devastated the island.
Wood may not solve that problem, but it's still what he's most
comfortable living in.

"I like wood. There's something special about wood. For me
it just speaks volumes about warmth and flexibility and change.
At the same time there's a strength about it, too."

In light of the twists and turns his life has taken, it's only fitting that the home Bill built should match a characteristic he has
spent a lifetime cultivating.

Epilogue

Early on I decided that I wanted this book to take me to new places and fill me with new experiences; I wasn't disappointed. I traveled from St. Louis to St. Thomas; from guitar shows to go-cart tracks; I drank home-brewed beer in Ray Hill's kitchen, and got a lesson in wine tasting in Tannie Stovall's living room; I met new-age entrepreneurs and old-line expatriates. Along the way, I was introduced to authors as dissimilar as Chester Himes and Krishnamurti; I studied up on Abraham Maslow's research into peak experiences and self-actualization, and hunkered down to learn some journalistic nuts and bolts from books like David J. Dent's *In Search of Black America*. Ivan Aranha, a young man I met while he was teaching in Japan, told me over lunch one afternoon how he'd been following Rick Warren's forty-day path to a "purpose-driven life"; Ellington Robinson would later tell me he was as well. Meanwhile, my father recommended a book entitled *A Theory of Everything* by Ken Wilbur that helped me integrate many of the amorphous ideas swirling in my head. Another book, Richard Florida's *The Rise of the Creative Class*, grounded my observations about an emerging economy of ideas with empirical data.

I also rediscovered a few things. The wonder of the zoo and the pageantry of the circus are the two obvious examples that come to mind. At the urging of more than one person whom I interviewed, I pulled *The Alchemist* off my bookshelf and reread it. I even researched First Amendment law. Deeply moved by the dynamism each person brought to the table, my mental tentacles stretched in all directions as I tried to do their stories justice.

Over the two years it took to write this book, I watched people quit jobs, leave the country, join communes, and even enlist in the U.S. Army. I saw writers publish, artists create, and musicians produce. Some folks, like Sariya Wilkens, for example, I had to hunt down. Others, like Michelle Luc, put me on their e-mail list so I always knew what they were up to. Some I consider dear friends now. Some I may never speak to again after this book is published. In all of the cases, I like to believe the exchange that took place when our paths crossed for that brief window of time was genuine and enduring.

But life moves on.

I am thrilled to have seen this thing through, but I lament the changes I now know are afoot. The ties that have traditionally bound black America together as a group are wearing thin as the collective experience of oppression gives way to a day when blacks are as free as their white counterparts to choose their destiny no matter how obscure, indulgent, or risky it may appear. For the most part, the lives within these pages have not been circumscribed by racism. These people have experienced the best that life has to offer. They are self-actualized human beings. They've gone to top schools, they've traveled extensively, they've had doors opened for them—in short, they are not oppressed.

What troubles me most, though, is that oppression has been in many ways the tie that's bound black America together for centuries. Without that oppression I wonder what African-Americans will have in common.

The black church? Well, for Kimson Albert, Buddhism is his faith of choice. For others it's Islam. Equally significant is the fact that more and more often I encounter people who are perfectly at ease being in tune with their spirituality without putting a label on it.

Our shared political viewpoints? Well, if this last presidential election (where a record number of black Americans voted Republican) is any indication, then I don't think we can count on that either. And after 2004's "Dream Team" debacle in Athens and a sudden influx of talented players from overseas, it's even debatable if African-Americans still corner the market in the sport that came to define black virtuosity in the Michael Jordan era.

And what of hip-hop, the so-called voice of the people? Can it be said that it represents the collective values of black America? A couple of generations perhaps, but an entire race, hardly.

What is left, then, is the stark reality of what Debra J. Dickerson calls the "end of blackness," where the essentializing characteristics of the black experience are few and far between; and where, as hyphenated Americans (rather than "coloreds" or "negroes"), African-Americans are now, more than ever, a part of the good, bad, and ugly that is the American Dream.

Still, as I contemplate the end of my twenties and the start of my thirties, I feel an optimism that I didn't feel two years ago. I know I'm not alone anymore; I know there is an army of seekers scattered about in this world; I know that if I just follow my bliss good (and some not-so-good) things will happen. The hundred or so tapes that fill a basket in my study will undoubtedly dust over, just as the thousands of pages of transcript I have stacked in my closet will curl at the edges. But nothing can change what I have experienced, and what I hope, to some degree, I have been able to share through this book.

Acknowledgments

To Candace, Leslie (Amina), Phillip, Jay, Joseph-Claude, Mia, Leila, and Joshua. It's taken me some time to see it, but ours is a strong and special family. Thank you for your patience and understanding. I've been saying, "It's coming," for a few years now. Finally, it's here!

To my wife, Candice. You have kept me sane, honest, humble, and hopeful these last few years. Thank you for understanding how important writing is to me, and for allowing me the space and time to pursue my dream.

To the Ebbesen family for inviting a stranger into your tight-knit fold and for trusting that a "writer" would take good care of your baby girl.

To my comrades in arms. Jeremy, whenever I thought you weren't listening you were. Your perceptive and progressive criticism keeps me honest. Darryl, I would have never had the courage to show my work to the world if it weren't for the inspiration you gave me so many years ago. Derek, we continue to grow in harmony. Everyone should be so fortunate to have a friend of your caliber. Thank you for the Web site and for your tireless ear. Sam, watching you and the guys go through all that you have these last four years with your book's success has been inspiring. You've handled it remarkably. Brendon, your encouragement through the years has been invaluable. G.G., without the discipline we learned on the hardwood together, I would've never finished this book. Stay strong and positive, brother. Chessa, we meet good friends at unexpected times. The last two years would have been unbearable without someone else who understood what I was going through and with whom I could always let off the steam. El, your dedication to creating keeps me creating.

Craig, thank you for blessing the cover of my book. I could think of no one else.

Byrd Leavell, my agent. It's hard to imagine that the only reason I even know you is because I happened to show up at the one and only reading I've ever gone to in New York. Just lets you know there's no such thing as chance. Things happen for a reason. Thank you for checking in, for showing love, for being honest.

Regine, I simply must thank you for opening the doors very early on. Meeting you jump-started this book. Even though you are not in the book, your spirit surrounds it. Thank you.

Stacey, the first editor to lay eyes on this book in its infant stage. You have no idea how validating your interest and excitement were. Before I met you I only wished; after I met you I believed.

Jason and Cecil, you held me down in Paris when you didn't have to. Robert, thank you for putting me up in London. That exchange rate was killing my pockets!

The Essence School family, thank you for allowing me to earn my stripes in your space and on your time.

To the people at Hyperion, thank you for giving an unpublished writer a chance.

Emily Gould, my editor. The third time is the charm. I am a better writer because of your red pencil.

Molly T, I don't know how you were able to listen to my voice for so many hours, but you did and there's no way I would have finished on time without your efforts.

There are a number of people whom I interviewed but whose stories don't appear in these pages. I apologize, I really do. You sat with me in some cases for three and four hours. Understand that just because your story isn't here doesn't mean your voice isn't. Thank you.

Finally, for all of the people whose stories appear in these pages, I only hope I've done some justice to you and that others will be touched by your lives and your words as I have been. Thank you immensely, immeasurably, infinitely.